Revenue Law in Uganda

David J. Bakibinga

FOUNTAIN PUBLISHERS
Kampala

Fountain Publishers Ltd
P.O. Box 488
Kampala, Uganda
E-mail:fountain@starcom.co.ug
Website:www.fountainpublishers.co.ug

Distributed in Europe, North America and Australia by African Books Collective Ltd (ABC), Unit 13, Kings Meadow, Ferry Hinksey Road, Oxford OX2 0DP, United Kingdom.
Tel: 44(0) 1865-726686, Fax: 44(0)1865-793298.
E-mail: abc@africanbookscollective.com
Website: www.africanbookscollective.com

First published 2006

ISBN-10: 9970-02-565-1
ISBN-13: 978-9970-02-565-7

Dedication

Dedicated to the memory of
DEBORAH NAOME MUSABE
An advocate and scholar struck down in her prime

Contents

Table of Cases

D

E

P

R

S

Table of Statutes

Preface

This work is a pioneering text on revenue law in Uganda. In its over 40 years of Independence, no text on revenue law has ever been produced. Yet, since 1991 when the Uganda Revenue Authority was set up, there has been increasing interest in revenue issues as the tax paying culture among Ugandans is revived. The importance of an appreciation of revenue law, which is the basis of taxation, is therefore, obvious.

The text examines theories and criteria for taxation as well as the critical distinction between income and capital for taxation purposes. It focuses on individual and business taxation in general and includes specialist analyses of taxation of companies, partnerships and trust income. The treatment of individual and business taxation closely focuses on the provisions of the Income Tax, 1997 as amended from time to time, as well as judicial decisions in England, on which our revenue law is based, and those from East Africa. The remaining chapters examine the relevance of taxation to investment, the concept of tax avoidance, and the practical administration of taxation based on statutory provisions as well as the tax appeal mechanism introduced by the Tax Appeals Tribunal Act.

Tax law is not static. The unease felt by lawyers about taxation partly stems from its dynamism and perceived volatility owing to its annual review through the finance legislation. The constant updating of any work on revenue law is, therefore, inevitable. This is not to suggest that works on revenue law are worthless, but to emphasize that while there are certain immutable principles of tax law, their operation depends in large measure on economic and political factors which are re ected in annual finance legislation.

I hereby express my gratitude to my former secretary, the late Ms Jane Sabano, who typeset the text; Mrs Florence Kasule, who reduced it to its present form and Ms Gertrude Kizito who typeset the tables of cases and statutes and index; my colleagues at the Faculty of Law and members of the legal profession who encouraged me to plunge into this virgin area; the former Commissioner General of Uganda Revenue Authority (URA), Mr Edward Larbi-Siaw, who permitted me to combine my work at URA with academic teaching and research; and the late Deborah Musabe, my former student and formerly with Tumusiime and Kabega Advocates, who provided research assistance. Finally, I appreciate the endurance of members of my family in the process of preparing this work.

The law is stated as at December, 2005.

D.J. Bakibinga
Office of the Deputy Vice Chancellor
Makerere University
February, 2006

1

Introduction

A. Definition of Taxation

Taxation is defined as "... the imposition of duties for the raising of revenue."[1] It is a device used by government to extract money or valuables from people and organisations by the use of law. In the words of Pinson, "All forms of taxation are imposed by Parliament. Taxation is a creature of the Statute."[2] Taxation, therefore, encompasses every charge or burden imposed by a sovereign upon persons and property rights for the use and support of government, thereby enabling it to support its functions and activities.

Taxation involves two phases. First the levying or imposition of taxes on persons and property and secondly the collection of the taxes levied. The first phase consists of provisions of the law which determine the persons or property to be taxed, the sums to be raised, the rate thereof, the time and manner of levying and the mode of receipt and collection of taxes. The second phase comprises legal provisions indicating the manner of enforcing the obligation to pay taxes on the part of the taxpayer.

Two attributes of taxation are, therefore, evident. First, there must be a requirement of public purpose to justify the exercise of the taxing powers since tax is an imposition for the supply of the public treasury and not for the supply of a private individual or enterprise. Second, tax operates as a forced charge and does not in any way depend on the will or contractual assent expressed or implied of the tax-payer. In other words it is a statutory liability.

B. Objectives of Taxation

The main objectives of taxation are first to raise revenue, second to achieve economic stability and development and third to bring about income distribution. Each of these will be examined brie y.

1. Raising Revenue

It has been observed that "the ability to raise revenue is the main factor determining the level of government expenditure."[3] Thus in a capitalist economy, where ownership of wealth is privatised, government needs to raise revenue through securing grants, loans,

1. *Osborn's Concise Law Dictionary* (8th ed. Sweet & Maxwell, 1993), p.320
2. PINSON on Revenue Law (1982), p.677
3. Walk, D. "Taxation and Taxable Capacity in Under-Developed Countries" in *Economic Development in Africa* (Blackwell, Oxford, 1965) p. 129

treasury bills and taxes. However, of these sources of revenue, taxation is the most reliable source of funds, when compared to the other sources which may be unreliable or could create heavy indebtedness for the country as is the case with loans. For instance the expected tax revenue for Uganda for the 1996/1997 financial year is Shs820 billion, which would constitute 60-70 percent towards government expenditure.[4]

2. Economic Stability and Development

The revenue function of taxation is important even for governments which have attained economic development or are free of financial constraints. It is significant in regulating private expenditures and stabilising employment and price levels. Thus during periods of insufficiency of funds within the economy, the government may allow revenue to fall automatically by taking steps to reduce effective rates of taxation with the objective of increasing private expenditure. Conversely, tax rates may be increased in order to mop up excess funds with the objective of controlling in ation.

In less developed countries revenue is collected in order to finance government expenditure thereby effecting economic development. In the words of John Due, "Taxation affects economic development in two ways: by altering the determinants of economic development and by permitting the financing of current governmental activities."[5]

Determinants of economic development include (1) levels of savings, (2) levels of investment, (3) balance of payments and (4) quality and quantity of available manpower. These are brie y examined.

(a) Level of Savings

Taxation may increase the level of savings in an economy because some taxes decrease consumption of various commodities, thereby leading to saving of incomes. It has in this vein been observed that "heavier taxes on income will reduce the tax-payer's spendable income."[6]

Furthermore, income tax is intended to divert resources from private consumption and investment to public use. Thus it has been stated:

> Much of interest in the expenditure tax can be traced to the belief that its substitution for the income tax would favour savings and therefore capital formation and growth. Under an expenditure tax, a person who foregoes a given amount of present consumption and lends or invests his savings can ensure a greater increase in future consumption than would be possible under an equal yield income tax. The gain in future consumption may be regarded as a reward for saving.[7]

It is thus evident that taxation has the effect of encouraging savings which are then diverted to public use, leading to capital formation and growth.

---

4. *Budget Speech* June 199.
5. Due, J.F. "Indirect Taxation in Developing Economies" in *Potential Effects of Taxation of Determinants of Economic Growth*, p.18.
6. Meade, J.E. *The Structure and Reform of Direct Taxation Report* of a Committee chaired by Professor Meade (1978), pp. 7-21.
7. Goode, R. *The Individual Income Tax: Studies of Government Finance*, p.38.

(b) Level of Investment

It should, however, be noted that savings can only contribute to growth if they are accompanied by rising investment. A country may be endowed with natural resources yet lack funds to exploit them effectively. Taxation can be used as a means of attracting investors and funds for investment by providing attractive tax incentives for investors.[8]

(c) Balance of Payments

Taxation can be used to redress the balance of payments deficit of less developed countries. This may be achieved by imposing heavy taxes on imports in an attempt to reduce imports and, conversely, decrease taxes imposed on exports.

(d) Capacity Building

Another economic determinant of taxation relates to the quality and quantity of manpower in a country. Thus through taxation, governments can finance the process of human capital formation at the expense of lavish consumption. This formation includes education and training programmes which reduce illiteracy and increase skills and quality of manpower. It also includes an improvement in productivity, technology, sanitation, health and nutrition build-up, thereby increasing the quantity of manpower available for economic growth and management.[9]

3. Resource Allocation

Taxation may alter the "product mix generator" within the private sector. This is achieved by rendering some commodities more expensive through the imposition of high taxes while others are made less expensive through the imposition of subsidies or negative taxes. The effect of this is that labour and capital are rendered redundant in fields which are heavily taxed so that they can be devoted to the production of other commodities which are not taxed or highly taxed. For instance the law provides for incentives to some investors in priority fields.[10]

Similarly, taxation can be used as a tool to fight dumping, especially of low-quality goods, technology and drugs. Recommended drugs may not be taxed or highly taxed while disapproved drugs and technology are heavily taxed. Taxation can, therefore, be used to limit dumping of goods on the market.

4. Income Redistribution

The role of fiscal policy relative to incomes and wealth distribution is to achieve a degree of redistribution of incomes and wealth through taxation. In the words of Birds and Oldman

> The role of redistributive finance in less advanced economies is investment in human beings who are an integral part of government programmes for improving productivity and technology, sanitation, health and nutrition build-up and thus increase the quantity of manpower available for economic development.[11]

---

8. See e.g. Investment Code Act Cap. 92
9. Bird and Oldman, *Readings on Taxation in Developing Countries* (John Hopkins 1967), p.23
10. Investment Code Act, Cap. 92, S.12 and First Schedule
11. *Supra* n.9. p.23

Taxation helps to check income inequalities through three main tax structures: (1) progressive taxes which increase with increasing incomes as is the case with income tax; (2) regressive taxes which decrease with increasing incomes, as is the case with indirect taxes such as Value Added Tax (VAT); and (3) proportional taxes which are neutral and are of a fixed percentage for all incomes, VAT again being an example.

It has, however, been observed that progressive taxation when combined with social security benefits and other elements of social expenditure, for instance on education or health, are designed to improve the relative position of poor members of society.[12]

It may be concluded that government, through taxation, is able to uplift every class of people and provide them with the basic requirements of life at the expense of lavish consumption. Apart from this, taxes also play a role in the management of demand in the economy.[13] It should be noted, though that while these are the aims and objectives of every government not all governments have succeeded in attaining them for one reason or another, such as failure to control inflation within the economy or to prioritise expenditure on public services.

C. General Theories, Criteria and Terminology of Taxation

1. General Theories and Criteria of Taxation

With the inevitable change in social structures of a particular economy, government policies and revenue requirements are bound to change, thereby necessitating changes in the tax regime, either through the imposition of new taxes or the abolition of old taxes. This is normally effected through annual finance legislation. For economies that have a narrow tax base, the changes encourage widening of the tax base by the imposition of new types of taxes. This happened in Uganda in the 1996/97 financial year when the Value Added Tax (VAT) was introduced. It is in this respect that changes must be critically examined not only in relation to the canons of taxation propounded by Adam Smith[14] but also to the workings and effect of the tax system as a whole and its interaction with the social security system.

Generally, as we have seen in relation to the definition of taxation, taxation is a tool by which the sovereign state extracts finances or funds from its people and property in order to provide public revenue for the support of governmental expenditures, administration of law or payments of public expenses. Additionally, it is a forced charge or extraction sanctioned by statute. Nevertheless, in order for government to effectively benefit from the imposition of any form or type of tax, it must ensure that the tax system is equitable and effective. It is in this respect that the canons of taxation proposed by Adam Smith[15] are relevant. Adam Smith postulated that a good tax system or principles of taxation are (a) certainty, (b) convenience, (c) economy (d) equality. Economists have subsequently added a fifth requirement: neutrality. These will be examined briefly.

---

12. Easson, *Cases and Materials in Revenue Law* (2nd ed. Sweet & Maxwell, London, 1990) p.4
13. Wilkinson, M. *Taxation* p.5
14. Smith, A. *An Inquiry into the Nature and Causes of the Wealth of Nations* (1776) Book V Chapter 11. See also Easson, *supra* n.12, pp. 1-2
15. *Ibid.*

(a) Certainty

The tax which every individual is bound to pay ought to be certain and not arbitrary. This means that the following features must be clear and plain to the contributor or tax-payer and any other person, particularly the collector.

First, the time of payment, that is, whether the tax is payable yearly, monthly or quarter yearly and if possible the deadline of payment of such a tax. Both the taxpayer and collector should be certain of the time when each tax shall fall due, and after how long it always falls due.

Second, both the taxpayer and collector should know the manner of payment, that is, whether it shall be by receiving cash or by cheque or some other form of credit, whether individually by each tax payer or deducted by his employer or whether it must be paid in instalment or lump sum or whether the taxpayer can pay for the whole year instead of every month, etc., and also the currency in which the payment must be effected.

Third, both the taxpayer and collector should be aware of the quantity to be paid, that is, how much a taxpayer is expected at every moment he is expected to pay.

The rationale for the requirement of certainty is to protect both the taxpayer and government interests against the tax collector. Thus certainty of a tax prevents aggravation of the tax upon any obnoxious taxpayer or extortion by the threat of aggravation by the tax collector. This explains for instance the annual gazetting of the trade tariffs under the finance legislation. Where a tax system or taxation is uncertain, it encourages "the insolence and favours the corruption, of an order of men [tax collectors] who are naturally unpopular,"[16] even when they are neither insolent nor corrupt.

(b) Convenience

Government should ensure that the taxpayer shall at a given time be in a position to pay the assessed tax. Consequently, every tax ought to be levied at the time, or in the manner, in which it is most likely to be convenient for the taxpayer to pay it. For instance, tax on income earned in employment is usually deducted at source as the employee is being paid, hence the acronym Pay As You Earn (P.A.Y.E.). Similarly, a tax upon the rent of land or houses is payable at the same time at which rents are usually paid, i.e. levied at the time when it is most likely to be convenient for the contributor to pay or when he is most likely to have the wherewithal to pay. Furthermore, taxes upon such consumable goods as articles of luxury are finally paid by the consumer, and generally in a manner that is very convenient for him. Since it is his/her choice to buy or not to buy, it would be his/her fault if he/she suffers any considerable inconvenience from payment of the taxes. Taxes upon incomes of individuals or corporations should be levied when such individuals or companies receive payment or profits, respectively.

It should be stressed that if the time or manner of payments is not convenient for the taxpayer, it is the government that loses or suffers the consequences.

16. Adam Smith, *Ibid*

(c) Economical

Every tax ought to be so contrived as both to take on and to keep out of the pockets of the people as little as possible, over and above what it brings in the treasury of the state. In other words every tax ought to be economical to collect, implement and enforce, if the government is to effectively benefit from its fiscal policies. There has been some debate as to whether the recently introduced Value Added Tax (VAT) is economical to collect by small traders, given the increased costs of book-keeping and engagement of accounting services.[17]

According to Adam Smith, a tax may either take out or keep out of the pockets of the people, a great deal more than it brings into the public treasury in four ways.[18] First, the levying of the tax may require a great number of officers, whose salaries may eat up the greater part of the produce of the tax, and whose perquisites may impose an additional tax upon the people. This may explain the abolition of the road toll tax in Uganda, which was found uneconomical in terms of staffing and accounting. Second, imposition of tax may obstruct the industry of the people and discourage them from applying certain branches of business which would provide maintenance and employment to many people. While it obliges the people to pay, it may diminish or even destroy some of the funds which might enable them move easily to do so. Third, forfeitures and other penalties incurred by unfortunate individuals who attempt unsuccessfully to evade the tax may frequently ruin them, thereby ending the benefit which the community might have received from the employment of their capital. Consequently, penalties must rise in proportion to the temptation. Fourth, subjecting the people to frequent visits and the odious examination of the tax collector may expose them to much unnecessary trouble, vexation and oppression; and though vexation is not strictly speaking expense, it is certainly equivalent to expense at which every man would be willing to redeem himself through bribery.

(d) Equality

The subjects of every state ought to contribute towards the support of the government, as nearly as possible, in proportion to the revenue which they respectively enjoy under the protection of the state. This is to protect the taxpayer from being over-taxed or under-taxed, and the government is enabled to extract tax from all its subjects who are liable.

(e) Neutrality

Neutrality requires that the tax system itself should influence as little as possible the way in which economic activities are carried out. For instance the tax system should not deter extra work being undertaken on the grounds that a lot of tax would be paid on the additional wages than on the slice of income immediately below them.[19]

17. *The New Vision* newspaper Vol 11, No. 248, p.13 (16th October, 1996)
18. Smith, *supra* n.14
19. Kay, J.A. and Keng, M.A. *The British Tax System* (4th ed., 1986) p.18

2. Terminology of Taxation

(a) Direct Taxes

Direct taxes are levied or imposed upon the individual according to his ability to pay or upon companies.[20] The impact of such taxes falls on the individual or the company concerned and cannot be easily transferred or passed to another person. Examples of such taxes are income tax, corporate tax, and estate duty.

(b) Indirect Taxes

Indirect taxes are levied on certain articles of popular consumption.[21] The taxpayer's liability varies in proportion to the volume of the particular goods sold or purchased. This type of tax is levied on expenditure or consumption of commodities. Examples of indirect tax include Customs Duty, excise duty and Value Added Tax (VAT).

D. The Structure and Administration of Tax in Uganda

Each country has its own unique tax structure which responds to whether tax capacity can be tapped without disrupting the economy, government policy or motivation.

It is intended to briefly examine the structure of the main taxes relative to the laws governing them. This entails discussion of the mode of collection and administration of the affected taxes.

In Uganda, the taxation system broadly encompasses (1) income tax, (2) taxes on services and transactions, (3) taxes on local production, (4) taxes on foreign trade and (5) graduated personal tax.

1. Income Tax

Income tax is defined as a tax payable on the income of a person or profits of a corporation over a period of time.[22] The structure, collection and administration of income tax in Uganda is governed by the Income Tax, Cap. 340.

Income tax is charged for each year of income (the calendar year preceding the year of assessment) in respect of any person, resident or non-resident, upon all the chargeable income of such person.[23] It is also charged upon the income of any business for whatever period of time covered as well as those from employment or and from any right granted to any other person for use or occupation of any property.[24] The tax is also chargeable upon income in respect of dividends or interest.[25] It is also charged on the total amount of any contributions made to a retirement fund during the year of income by a tax-exempt employer.[26] It is also chargeable on the value of any gifts derived by a person in connection with the provision, use, or exploitation of property.[27]

20. *Osborn's Concise Law Dictionary, supra* n.1, p.320
21. *Ibid*
22. Musgrave, R.A. *Theory of Public Finance*, p. 165
23 Income Tax Act 1997, S.4(1) read together with Ss 15-20
24. *Ibid* SS.4(1), 17(1), 18, 19, 20
25. *Ibid* S20(1)(a)
26. *Ibid* S.20(1)(c) as modified by Article 254 of the Constitution, 1995
27. *Ibid* S.20(I)(b)

It is also chargeable on income in respect of any amount deemed to be income of any person under the Act.[28]

The Income Tax Act is administered by the commissioner general appointed under the Uganda Revenue Authority Act.[29] In practice the commissioner general delegates his powers to the Commissioner for Internal Revenue, who administers the Act. The commissioner is in turn assisted by two deputies, respectively for assessment and collection and an assistant commissioner in charge of regional and technical matters who are in turn assisted by various revenue officers (assessors and collectors), some of whom man regional and district revenue stations all over the country. While the commissioner operates from the headquarters of the Uganda Revenue Authority, the main revenue offices in Kampala are located at Crested Towers premises on Nile Avenue, Nakawa, Makindye, Bwaise and Jinja Road.

2. Taxes on Services and Transactions

(a) VAT

Until 1st July 1996, there existed sales tax[30] and Commercial Transactions Levy.[31] These have since been replaced by Value Added Tax (VAT).[32] VAT is a consumption tax which is imposed at each stage of distribution on the value added at each of those stages. The recognised stages are importation, manufacturing, wholesale, retail and consumer.[33]

Assuming a VAT rate of 20 percent, the table below shows the incidence of VAT at the various stages in the production and distribution chain:

Stage of Produce Charged	Value Added (Shs) (%)	Tax Rate	Tax (Shs)
1. Pitsawayer	110,000	20	22,000
2. Timber Dealer	16,500	20	3,300
3. Carpenter	25,300	20	5,060
Total	**151,800**		**30,360**

28. *Ibid* S.20 (1)(d)
29. Income Tax Act Ibid, Ss.2, 156 read together with the Uganda Revenue Authority Act, Cap. 196, S.10
30. Sales Tax Act 1970
31. Finance Decree 1972
32. Value Added Tax Act, Cap. 349
33. See further, Bakibinga, *Value Added Tax: Introduction, Rationale and the Law in Uganda* (Professional Books Publishers, 1996) pp. 1-3

In the above table it is significant that the price exclusive of the tax (final product of the timber) is Shs151,800/=. The tax inclusive value is Shs182,160/= (Shs151,800 + Shs30,360/=). The carpenter, therefore, sells the furniture to the final consumer at Shs182,160/= after adding a VAT of Shs30,360/= to the final value of Shs151,800/=. The consumer therefore bears the final tax, which is remitted to the Uganda Revenue Authority (URA). A consequence of this is that the pitswayer, timber dealer and carpenter are entitled to a refund of the VAT paid to URA of Shs22,000/=, 3,300/= and 5,060/=, respectively, after submitting necessary returns.[34]

A major feature of VAT is the need for taxable persons to keep records of their transactions[35] and to register with the commissioner general for purposes of claiming refunds.[36] A threshold of Shs50,000,000/= of turnover value of a business has been set for registration or, alternatively, demonstrable turnover of Shs12,500,000/= over a period of three months.[37] Voluntary registration mainly for claiming refunds on VAT paid on business inputs is available, regardless of the threshold being met.[38] All public authorities are required to register for VAT.[39]

Certain items are exempted from VAT.[40] The effect of this is that persons dealing in those products cannot claim refunds of VAT in respect of business inputs for those items. Other supplies are zero rated.[41] This in effect means that no VAT is paid on them. A main example is exports. However, VAT paid on inputs for exports and other zero-rated goods can be refunded.

The VAT statute is administered by the commissioner general of URA who in practice has delegated his powers to the commissioner for VAT. The commissioner for VAT works closely with the commissioner for Customs and Excise in monitoring the collection of VAT at importation and manufacturing points and in verifying claims for refunds of VAT. The main VAT office is presently located at Impala House on Kimathi Avenue and Customs House on Parliament Avenue, Kampala. The commissioner for VAT is presently assisted by a deputy commissioner and an assistant commissioner in charge of inspections and audit. These are in turn assisted by various revenue officers.

(b) Stamp Duty

Certain instruments of transfer of title, property or interest are charged with payment of stamp duty. The rate of duty presently stands at 1 percent.[42]

Stamp duty collection is presently administered by the Commissioner for Internal Revenue and in most cases through the agencies of the Registrar General, Registrar of Titles and Registrar of Motor Vehicles.

---

34. Value Added Tax Statute, Cap 349, Ss. 31-2, 53, Schedule IV
35. *Ibid.* Ss 46-7
36. *Ibid.* Ss 7-8, 53
37. *Ibid.* S. 7(1), (2)
38. *Ibid.* S. 7(4)
39. *Ibid.* S. 7(5)
40. *Ibid.* S.19 and Schedule II
41. *Ibid.* S. 24 (4)
42. Stamps Act, Cap. 342, S.2 and Schedule Item 42 as amended

3. Taxes from Local Production

Taxes which are imposed on local production are called excise duty. Excise duty is defined as a duty charged on the production or use of any goods whether meant for local consumption or export or on a licence to deal in certain products.[43] The structure, collection and administration of excise duty in Uganda is governed by the East African Excise Management Act[44] and the Excise Tariff Act[45] as amended from time to time.

Essentially every manufacturer of excisable goods must be licensed in the manner provided by the Excise Management Act.[46] The licensee must pay excise duty at the rates and under circumstances provided for under the Excise Tariff Act.[47]

Excisable goods include beer, spirits, soda, mattresses, and plastics. Recently excise duty has also been imposed on imports such as textiles and second-hand clothes.[48] Excisable goods may be increased or reduced depending on the demands of the economy and government policy.

The excise legislation is administered by the Commissioner General of URA through the Commissioner for Customs and Excise.

4. Taxes from Foreign Trade

Taxes from foreign trade comprise duties on imports or exports principally excise and customs duties. Customs duty is defined as duties or tolls payable upon merchandise imported into the country.[49] Trade taxes are governed by the Customs and Excise Act[50] which provides for the application of the East African Customs and Transfer Management Act[51] and the Excise Management Act.[52] Both legislation regulate the collection of Customs and excise duty while the Customs Tariff Act, Cap. 337 and the Excise Tariff Act provide for imposition of fiscal entry, suspended fiscal entry and import duty on goods, the rates of customs duty and goods or imports liable to customs duty.

Customs duty legislation is administered by the Commissioner General of the URA through the Commissioner for Customs and Excise.

5. Graduated Personal Tax

Graduated tax is defined as "a crude form of income tax levied in Uganda upon the entire population of able bodied adult males and some women by the District Administration and Urban Authorities where they reside."[53] It is a form of direct personal tax and local income tax adopted to the economic circumstances of the country. It is "levied on income, actual or presumed, from all sources, including land and other assets used for subsistence."[54]

Graduated tax is administered by local authorities under powers conferred by the

43. *Osborn's Concise Law Dictionary* (8th ed. 1993), p. 138
44. Cap. 28 *Laws of East African Community* (1970)
45. Cap 338 *Laws of Uganda* (2000 ed.)
46. SS. 8-15
47. *Ibid.* S.39
48. Finance Bill, 1996
49. *Osborn's Concise Law Dictionary*, supra, p.105
50. Cap 335 (*Laws of Uganda*, 2000 ed.)
51. Cap. 27 *Law of the East African Community*, 1970
52. *Supra* n.44
53. Davey, K. J. *Taxing a Peasant Society* (Charles Knight & Co Ltd., London 1974), p.31
54. Ghai, *Taxation for Development: A Case Study of Uganda* (E.A.P.H. 1966) p.19

Local Government Act.[55] Assessment of the tax is made by a tax assessment committee or assessment officer appointed by the District Local Council for that purpose for that subcounty. For urban areas the assessment committee or officer is appointed by the Urban Local Council.[56] Only adults of 18 years of age or above residing in the particular area are assessed.[57] Certain persons, who include visitors to the particular local council, students, and diplomatic and consular personnel, are exempted from payment of the tax.[58]

The tax is due and payable on January 1 in each year, although in practice a grace period of up to 30th June is given. There is also provision for appeal against assessment of graduated tax.[59]

6. Uganda Revenue Authority

The Uganda Revenue Authority (URA) was established by the Uganda Revenue Authority Act, Cap. 196, and commenced activities on 5th September, 1991. Its major role was to optimise tax collection by administering and enforcing the law relating to revenue assessment and collection. It replaced the defunct tax collecting departments of the Ministry of Finance in response to the low ratio of tax revenue to GDP collected in Uganda in comparison to other developing countries, particularly in Africa.[60]

Rationale for a Revenue Authority

The causes of poor tax collection in Uganda by the defunct tax collecting departments in the Ministry of Finance included poor management; lack of motivation of workers in terms of remuneration package; poor accommodation; lack of training programmes; inadequate collection facilities, such as transport, equipment and stationery; revenue collection stations; and lack of funds. Other causes were inadequate manpower in terms of quantity and quality, poor record-keeping, ineffective tax collection due to poor assessment, insufficient auditing systems, low compliance of tax payers due to lack of effective legal enforcement system, and lack of banking facilities.

It was initially proposed that the defunct revenue collection departments should be improved instead of setting up a new revenue collection body. However, studies by British tax consultants Coopers & Lybrand Deloitte concluded that the best solution was the establishment of an autonomous body free from civil service terms and conditions of service and management practices. A major reason for poor performance was the neglect of the civil service[61] and the fact that many of the prevailing civil service rules and procedures prevented many improvements in the departments which had no capacity to discipline their staff. When disciplinary cases were referred to the Public Service Commission, there was excessive delay and staff members were rarely dismissed. As a result, problems such as embezzlement of taxes, corruption of officials, and lack of

55. Cap. 243, S. 81 (1)
56. Local government revenue regulations made under the Local Government Act (Fifth Schedule), Ibid.
57. Regulation 2 (1) *Ibid*
58. Regulation 2 (9) *Ibid*
59. Regulation 2 (2),(7) *Ibid.* See further, Bwengye, F.W. *Local Government Taxation in Uganda* (Makerere University LL.M. Dissertation 1996) Chapter 3
60. Coopers & Lybrand, Government of Uganda Planning for a Revenue Authority for Uganda (1991) p.1
61. *Ibid,* para. 206

commitment to work were never checked. In contrast, the new body would possess autonomy in handling disciplinary matters and taking firm action, including dismissal of staff when appropriate.

It was further argued that an overhaul of the revenue collection system would permit a salary structure set at levels which would discourage staff from corrupt practices.[62] In this respect, performance of the revenue collection body would determine promotion and increase of salary neither of which could be accomplished under civil service rules and procedures.

Inefficiency in the defunct revenue collection departments was blamed on the civil service structure, which did not permit autonomous control over resources allocated to their budgets. Instead the departments had to request release of funds and vehicles from the Ministry of Finance, which often created delays, and some budgeted funds were withheld.[63]

The decay of the civil service necessitated the establishment of a separate Revenue Authority which would introduce a clear break with the past standards of performance, ethics and working practices, thereby creating an advantage in the recruitment of high-quality staff and greater management control.[64]

The URA is not an independent entity but more in the nature of a government revenue collection agency. It is not a conventional public parastatal or privatised corporation but rather part of the public sector reporting to the Ministry of Finance. It operates within an expenditure budget voted by Parliament and is accountable for that expenditure and revenue collection.

After five years of operation, URA had realized many advantages. It is a body corporate capable of suing and being sued and owning property.[65] It operates under the general guidance of a board of directors which is answerable to the Minister of Finance through the Commissioner General. It has power to hire and fire staff and to determine the terms and conditions of service.[66] It retains a portion of the revenue for operational expenses within approved budget limits and thereby is enabled to acquire facilities for its operations. It also has a salary structure independent of the civil service. The result of this is that revenue collection rose from an average of Shs9-11 billion per month in the 1990/1991 fiscal year to Shs53 billion in the 1995/1996 fiscal year.[67] In the year 2004/05 revenue was over a trillion shillings.

The success of the URA has spearheaded establishment of revenue authorities in Zambia, Kenya and Tanzania, and others are planned elsewhere in Africa.[68] The new authorities have benefitted from discussions with and information from management of URA. A delegation from Pakistan has visited Uganda to study the preparations for starting up the Value Added Tax.

However, while the problem of corruption has persisted, the most notable achievement

62. *IMF, Uganda : Possibilities for Tax Reform Aide Memoire,* (1991) para 1.3
63. Coopers & Lybrand, *supra* n.60, para 206
64. *Ibid.* para 208
65. URA Act, Cap. 196, S.2
66. *Ibid* S. 11 (3)
67. URA Revenue Statistics, Department of Finance & Administration
68. Zimbabwe and South Africa are contemplating setting up a similar body.

of the URA has been the setting up of controls to curb malpractices. These are evident in the form of the work of the Internal Audit Department, the Tax Audit and Investigation Division of the Department of Management Services, and the Mobile Task Force in the Department of Customs whose work is supplemented by the Anti-Smuggling Unit. Malpractices which would otherwise have gone undetected have been unearthed by these units either separately or acting together. Interestingly, even the alleged excesses of the Special Revenue Protection Services Unit have been detected through claims by the public addressed to the Legal Division!!

2

Concept of Income

A. Definition and Concepts of Income

It has been observed that income tax is a tax upon what is properly regarded as "income" for the purposes of the taxing legislation, that is "taxable income."[1]

There are two concepts of income: (1) the traditional view which holds that income as distinguished from capital is the fruit from the tree and (2) the modern approach which regards incomes as accretions to wealth or to economic power.
Adam Smith defined income thus:

> Revenue is drawn from either labour, stock or land. That derived from labour is **wages**; that derived from stock by the person who employs or manages it is called **profit**; that derived from it by the person who does not employ it, himself but lends it to another is **interest** on the use of money. Revenue from land is **rent** belonging to the landlord.[2]

Smith defined stock thus:

> Stock is distinguishable into two. First, the part which a person expects to afford him revenue is **capital** and secondly, that which is reserved for purpose of revenue is *reserve*. In this vein, stock in trade is **circulating capital**, while investment in improvement of land, purchase of useful machines and instruments of trade or things which yield revenue or profit without changing masters is **fixed capital**.[3]

In *John Smith & Sons v. Moore,*[4] a taxpayer bought a coal business which included certain forward contracts worth 30,000 to supply colliery owners. He claimed to be entitled to deduct the cost of the contracts from the profit of the business. It was held that the deduction, being of a capital nature, was not permitted Viscount Haldane stated that assets of a business, including its goodwill and inherited contracts by which to employ circulating capital, constituted fixed capital. In *Eisner v. Macomber,*[5] the U.S. Internal Revenue Service claimed tax in respect of certain stock dividends (bonus issue of shares) received by Macomber. The taxpayer argued that the dividends were not "income" and that tax could not be raised in respect of them. The court accepted the plea. Pitney J. thus stated:

1. Wheatcroft, 9. "What is Taxable Income" (1957) *British Tax Review* 310
2. Smith, A. *The Wealth of Nations* (1776) Book 1 Chapter 6. Emphasis supplied.
3. *Ibid* Book II Chapter 1. Emphasis added.
4. [1921] A.C. 13; 12 T.C. 266. See also *Taxes Commissioner v. Nchanga Consolidated Copper Mines Ltd.* [1964] A.C. 948; *Kauri Timber Co. Ltd. v. Commissioner of Taxes* [1913] A.C. 771; *Law Shipping Co. Ltd. v. IRC* (1924) 121.C.621.
5. 252 U.C. 189 (Supreme Court, U.S.A.) (1919) his emphasis.

> Income may be defined as the gain derived from capital from labour or from both combined provided it be understood to include profit gained through a sale or conversion of capital assets ....

It is further stated that

> "The essential connotation of income ..... is gain to someone during a specific period and measured according to objective standards."[6]

B. Taxable Income

It has been suggested that taxable income is the value of what a taxpayer could have consumed during the year without diminishing his or her capital wealth in the process.[7] [7]Additionally, it is suggested no income would be recognised as arising unless an actual receipt had taken place, although a receipt may take the form of a benefit having money's worth received in kind as well as money or of a payment made to a third party in discharge of another's legal debt.[8] Nevertheless no mere improvement of a person's financial or material position is recognised as constituting income. Thus an increase in value of property that he owns, even a net increase in value of his total resources, is excluded from the computation of his income. This view would in modern circumstances be limited to income tax **simpliciter** and would probably not be valid in the case of capital gains tax.

Examples of receipts of an income nature are interest, annuity, and public revenue dividends. Sources of income include land, trade, profession, securities, and employment. Thus tax charges the income from the source.

C. Distinction between Capital and Income

1. Concept

The tendency in English Law has been to prefer "the fruit of the tree" concept of income rather than "accretion to economic power" concept.[9]

The distinction is normally too fine[10] and in Britain since 1988-89 has been reduced in importance as capital gains are taxed as if they were top slice of the individual's income. However the distinction is still important in the following instances:

(a) Income from Land. A distinction is made between rental payments and "capital" payments such as lease premiums.

---

6. Simons, H.C. *Personal Income Tax* (1938), pp. 50-51. Emphasis supplied.
7. Meade, J.F. *The Structure and Reform of Direct Taxation* (1976) pp 30-33
8. Final Report of the Royal Commission on the Taxation of Profits and Income (cmnd 9474 (1955) U.K.)
9. *Ryall v. Hoare* [1923] All E.R. Rep. 528; *Riches v. Westminster Bank Ltd.* [1947] A.C. 390, 398; *John Smith & Son v. Moore* [1921] 2 A.C. 13, 34
10. Whiteman, P.G. "The Borderline between Capital and Income" [1966] *British Tax Review* 115

(b) Trading Income. A distinction is made between a trading profit and an isolated capital gain and between receipts or expenditures of revenue nature which enter into the computation of profits of the trade and those of a capital nature which do not.
(c) "Annual" income. A distinction is made between instalments of capital and income payments.
(d) Income from Foreign Possessions.
(e) Tax Avoidance. Many avoidance schemes depend upon the successful conversion of income into capital or vice versa.

In *Ryall v. Hoare,*[11] an isolated commission paid to a company director in consideration for guaranteeing the company's bank overdraft was held to be properly assessed under case VI of Schedule D of the British Income Tax Act.[12] Furthermore, in *IRC v. Mallaby Deeley,*[13] payments made to a publishing firm under a seven-year covenant, replacing a previous obligation to pay a lump sum to finance the publishing of a literary work, were held to be payments of a capital nature. The covenantor was not permitted to deduct tax from the payments. In *Golden Horse Show (New) Ltd v. Thurgood,*[14] the taxpayer company claimed to be entitled to deduct, in computing profits, the purchase price of dumps of tailings from gold mines. Its claim that the dumps were not capital assets but instead formed part of the stock-in-trade was upheld by Romer L.J. who stated:

> The question to be decided in this case is whether the dumps are to be regarded as fixed capital or as circulating capital. If they are the former, it is conceded by the appellants that the assessment made on them is correct. If, on the other hand, they are floating or circulating capital it is conceded that the cost of them to the appellants must be debited in the profit and loss account, the account being credited with the cost price of what was left of the dumps at the end of the year of assessment.

Concerning the distinction between fixed capital and circulating capital, Romer L.J. observed:

> The determining factor must be the nature of the trade in which the asset is employed. The land upon which a manufacturer carries on his business is part of his fixed capital. The land with which a dealer in real estate carries on his business is part of his circulating capital. The machinery that a dealer in machinery buys and sells is part of his circulating capital, as is the coal that a merchant buys and sells in the course of his trade.

In *B.P. Australia Ltd v. Court of Taxation of Commonwealth of Australia,*[15] it was stated that in distinguishing between capital and revenue payments the following matters should be considered:

(a) the character of the advantage sought and in this its lasting qualities may play

---

11. *Supra* n.9
12. equivalent to Income Tax Act, Cap. 340 (Uganda), S. 18
13. [1938] 4 All E.R. 818
14. [1934] 1 K.B. 548; [1933] All E.R. Rep 402. See also *Whitehead v. Tubbs* (Elastics) Ltd. [1983] 57 T.C. 472; [1984] S.T.C.1. following *San Newspapers Ltd. v. Federal Commissioner of Taxation* (1938) 61 C.L.R. 337, 363; *Modern Buildings Ltd v. C.I.T.* [1962] E.A. 275; *Commissioner General of Income Tax v. Robson* [1970] E.A. 213; *Income Tax v. Kotecha* [1971] E.A. 63 (U); *D. Ltd v. Income Tax* [1971] E.A. 455 (Kenya)
15. [1966] A.C. 224, 281 approved in *Whitehead v. Tubbs* (Elastics) *Ltd* [1984] S.T.C.1. (C.A.)

a part;

(b) the manner in which it is to be used, relied upon or enjoyed and in this and under the former head recurrence may play a part;

(c) the means adopted to obtain it; that is by providing a periodical reward or outlay to cover its use or enjoyment for periods commensurate with the payment or by making a final provision or payment so as to secure future use or enjoyment.

2. Application of the Distinction between Capital and Income

Having laid down the salient ingredients of the distinction between capital and income, a brief illustration of the application thereof is apposite.

In *IRC v. Biggar*,[16] the taxpayer carried on a dairy farming business in partnership. Later, they decided to participate in the EEC Dairy Herd Conversion Scheme and, in return for agreeing to cease commercial production of dairy produce and to convert the dairy herd to a meat-producing herd within four years, received a grant of £11,165. The Revenue assessed the payment as "annual profits or gains arising or accruing" from a trade, profession or vocation under the Tax Act, 1970, S. 107 (1) (a) (ii). On appeal to the General Commissioners, it was held that the payments were capital receipts and not taxable. The Revenue appealed to the Scottish Court of Session arguing that the payment was intended to make good a potential loss of income and should, therefore, be treated as income.

The Court held that the true test is to ask, first, what the payment is for and, secondly, whether it is of a revenue or capital nature. Since entry into the scheme was purely voluntary and was not conditional upon expenditure on new machinery, buildings, and so on, the payment could not be regarded as the "price" for the reorganisation of the farm. Rather "the premium was payment designed to make good a possible loss of income" and since that income, "if it had been received, would have been taxable in the hands of the taxpayers," the premium was accordingly to be taxed.[17]

The case has been described[18] as useful in reiterating the two-fold test to be applied in considering the taxability of compensation payments. First, does the sum arise in the ordinary course of the trade and, if so, second, is it revenue or capital?

Furthermore in *A.L. et al v. Commissioner of Income Tax*,[19] the appellants were brothers who were registered proprietors as tenants in common of certain premises and buildings (which were divided into shops, offices, and residential accommodation) thereon. The land was held on a 99-year lease from the Crown (Government) of which there were approximately 50 years to run. Four of the shops in the building were leased, each for a period of 10 years and each on payment of a premium together with a monthly rental. The total of the premium payable was Shs112,000/= of which Shs25,000/= was paid to the appellants in 1951 and Shs87,000/= in 1952. Each appellant was assessed income tax in respect of the years of income, 1951 and 1952 for half his share received in those years. They appealed to the Local Committee in respect of the assessments for

---

16. [1982] S.T.C. 677
17. distinguishing *Higgs v. Olivier* [1952] Ch. 311 and *Vanden Berghs Ltd v. Clark* (1935) 19 TC 390 and following *London & Thames Haven Oil Wharves Ltd v. Atwool* [1967] Ch. 772
18. White P. *Leading Cases in Personal Taxation* (Longman, 1991) p. 317
19. 2 E.A.T.C. 148 (Case No. 37) (Kenya)

1952 on the ground that the amount of the premiums should be spread over the period of the lease and taxed accordingly. The Committee rejected the appeals and confirmed the assessments. Both appellants appealed to the Supreme Court on the grounds that the premiums were capital and not income receipts and, alternatively, that if they were income receipts, they should be spread over the period of the leases and taxed accordingly. The Supreme Court held that the premiums were income and not capital receipts and they were taxable in the year of receipt and no other year.

On further appeal to the Court of Appeal for Eastern Africa, the Court held that if the premiums were capital receipts they were not taxable even though premiums were expressly included in Section 8 (1) of the East African Income Tax Management Act, 1952.[20] However, the premiums were received for the user of a capital asset and not for its realisation and they were, therefore, income receipts and taxable in the year of receipt. Furthermore, in the absence of an express power, spreading over was not permissible.

In contrast, in *Mamor Sendrian Berhad v. Director of Inland Revenue*,[21] the taxpayer company, which was incorporated in 1968, had power in its memorandum of association to carry out the business of planters and cultivators of inter alia oil palm. Other clauses of the memorandum included many objects including carrying on the business of timber merchants. The taxpayer applied for and was granted about 7,000 acres of jungle land in Kluang by the government of the State of Johore at a price of $100 an acre which was calculated by the government to include $47 an acre for the right to extract timber. No evidence was given as to whether the method of calculation was known to the taxpayer company.

The company entered into an agreement with the state government to develop the area for the purpose of planting oil palm, and to fell and log timber and to remove such timber from the area where it was felled. Logging operations started in 1970. The company arranged for a contractor to extract marketable timber and appointed a Singapore agent to arrange its sale. By 1976 nearly all the land had been planted with oil palm.

The taxpayer company was assessed income tax, timber profits tax and development tax for the assessment years 1971, 1972, and 1973, and it appealed to the Malaysian Special Commissioners. The issue was whether the receipts from the extraction and sale of timber were received by the taxpayer company in the course of developing the land into an oil palm plantation and thus were capital, or were income from a separate business of timber operators and thus liable to income tax. The Commissioners held that the receipts were the income of a separate trade. On further appeal to the High Court of Johor Bahru, the taxpayer's appeal was upheld. However the Revenue successfully appealed to the Federal Court of Malaysia. The taxpayer company then appealed to the Privy Council.

In allowing the appeal, Lord Keith reasoned that the taxpayer company was obliged to develop the 7,000 acres as an oil palm plantation and that the felling and extraction of timber was a necessary and obligatory step in that process, which was an expensive one. The sale of timber was a prudent and reasonable means of mitigating that expense.

20. Like Income Tax Decree 1974 (Uganda), S.10 (d) is now repealed. See now Income Tax, Cap 340, S.18(1)(a) and 20(1) (a).
21. In White P, *supra* n. 18 P. 319 (Privy Council On appeal from Malaysia) (1985); [1985] STC 801

Additionally, the Commissioners were not entitled to infer[22] from the facts that the extraction and sale of timber constituted the carrying on of a business of timber operators since the extraction of timber was inseparable from the process of developing the land as an oil palm plantation as that development was impossible without such an extraction. Furthermore, the taxpayer's operations resulted in the transformation of one capital asset, 7,000 acres of virgin forest into a capital asset of a different character, namely that of an oil plantation. The taxpayer company's receipts from the sale of timber were, therefore, capital receipts.

However, where it is clear that the transaction is a purely commercial or trading activity, income accruing therefrom is taxable,[23] although a distinction can still be made between activities of a capital and income nature based on the same transaction,[24] which will determine the taxability of the proceeds. Thus in *McClure v. Petre*,[25] Captain Petre received £50,000 from MacAlpines for allowing it to deposit soil on his land, provided that having done so it restored the land to agricultural use. The Revenue argued that as Captain Petre still owned his land before and after the transaction he had not disposed of anything, and the £50,000 was, therefore, fruit from the exploitation of the land and thus income. The taxpayer appealed and maintained that the payment was of a capital nature. The Commissioners allowed the appeal, but the Revenue appealed. In dismissing the appeal, the Commissioners held that when the value of an asset is attributable to many different characteristics, the consideration received for a transaction which realises once and for all the capital value of one of those characteristics (thereby diminishing the remaining value of the whole asset) is capable of constituting capital, not income, and that is so notwithstanding that the asset itself and all the rights in it remain throughout the property of the taxpayer.[26] In this case, the payments were received by the taxpayer as a consideration for a once-and-for-all disposal of a right or advantage of using it for dumping. It was in truth a realisation of part of the value of the freehold. It was a disposal of a capital nature.

In *Kirkham v. Williams* (Inspector of Taxes)[27] the taxpayer demolished some buildings and eventually erected a new four-bedroom residence on the site. He then sold the whole site. He was assessed income tax for the whole profit, an assessment which was upheld by the Commissioners. On appeal to the High Court, he argued that the proceeds were of a capital nature and at least should qualify for roll-over relief in that his business had continued, and he had bought another site. The request for apportionment of the proceeds in income and capital was rejected by Vinelott J., who explained that to succeed the taxpayer needed to establish "that he had bought part of the land to provide a site for his demolition and plant hire business and part for development and resale as a

22. Following *Edward v. Bairstow* [1956] A.C. 14. See also *Y. Co. Ltd v. Commissioner of Income Tax* 2 E.A.T.C. Case No. 25 (1955, Tanganyika); *A.G. et al v. Commissioner of Income Tax* 2 E.A.T.C. Case No. 33 (1955, Kenya); *Commissioner of Income Tax v. A.M. Ltd.* 2 E.A.T.C. Case No.38 (1956, Uganda)
23. *Z. Co. Ltd v. Commissioner of Income Tax* 2 E.A.T.C. Case No. 26 (1955, Kenya); *The Trustees of A.D. Charitable Business Trust v. Commissioner of Income Tax* 2 E.A.T.C. Case No. 30 (1955, Kenya); *A.J. v. C. I.T.* 2 E.A.T.C. Case No. 35 1956 (Kenya)
24.. *The A.E. Investment Trust Ltd v. C.I.T.* 2 E.A.T.C. Case No. 31 (1955, Kenya)
25. [1988] S.T.C. 749 (Ch.D. England)
26. per Browne-Wilkinson, V.C.
27. in White P. *supra* n.18, p.324; [1991] STC 342 C.A.

separate trading transaction." However, Vinelott J. was overruled by the Court of Appeal by a majority.[28]

Similarly, in *The A.E. Investment Trust Ltd v. Commissioner of Income Tax*,[29] the company was incorporated with objects inter alia which included power to deal in land. Its principal business was to work as managing agent for a group of companies and trusts. In 1947 it acquired two properties, one in Eldoret and one in Nairobi and in 1948, one property in Mombasa. The Eldoret property was undeveloped and after purchase, the company took steps to develop it but for certain reasons sold it at a profit in 1949 still undeveloped. The Nairobi property was subdivided and an unsuccessful attempt was made in 1949 to sell a part of it. The Mombasa property was undeveloped and was sold at a profit in 1949 still undeveloped. The company was assessed income tax on the profits from the Eldoret and Mombasa properties and appealed to the Supreme Court of Kenya on the ground that the profits were capital profits derived from the realisation of investments. It was held that the proceeds from the sale of the Mombasa property were revenue profit liable to income tax. However those from the Eldoret property were capital profit resulting from the realisation of a capital asset since there was genuine intention to develop it when it was acquired.

The cases also emphasize that receipts are of a revenue nature for the purpose of income tax rather than that the frequency of transactions gives rise receipts.[30] To avoid taxation, one must show that the relevant sale was simply the realisation of a capital asset and consequently the profits therefrom are not liable to taxation[31] or deductible as a business expense.[32]

It may be concluded that, whether proceeds from a sale or transaction are of a revenue or capital nature depends on the particular circumstances of the transaction.[33]

---

28. [1991] S.T.C. 342
29. *Supra* n.24. See also *H. Co Ltd v. Commissioner of Income Tax* 1 E.A.T.C. 65 (Case No. 8) (1950) (Kenya); *N v. Commissioner of Income Tax* 1 E.A.T.C. 118 (Case No. 14) (1952) (Kenya); *R.v. Commissioner of Income Tax* 1 E.A.T.C. 172 (Case No. 18) (1953) (Kenya); *O. et al v. C.I.T.* 1 E.A.T.C. 124 (Case No. 15) (1953) (Kenya)
30. *H. Co v. C.I.T.* Ibid; *O et al. v. C.I.T. Ibid; A.E. Investment Trust Ltd v. C.I.T. Ibid.*
31. *Commissioner of Income Tax v. Sydney Tate* [1963] E.A. 671 (C.A. Kenya); *B.N. Ltd v. C.I.T.* 3 E.A.T.C. 456 (Kenya); *C.I.T. v. Overland Company Ltd.* 3 E.A.T.C. 307 (Kenya); *Ralli Estates Ltd v. C.I.T.* 3 E.A.T.C. 203 (Tanganyika)
32. *Income Tax v. Kotecha Estates Ltd* [1971] E.A. 63; *M.v. Income Tax* [1971] E.A. 338
33. *Harry Ferguson (Motors) Ltd. v. I.R.C.* 33 T.C. 15 approved in *D. Ltd. v. Income Tax supra* n.14 (Kenya)

3

Personal Taxation

A. Charge to and Definition of Personal Taxation

Income tax is imposed by Section 4 (1) of the Income Tax Act[1] which provides thus:

> subject to, and in accordance with this Act, a tax to be known as Income Tax shall be charged for each year of income and is hereby imposed on every person who has chargeable income for the year of income.[2]

The effect of the provision is to charge income tax on every person for the relevant year of income. "Person: includes an individual, a partnership, a trust, a company, a retirement fund, a government, a political sub-division and a listed institution (under First Schedule to the Income Tax act)."[3] "Each year of income" refers to "the period of twelve months ending on 30th June, and includes a substituted year of income and a transitional year of income."[4]

In contrast to the repealed law,[5] the ITA has introduced worldwide income taxation. In this vein, chargeable income, which is defined as the gross income of the person for the year less total deductions allowed under the ITA,[6] is calculated by reference to the gross income, in the case of a resident person derived from all geographical sources, while in the case of a non-resident, it is income derived from sources in Uganda.[7]

It is significant, in this respect that the chargeable income must have been received or be in possession of the taxpayer before income tax is imposed on it. Thus in *Brown v. National Provident Institution,*[8] it was held that a source of income is chargeable to income tax for a particular year if a person possesses that source in that year. The sources of income included business income, employment income, property income and any other income derived by a person.[9]

1. Cap 340 hereinafter referred to as ITA
2. Emphasis supplied
3. ITA, S.2
4. *Ibid*
5. Income Tax Decree, 1974
6 ITA, S.15
7 *Ibid.* S.17(2)
8. [1921] 2 A.C.222 (H.L.(E). See also *Dupe Motor Bodies v. Ostime* (1961) 39 T.C.537
9. ITA, ss.17(1) (a), 18, 19, 20

B. Ascertainment of income

1. Business Income

a) General

Business income refers to any income derived by a person in carrying on a business and includes the amount of any gain derived by a person on the disposal of a business asset, or on the satisfaction or cancellation of a business debt, whether or not the asset or debt was on revenue or capital account.[10] Business income also includes: income of a person derived as consideration for accepting a restriction on the person's capacity to carry on a business[11] (sometimes described as good will); the gross proceeds derived by a person from the disposal of trading stock;[12] any amount included in the business income of the person under the ITA;[13] the value of any gifts derived by a person in the course of, or by virtue of, a past, present, or prospective business relationship;[14] interest derived by a person in respect of trade receivable or by person engaged in the business of banking or money lending;[15] and rent derived by person whose business is wholly or mainly the lending or letting of property[16].

For purposes of the above transactions, "business" includes any trade, profession, vocation or adventure in the nature of trade, but does not include employment."[17] In practical terms for a person to carry on a business he or she must be trading. "Trade" has been defined as a regular business of buying and selling or rendering services.[18] However, even without such regularity, any activity may constitute a trade if it is sufficiently systematic. In *Smith v. Anderson*[19] Brett L.J. was of the view that "carrying on business" in the context of the definition business in the Partnership Act implied "a repetition of acts and excludes in the case of an association for doing one particular act which is never to be repeated. That series of acts is to be a series of acts which constitutes a business."[20] However, in *Re Abbeinheim*[21] the expression "every trade, occupation or profession" in section 45 of the British Partnership Act, 1890[22] was understood to cover a single venture. Furthermore, in *Ojemen v. Okoafuda,*[23] it has been held that the word "business" incudes on isolated business transaction and that the profits from an isolated business transaction are, unless they are capital profits liable to income tax.[24]

10. *Ibid,* S.18(1)(a) read together with ss.49-54
11. *Ibid* S.18(1)(b)
12. *Ibid* S.18(1)(c)
13. *Ibid* s.18(1)(d)
14. *Ibid* s.18(1)(e)
15. *Ibid,* s.18(1))f)
16. *Ibid* s.18(1)(g)
17. *Ibid* s.2
18. Beettie, C.N. *Elements of the Law of Income and Capital Gains Taxation* (9th ed.) pp.54-55
19. (1880) 15 Ch.D.247, 277-278
20. Cap.114, S.2
21. (1913) 109 L.T.219
22. Equivalent to s.2 Partnership Act, Cap.114 (Uganda)
23. 1977 N.C.L.R.192 (High Court of Bendel State Nigeria). See also S.36(b) Partnership Act.
24. *H. Co. Ltd. v. Commissioner of Income Tax* 1 E.A.T.C.65 (Kenya)

Apart from trading, the individual must have traded within the year of income or expressed a desire to profit by trading.

b) Partnership

The income and losses arising from partnership activities is taxable (ITA, s.66(1)). For this purpose, partnership income refers to the gross income of the partnership for the relevant year as if the partnership were a resident taxpayer less the total amount of deductions allowed under the ITA for expenditures or losses incurred by the partnership in deriving that income other than the deduction allowed for carry-over losses to the following year.[25] In this vein, the gross income of a resident partner for the relevant year of income includes the partner's share of the partnership income for that year.[26]

c) Concession from Arrangement with Creditors

If, as a result of any concession of, granted by, or compromise made with, a taxpayer's creditors in the course of an insolvency, the taxpayer derives a gain on the cancellation of a business debt, such gain shall be deemed to be part of the business income of the taxpayer and chargeable to tax.[27]

2. Employment Income

The income derived by an employee from any employment is taxable.[28]

At this stage it is necessary to consider what amounts to "employment" or "services rendered," expressions which will be compared to "vocation" and "profession" for purposes of taxation.

(a) Meaning of "Employment," "Services Rendered," "Profession" and "Vocation"

In Great Britain, employment income is charged under Schedule E of the Income and Corporation Taxes Act, 1988, while income from a vocation or profession is taxed under Schedule D. Uganda charges income from employment under Section 19 of the Income Tax Act. Presumably, income from a profession or vocation would be regarded as arising from a business and therefore would be taxable under sections 17 (1) (a) and 18 of the Income Tax Act Cap 340.

In *Mitchell and Edon v. Ross*[29] Viscount Simmonds described the relationship between the schedules under the British Income Tax Act:

> I regard it as fundamental and well established Law that the Schedules to the Income Tax Acts are mutually exclusive and that the specific Schedules A, B, C, D and E and the rules which respectively regulate them afford a complete code for each class of income, dealing with allowances, deductions and exemptions relating to them respectively.

---

25. ITA, S.66(1) read together with S.38
26. *Ibid.* s.67(1). For further discussion of taxation of partnership, see chapter 6 *infra*
27. *Ibid* s.18(3)
28. *Ibid* s.19 (1)
29. [1962] A.C. 813; [1967] 3 All E.R. 49

In the British context, therefore, before an individual is assessed income tax, the commissioners and courts of law must distinguish employment from vocation and profession so as to determine the schedule under which he can be fairly taxed. Presumably, Uganda would adopt the same approach to determine whether the taxpayer should be assessed under ITA, Ss 17(1)(a), 18 in respect of business income or ITA, ss.17(1)(b), 19 in respect of income from employment. That such a determination is often necessary indicates that the distinction between employment on the one hand and vocation and profession on the other hand, may in some cases be blurred or not clear. The following discussion attempts to draw a distinction between the two by reference to decided cases.

In *Davies v. Braithwaite,*[30] Miss Braithwaite was a well known actress who in the year of assessment in question, appeared on stage, film and radio in the United States. and United Kingdom. The issue arose as under which of the Schedules D and E of the British Income Tax Act she should be assessed for income tax. Rowlatt J. answered the issue thus:

> The question of principle in this case is whether the Respondent ought to be assessed under Schedule D of the Income Tax Act of 1918, as following her profession of an actress, or whether she ought to be assessed under Schedule E as exercising certain employments under the particular engagements which she makes. The question is a difficult one mainly because of the want of precision in the meaning of the term 'employment' as it comes into controversy.
>
> When the word 'employment' is used in connection with a profession or vocation in Schedule D it means the way in which a man employs himself. But 'employment' in Schedule E means ..... something analogous to an office and which is applied to offices as opposed to the earnings of a man who follows a profession or vocation.[31]

In *Great Western Rly Co. v. Bater*,[32] Rowlatt J. observed that the term "office" or "employment" has been judicially described as a subsisting, permanent, substantive position which has an existence independent of the person who fills it, which goes on and is filled by successive holders — for example, a director of a company, a consultant with a part-time appointment, trustees, executors, and so on hold offices.

It is notable, though, that not all professions are businesses, and some professions can be assessed under Schedule E of the British Income Tax Act. Thus in *Fall v. Hitchen,*[33] H. the taxpayer was a professional dancer employed under a standard form of contract. He was assessed under Schedule E in respect of earnings under the contract. He appealed to the General Commissioners, who decided that these sums were assessable under Schedule D. The Inland Revenue appealed. In delivering his judgment, Pennycuick V.C. observed, "The first matter which falls to be considered is whether the relation created by the contract was that of service or a contract for services."[34]

30. [1931] 2 K.B. 628; [1931] All E.R. Rep. 792
31 Emphasis supplied
32 [1920] 3 K.B. 266 at 274
33 [1973] Ch.66; [1973] 1. All E.R. 368
34. *Ibid.* following Cooke J. in *Market Investigation Ltd v. Minister of Social Security* [1969] 2 Q.B. 173, 184

In the words of Cooke J:

> The observations of Lord Wright, of Denning L.J. and of the judges of the Supreme Court suggest that the fundamental test to be applied is this "Is the person who has engaged himself to perform those services performing them as a person in business on his own account?" If the answer is "Yes," then the contract is a contract of services. If the answer is 'No' then the contract is a contract of service.[35]

Pennycuick V.C. continued:

> Once it is accepted that this is a contract of service it seems to me to follow that it must equally represent an employment within the terms of Schedule E. Indeed, unless some special limitation is to be put upon the word 'employment' in any given context, the expression 'Contract of Service' appears to be coterminous with the expression 'employment.'

It can be concluded that in the English context any professional who is under a contract of service is chargeable under Schedule E (the equivalent of ITA, Ss 17(1)(b), 19) in respect of profits of employment under a contract of service. He can also be charged under Schedule D (equivalent to ITA, ss.17(1) (a),18) in respect of profits from a business or profession under a contract of services.

It has been seen that income from a profession or vocation is chargeable under Schedule D of the British Income and Corporation Taxes Act 1988. What then distinguishes these expressions from employment? The term "profession" was defined in *IRC v. Maxse:*[36]

> There is no definition in the Income Tax Acts, but it has been judicially indicated that it involves the idea of an occupation requiring either intellectual skill or any manual skill controlled by the intellectual skill of the operator, as distinguished from an occupation which is substantially the production or sale, or arrangements for the production or sale of commodities.[37]

The word "vocation" was defined to be "analogous" to "calling a word of wide signification meaning the way in which a person passes his life."[38] It is notable though, in the English context that the words "trade" and "trading" are used to include a "profession" or "vocation"[39] and income thereof charged is under Schedule D of the British Income and Corporations Taxes Act 1988.

In Uganda "business" is defined to include "any trade, profession or vocation and every manufacture, adventure and concern in the nature of trade, but does not include employment."[40] This clearly places profession and vocation outside employment and

---

35 *Ibid*

36. [1919] 1K.B. 647

37. *Ibid* per Scrutton L.J.

38. *Patridge v. Mallandine* (1886) 18 Q.B.D. 276 per Denman J.

39. Partnership Act 1890, S.45

40. ITA, S.2 compare with Income and Corporations Taxes Act, 1988 (UK) S. 832 (1) which defines "trade" to include "every trade, manufacture, adventure or concern in the nature of trade"

makes income thereof chargeable under Sections 18(1)(a) and 19(1) ITA.

Thus in *Edwards v. Clinch*,[41] a consultant civil engineer was held assessable under Schedule D rather than Schedule E in respect of the exercise of his profession. In this regard, Lord Salmon observed that the separate public inquiries over the years held by Mr Clinch (the engineer) did not constitute one continuing office rather

> It was a temporary, ad hoc appointment confined to the taxpayer. He was not appointed to a position which had an existence of its own. It had no quality of permanence about it. It was a transient, indeterminate once only, execution of a task to which the taxpayer was peculiarly qualified.[42]

(b) Emoluments Liable to Income Tax

(i) Wages, Salary, Leave Pay, Payment in Lieu of Leave, Fees, Commission, Bonus, Gratuity, Sick Pay Etc.

Employment income include any wages, salary, leave pay, payment in lieu of leave, fees, commission, bonus, gratuity or any subsistence, travelling, entertainment, utilities, cost of living, housing, medical or other allowance.[43] However, where the Commissioner General is satisfied that any such subsistence, travelling, entertainment or other allowance represents solely the reimbursement to the recipient of an amount expended by him wholly and exclusively in the production of his income from the employment or services rendered, then calculation of the taxable income shall exclude any such allowance or expenditure.[44] In English terminology the gains or profits described here are termed emoluments.[45]

In *Hamblett v. Godfrey*,[46] the right to belong to a Trade Union and certain other rights under the employment protection legislation were withdrawn from civil servants working with the Government Communications Headquarters (G.C.H.Q.) including the taxpayer, H. A payment of £1,000 was paid to those employees who wished to continue to be employed at G.C.H.Q. in recognition of the withdrawal of those rights. H received the £1,000 but appealed against assessment under Schedule E. (ITA S.18(1)(b)) made on the sum contending that it was neither an emolument nor chargeable under the British Income and Corporations Taxes Act 1970, but a solatium. It was held that the payment was an emolument within the Act and taxable since it was made for loss of rights within the employment protection legislation and was thus a recognition of changes in the contract of service. The source of the payment was the employment and was referable to employment and nothing else.

Similarly, in *Wicks v. Firth*,[47] a trust fund established by the employer company paid a

41. [1982] A.C. 845; [1981] 3 All E.R. 543 H.L.
42. Adopting the words of Ackner L.J. in the Court of Appeal [1981] Ch.D.1 at pp. 17-18. Consult also *Ready Mixed Concrete (South East) Ltd. v. Minister of Pensions & National Insurance* [1968] 2 Q.B. 497; *O'Kelly v. Trusthouse Forte* [1984] Q.B. 90; *Edwards v. Bairstow* [1956] A.C. 14; [1955] 3 All E.R. 48
43. ITA, Ss.17 (1) (b), 19(1)(a)
44. *Ibid.* S.19 (1) (c)
45. Income and Corporation Taxes Act, 1988, S. 131 (1)
46. [1987] 1 All E.R. 916

scholarship to the employee's undergraduate child to supplement the maintenance grant paid to the child by the Local Education Authority. It was held that the "scholarship" was a benefit (under the equivalent of ITA, S.20(1)(b)) but was exempted from tax as income arising from a scholarship.

In *Glantre Engineering Ltd v. Goodhand,*[48] the taxpayer company offered a lump sum payment of £10,000 to Wells as an inducement to him to leave the firm for which he was then working and take up employment with the taxpayer company. Wells accepted the offer and was paid the £10,000 on taking up employment with the company. Wells was assessed tax on this "inducement." The issue arose as to whether this payment was an "emolument" within the Income and Corporations Taxes Act 1970.[49] It was held that the payment was an emolument.

However, in *Durga Dass Bawa v. Commissioner of Income Tax,*[50] a company offered to the appellant in appreciation of his long and loyal service personally rendered to the company by him a personal *ex gratia* monetary gift payable in four quarterly installments all after the termination of his agency as distributor of tobacco for the company. He was assessed tax and appealed. It was held that in considering whether a payment is truly voluntary and not in the nature of extra remuneration arising out of employment, the fact that it was made after the completion of the service and without legal obligation is of high importance. Furthermore, a payment is not taxable merely because it had "something to do" with one's employment, if "the occasion of making it arises out of his past services." Finally, that the payment was a personal gift made after the termination of employment and was not taxable as gains or profits from employment or services rendered.

(ii) Allowances

It is possible for an employee to receive a stated sum less some deduction or a stated sum plus some benefit received in a form other than cash. The allowances currently cover travelling, lunch and entertainment, accommodation and provision of an official car.

In *Machon v. McLoughlin,*[51] the taxpayer was a male attendant at an asylum. He received a weekly salary subject to fixed deductions, before payment, for board and lodging and for laundry. He contended that only the net amount of salary was assessable. It was held that he was assessable in respect of the gross amount. Rowlatt J. stated:

> If a person is paid a wage with some advantage thrown in, you cannot add the advantage to the wage for purpose of taxation unless the advantage can be turned into money. That is one proposition. But when you have a person paid a wage with the necessity – a contractual necessity if you like – to expend that wage in a particular way, then he must pay tax upon the gross wage and no question of alienability or inalienability arises.

---

47. [1982] 56 T.C. 318 H.L.
48 [1983] 1 All E.R. 542
49 S. 183 (1)
50. [1963] E.A. 659; 3 E.A.T.C. 437 (C.A. 8 H.C. (Uganda)) following the dictum by Rowlatt J. in *Cowan v. Seymour* 7 Tax Cas. 372. See also *Moore v. Griffiths* [1972] 3 All E.R. 399; *Shilton v. Wilmhurst* [1989] 1 W.L.R. 179 . The decision in *Durga Dass* case has been reversed by ITA, S.18(1)(e)
51. (1926) 11 T.C. 83 (C.A. (E))

Similarly, in *Heaton v. Bell*,[52] the taxpayer agreed to participate in a car loan scheme initiated by his employers. In return for the use of a car he was to receive an amended lower wage. Two issues were considered: (1) whether this was merely a deduction from his gross wage, the gross wage remaining taxable, and (2) whether the benefit of the car loan scheme was a taxable perquisite and, if so what was the value. It was held that the amendment was a deduction and the gross wage was taxable. In any event the benefit was a taxable perquisite.

Section 19(1) (a) of the Income Tax Act describes "employment income" under Section 17 (1) (b) to include any other subsistence, travelling, entertainment or other allowances. However, such allowance is not taxable if it represents solely the reimbursement to the recipient of an amount expended wholly and exclusively in the production of his income from the employment or services rendered.[53]

In *Fergusson v. Noble*,[54] the taxpayer, a detective sergeant in the police force, was assessed tax on £11 paid to him in cash as an allowance for clothing. He was obliged to spend this sum to provide "plain clothes." The payment was held to accrue to him by reason of his office and to be assessable under Schedule E of the British Income Tax Act.[55] Lord Salvesen thus stated:

> It appears to me that such money allowance is in a totally different position from the case where the employer supplies a uniform to be worn only when the man is on duty and which remain the employer's property.... We are dealing with a payment of money... but it seems to me that once we have reached the conclusion that this money allowance is part of the salary or wages, perquisites, profits or other emoluments which are derived from his office, we must hold that it is assessable to Income Tax whatever deductions may be claimable by the respondent.

With regard to allowances constituting reimbursements to an employee, the case of *Owen v. Pook*[56] is apposite. In that case, the taxpayer, a general medical practitioner in practice in Fishguard, also held 2 part-time appointments at a hospital in Harrefordwest, 15 miles from Fishguard. Under the terms of service of the Hospital staff, the taxpayer was paid travelling expenses of 10 miles at a fixed rate per mile, limited to a single journey of 10 miles, for journeys between Fishguard and the Hospital. He paid the cost of the additional five miles himself. The travelling expenses he received were included in his income tax assessment. The issues in the House of Lords to which the taxpayer had appealed against assessment were (1) whether the travelling allowance was properly included in the appellant's emoluments for income tax purposes under Schedule E (ITA Ss.17(1)(b),20), (2) whether the actual cost of the journeys was deductible from his emoluments under the relevant rule. The House of Lords held that the payments to the taxpayer were reimbursements and therefore not taxable. Lord Pearson stated:

---

52. [1970] A.C. 728; [1969] 2 All E.R. 70. See also *Bird v. Martland* (1982) 56 T.C. 89: *Wicks v. Firth*, supra n.46
53. ITA, S.19(1)(a),(c)
54. (1919) 7 T.C. 176 (Court of Session, Scotland)
55. equivalent to ITA, Ss. 17 (1) (b), 19
56. [1970] A.C. 244; [1969] 2 All E.R. 1 (H.L.) distinguishing *Fergusson v. Noble* supra

> When the employee incurs an expense in performing the duties of his employment – e.g. making a journey from head office to branch office and back to head office, or buying stamps and stationery for the firm – and has it reimbursed to him. In such a transaction, there is no benefit – no profit or gain – to the employee. He does not receive any emolument.

(c) Benefits In Kind

Employment income under Section 17(1)(b) of ITA also includes "the value of any benefit granted.[57]

While the detailed provision for computation of benefits in kind for purposes of taxation is found in the ITA, Schedule V, the legal effect of such benefits is considered here briefly.

A payment in kind and a benefit received in a form other than money may be taxable but only if such benefit is "convertible" into cash. Hence the significance of the ITA, S.19(3), Schedule V.

(i) Convertibility of Benefits

In *Richardson v. Lyon*,[58] a company paid premiums on an endowment policy on the life of its manager to secure an annuity on his retirement. The policy belonged to the manager. It was held that the manager was properly assessed on the payments made by the employer to the insurance company. Similarly, in *Brown v. Bullock*,[59] subscriptions to a club paid by a bank on behalf of its manager were considered to be "remuneration." In *Richardson v. Worral*,[60] an employer provided his employee with credit card facilities to obtain petrol for private motoring and discharged the indebtedness produced by the employee's use of the card. It was held that this was a discharge of the employee's debt which represented money's worth to the employee and was, therefore, a taxable emolument.

In *Heaton v. Bell*,[61] Lord Morris observed thus:

> In my view his free use of a car was a perquisite which represented money's worth and was taxable...The right to use the car could be converted into money.

In *Abbott v. Philbin*,[62] the taxpayer A was secretary to a company. For a small consideration, he was offered an option to purchase shares in the company at the then market price of £3 8s 6d per share. About 18 months later he exercised the option, at which time the shares were worth £4 2s each. He was assessed on a sum equal to the difference. He contended that any benefit he had received had been conferred at the time he acquired the option and that any excess in value was not an emolument but represented an appreciation in the value of the property (i.e., the option) owned by him. His contention was upheld. It was

---

57. ITA, S.19 (1) (b)
58. [1943] 25 T.C. 497
59. [1961] 1 W.L.R. 1095 (C.A. (E))
60. [1985] S.T.C. 693
61. *supra* n.52 and text thereof for facts
62. [1961] A.C. 352; [1960] 2 All E.R. 763. See also *Tyrer v. Smart* [1979] 1 WLR 113

held that the benefit of the option contract was a perquisite which fell to be taxed only in the year in which it was granted. In delivering his judgment, Lord Radcliffe stated:

> ... this decision does impose a limitation upon the taxability of benefits in kind which are of a personal nature, in that it is not enough to say that they have a value to which there can be assigned a monetary equivalent. If they are by their nature incapable of being turned into money by the recipient, they are not taxable even though they are in the ordinary sense of the word of value to him.

In *Tyrer v. Smart*,[63] a company offered its shares to its employees at a preferential price. It was held that the difference between the price paid by the employee and their market value on the date when the employee's application for shares was accepted was a taxable emolument.

Finally, is a case on living accommodation. In *Vertigan v. Brady*,[64] Vertigan was employed as a nursery foreman. It was important that he should live near his work, but there was no suitable council accommodation, and he could not buy. His employer provided him with a rent-free bungalow three miles from the nursery. He was assessed to tax on the annual value of the bungalow under the Finance Act 1977, Section 33.[65] He argued that there should be no liability to tax either because the accommodation was necessary for the proper performance of his duties (S. 33 (4) (a)) or that it was customary for accommodation to be provided for his kind of employment (S. 33 (4) (b)). It was held that Vertigan's situation fell outside Section 33 (4) (a)) which was directed to a necessity based on the relationship between proper performance of duties and the dwelling house and not to a necessity based on personal exigence of the taxpayer and his ability to buy suitable accommodation.

(ii) Valuation of Benefits

The requirement that a benefit be monetised for taxation purposes inevitably gives rise to the issue of valuation of the benefit in question. In view of the valuation guideline contained in Schedule V of the ITA, the following cases are only of persuasive value.

In *Wilkins v. Rogerson,*[66] the company employing the taxpayer, Rogerson, wrote to him stating that it had decided to make a Christmas present of clothing suitable for wearing at the office to all male members of staff. He was instructed to obtain the garments of his own choice up to a total of £15 from a specified branch of a men's outfitter and to take the letter with him. The bill was to be sent directly to his employer, and no cash payment would be made to the taxpayer should he select clothes of a total value of less that £15. Burton's (the outfitter) had also received a copy of the letter. The Crown claimed that the £14 15s should be treated as part of the taxable income of the taxpayer for the taxpayer in question. It was held that Rogerson had acquired a suit from his employer on which value could be attached and was taxable.

Similarly in *Rendell v. Went*,[67] the appellant taxpayer was a full-time company director.

---

63. *Ibid*
64. (1988) S.T.C. 91 (Ch.D. (E))
65. now I.C.T.A. 1988, S 145 (a) and (b) (U.K.)
66. [1961] Ch.133; [1961] 1 All E.R. 358

While driving on company business, he struck and killed a pedestrian. He attempted to obtain legal advice himself, but the company's managing director countermanded the taxpayer's instructions and consulted the company's solicitors who advised that if convicted, the taxpayer might be imprisoned and that the company might be involved in liability. The absence of the taxpayer would have had a deleterious effect on the company's business. So the managing director instructed the company's solicitor to spare no reasonable expense in the taxpayer's defence. This was accepted by the taxpayer who was ultimately acquitted. The company paid £641 for his defence. The taxpayer was then assessed on the payment. He appealed arguing that although he had received a benefit, it was not worth £641 and that the sum should be apportioned between the company's benefit and his benefit. Lord Reid answered this contention thus:

> I could understand a case being made for apportionment if the expenditure had been made for two objects, only one of which was of benefit to the director. But here there was only one object – to prevent conviction of the appellant.

(d) Compensation for Termination of Contract of Employment

Employment income also includes compensation for termination of any contract of employment or services.[68] The compensation could be on or after the termination, whether or not such compensation was provided for in the contract of employment. In *Comptroller General of Inland Revenue v. Knight*,[69] Lord Wilberforce observed:

> Where a sum of money is paid under a contract of employment, it is taxable, even though it is received at or after the termination of the employment ... where a sum of money is paid as consideration for the abrogation of a contract of employment, or as damages for the breach of it, that sum is not taxable.

Unlike the complicated provision on compensation for termination of employment under the repealed law,[70] the ITA has simplified the position by providing for the taxation of 75 percent of the compensation paid.[71]

e) Premium for Life Insurance of Employee

Employment income also includes any amount paid by a tax-exempt employer as a premium for insurance on the life of the employee and that is for the benefit of the employee or any of his or her dependants.[72] The provision envisages that a premium paid by a taxpaying employer would not be regarded as part of the employee's income.[73] However, the taxpaying employer would not be allowed to deduct such payments from his income for purposes of taxation.[74] This means that the premium is taxed indirectly

67. [1964] 2 All E.R. 464. See also *Westcott v. Bryan* [1969] Ch. 324 Nock, R.S. "Company Houses" [1969] B.T.R. 253
68. ITA. S. 19 (1) (d), (4)
69. [1973] A.C. 428, 433. See also *Henry v. Foster* (1932) 16. T.C. 605; *Henley v. Murray* [1950] 1 All E.R. 908
70. Income Tax Decree, 1974 S.5(2)(c)
71. ITA, S.19(4)
72 *Ibid* s.19(1)(e) See also *Richardson v. Lyon, supra* n.58
73. *Ibid* s.19(2)(c)

in the hands of the employer.

f) Payments upon Variation of Agreement

The employment income includes any amount derived as consideration for the employee's agreement to any conditions of employment or to any changes in his or her conditions of employment.[75]

g) Issue of Shares at a Discount

The employment income of an employee includes the amount by which the value of shares issued to an employee under an employee share acquisition scheme at the date of the issue exceeds the consideration, if any, given by the employee for the shares including any amount given as consideration for the grant of a right or option to acquire the shares.[76]

h) Gain from Disposal of Right or Option to Acquire Shares

The employment income of an employee also includes the amount of any gain derived by an employee on the disposal of a right or option to acquire shares under an employee share acquisition scheme.[77]

i) Housing

The cost of housing provided by an employer to an employee is taxable.[78] However, where the employer provides accommodation or housing other than where Section 20(1)(a) or (c) applies (relating to the value of housing and reimbursement of expenses related to housing), the value of the benefit is computed to be the less of (1) the market rent of the accommodation or housing reduced by any payment made by the employee for the benefit, or (2) 15 percent of the employment income, including any payment made by the employee for the benefit for the relevant year of income in which the benefit is provided.[79]

3. Non-Taxable Benefits

For taxation purposes there are some benefits which are excluded from computation of taxable income.[80] These include expenditure by an employer on the passage to or from Uganda in respect of the employee's appointment or termination of employment.[81] However this is restricted to a situation in which the employee was recruited or engaged outside Uganda, is in Uganda solely for the purpose of serving the employer and is a non-Uganda citizen. Other benefits which are excluded from computation of income are: any reimbursement or discharge of the employee's medical expenses,[82] any amount paid

74. *Ibid* s.22(2)(j)
75. *Ibid* s.19 (1)(f). See also *Hamblett v. Godfrey supra* n.46 and Glantre *Engineering Ltd. v. Goodhand, supra* n.48
76. ITA, S.19(1)(g) (s) See also *Tyrer v. Smart supra* n.62 cf. *Abbott v. Philbin* [1961] A.C.352
77. *Ibid* s.19(1)(h). See also cases at note 76 *ibid*
78. *Ibid* s.19(1)(a)
79. *Ibid* Fifth Schedule Item 10
80. *Ibid.* s.19(2)
81. *Ibid* s.19(2)(a)

as a premium for the insurance of the life of the employee for the employee's benefit or any of his or her dependant,[83] and allowances given for costs actually incurred or likely to be incurred or reimbursement or discharge of expenditure incurred by the employee on accommodation and travel expenses or meals or refreshment while undertaking travel in the course of performing duties of employment.[84] Excluded income includes the value of any meal or refreshment provided by the employer to the employee in premises operated by or on behalf of the employer solely for the benefit of employees and which is available to all full-time employees on equal terms.[85] The other benefits which are excluded from computation of taxable income are: any benefit granted by the employer to the employee during a month which does not exceed in value shs 10,000/=[86] and any contribution or similar payment made to a retirement fund for the benefit of the employee or any of his or her dependants.[87]

The value of the excluded benefits is determined in accordance with the Fifth Schedule to ITA.[88]

4. Income from Use of Property

Income from use of property is also taxable.[89] Income in this context includes royalty, rent, premium, dividend, interest, annuity or similar consideration received for use or occupation of property.[90]

(a) Rent

In *Jeffries v. Stevens*,[91] the respondent and his wife conceived the idea of acquiring premises for the business of letting holiday accommodation. This was to be carried out through a company. However, the company did not have sufficient funds to buy the property in question and could not raise the amount of £60,000 through a loan. The couple therefore executed a legal charge to secure both that sum and other money which would, thereafter, be advanced by the Lombard Bank. The couple then charged by way of legal mortgage as beneficial owners, the property acquired. Furthermore, the couple took out a life insurance policy on the life of the husband to the tune of £45,000 with an insurance company. This was charged on the Lombard Bank by way of collateral security. The issue arose as to whether the payments by the company which was owned by the couple to the couple and from the insurance company to the couple were taxable under Schedule A of the British Income and Corporation Taxes Act, 1970 (equivalent to Section 5 of the ITA of Uganda). It was held that they were taxable since they were made to the husband as the owner of the property. Similarly, in *Dhanji Govind v. Commissioner of Income Tax*,[92] it was held that deposits under a lease were payments of advance rent and were

82 *Ibid* s.19(2)(b), which includes a premium or there amount paid for medical insurance
83. *Ibid* s.19(2)(c)
84. *Ibid.* s.19(2)(d)
85. *Ibid* s.19(2)(e)
86. *Ibid* s.19(2)(f)
87. *Ibid* s.19(2)(g)
88. *Ibid* s.19(3)
89. *Ibid* Ss.5, 17(1)(c); 20(1)(a)
90 ITA S.20(1)(a)
91 [1982] S.T.C. 639

taxable. Furthermore, in *Commissioner of Income Tax v. the S. Golf Club*,[93] it was held that the club was capable of occupying the land and that it was used for the purpose of residence or enjoyment and not for the purpose of gain or profit and, accordingly, that it was assessable on the net annual value of the land. Rental income is charged to tax separately from other income at a rate of 20 percent of gross value.[94]

(b) Premium

In *Banning v. Wright*,[95] a tenant sublet his premises in breach of covenant. The breach entitled the landlords to prevent the tenant from exercising an option to renew the lease. The tenant paid a sum of money to the landlords in consideration of the landlords' waiving of this right. The House of Lords (one law lord dissenting) held that the payment should be treated as a premium. In *B.R. Ltd v. Commissioner of Income Tax*,[96] a premium was paid by an oil company to a parent company which held majority shares in the appellant company. The parent company passed on the payment to the appellant. The issue arose as to whether the payment was a premium and therefore capital in the hands of the appellant and not liable to tax. It was held that as the premium was in fact paid to the appellant company, the appellant was liable to tax thereof since it was by way of prepayment of a discount and not a capital sum.

5. Dividends or Interest

Payments received as dividend or interest are taxable.[97] The ITA describes these as property income.[98]

With regard to interest, in *B.P. v. Commissioner of Income Tax*,[99] it was held that interest paid on compensation received by the appellant was additional payment and despite compensation per se being exempted from taxation, the interest thereon was taxable.

In *Re Euro Hotel (Belgravia) Ltd*,[100] Megarry J. explained the meaning of interest thus:

> ... as a general rule two requirements must be satisfied for a payment to amount to interest, and a fortiori to amount to 'interest of money.' First there must be a sum of money by reference to which the payment which is said to be interest is to be ascertained. A payment cannot be 'interest of money' unless there is the requisite 'money' for the payment to be said to be 'interest of' ... Second, those sums of money must be sums that are due to the person entitled to the alleged interest ...

92. 4 E.A.T.C. (Pt 1) 225; [1957] E.A. 153
93. 1 E.A.T.C. 193 (Case No. 19) (Kenya). See also *Sunni Muslim Jamat V. C.I.T.* 4 E.A.T.C. Pt 1 66
94. ITA, Ss.6(2), 22(1) (c), Schedule 3 Part VI
95. [1972] 2 All E.R. 987
96. 4 E.A.T.C. (Pt 1) 118 (Tanzania). See also Beattie, C.N. "Premiums or Leases" [1963] B.T.R. 243; Park, A.E.W. & Landau, D.A. "The Taxation of Leases" [1969] B.T.R. 265, 268; *A.L. et al.v. C.I.T.* 2 E.A.T.C. (Pt II), 148
97. ITA, S 20 (1)(a)
98. See *infra* Chapter 5
99. 4 E.A.T.C. (Pt I) 76 (Tanganyika)
100. [1975] 3 All E.R. 1075; [1975] S.T.C. 682. For statutory definition of interest, see ITA S.2.

Megarry J., however, explained that these requirements were not "exhaustive" or "inescapable." Consequently interest would be said to arise "if A lends money to B and stipulates that the interest should be paid not to him but to X." It follows that an objective test of what constitutes "interest" would be employed regardless of the language used by the parties to an instrument describing the payments to be interest.[101]

6. Pension Payments and Annuity

(a) Pension

While the repealed law previously taxed income from any pension,[102] this was superseded by the Constitution of 1995 which exempts "pension payable to any person ... from tax."[103] This overrides the ITD by virtue of Article 2 (2) of the Constitution which invalidates laws or customs which are inconsistent with the Constitution. The term pension has been strictly interpreted by reference to the Pensions Act[104] definition thereof, thereby excluding annual payments or gratuity.[105] This probably reflects concern by the International Monetary Fund that the constitutional provision has the effect of eroding the income tax base and consequently all deductions for contributions to pension schemes should be eliminated.[106]

(b) Annuity

In *IRC v. Church Commissioners of England*,[107] Stamp L.J. thus described annuity:

> The taxpayer parts with a capital sum which is then lost to, and invested by, the recipient. In return, the recipient agrees to pay the taxpayer a certain sum (annuity) for a given period, which may be the rest of the taxpayer's life or a predetermined period. The annuity is treated as wholly income when received by the annuitant.

It is in this light that the taxation of income from annuity[108] may be understood. It should be noted that although calculation of annuity may be based on the return of the capital sum with interest, no account of this is taken on the basis of general principles. In this regard Sir Wilfred Greene M.R. (as he then was) stated:

> If the law were that, in the ordinary case of annuity for a term of years, the nature of the financial calculation involved stamped part of the payment as a capital payment, leaving only the interest element to be taxed, on the ground that an annuity is taxable only in so far as it is profit, the position would be simple and perhaps not unjust ....

---

101. *Ibid.* See also *Lomax v. Peter Dixon & Sons Ltd* [1943] 1 K.B. 671; [1943] 2 All E.R. 255
102. ITD, S.3 (2) (c) and 8. Now see ITA, S.22(2)(k) which has implemented the IMF recommendation.
103. Article 254. See now ITA, S.22(1)(n) which exempts pension from tax.
104. Cap 281 Laws of Uganda (1964 Edn), S.2
105. Head, Legal Services, URA, to Commissioner, Internal Revenue: Internal Memo 1995. See also *A.B. v. Commissioner of Income Tax* 2 E.A.T.C. 70 Kenya
106. IMF, *Uganda: A Program for Reform of Income Tax: Aide Memoire* (July 1996), pp 3, 57-60. See now ITA, S.22(2) (k) which prevents deductions in respect of payments by employers of pension.
107. [1957] 3 All E.R. 614; See now ITA, S. 20 (1) (a).
108. ITA, S.20(1)(a)

However, I do not feel myself at liberty to adopt such principle...[109]

The position has been simplified in Britain by the Income and Corporations Taxes Act 1988, Section 656, and in Uganda by S.20(1) ITA, which allows an annuity to be divided into a capital and an income element, with only the latter being subject to income tax, as the following example shows: A pays Shs9,000,000 in return for an annuity of Shs900,000. At the time the first annuity payment becomes due, A's life expectancy is 12 years. The capital element of each annuity payment would be one-twelveth of 9,000,000/= which is Shs750,000/=. The income element of the annuity payment would be Shs900,000 -750,000/= Shs150,000=.

7. Alimony or Allowance under Judicial Order or Separation Agreement

The ITA exempts any amount derived by way of alimony or allowance under any judicial order or written agreement of separation from taxation.[110] While the payee of such alimony or allowance does not bear tax, the payer is not allowed to deduct such payment for the purpose of computing chargeable income.[111] Effectively, therefore, he or she bears the tax.

8. Income from Non-Resident Persons

A non-resident person [112] is only taxed on income derived from sources in Uganda.[113]

9. Allowable Deductions in Computing Chargeable Income

The Income Tax Act provides for deductions of any expenditures and losses which are incurred in generating or production of income in such year of income.[114] This enables determination of the total income chargeable to tax after making the deduction.

It has been observed[115] that if a holder of an office or employment is necessarily obliged to incur or defray the emoluments thereof or to expend money wholly, exclusively and necessarily in the performance of the duties of the office or employment, these monies may be deducted from the emoluments to determine the total income chargeable.

A detailed discussion of the specific deductions which may be made in the context of a business is undertaken later in this text.[116] However a few examples may be given here which impinge purely on individual taxation.

In *Commissioner of Income Tax v. D*,[117] the respondent, a surveyor, suffered from arthritis and so as to enable him to carry on his profession he visited South Africa for specialist medical treatment in 1941, 1943 and 1944.

In his income tax assessments for those years, he was granted neither deduction of

109. *Southern Smith v. Clancy* [1941] 1 K.B. 276. See Section S. 21 (1) ITD, 1974, which exempts the capital element of the annuity from taxation.
110. ITA, S.21(1)(h)
111. ITA, S.22(2)(l)
112 See *ibid* s.14 read together with S.9
113. *Ibid* Ss.18(2)(b), 80. For detailed discussion, see chapter 7 *infra* dealing with ITA, Part IX, Ss 78-79.
114. ITA, S.22(1)
115. Easson, *Cases and Materials on Revenue Law* (Sweet & Maxwell, 2nd ed. 1990) p. 180
116. See *infra* Chapter 4

his medical treatment expenses in South Africa nor the expenses of travelling to South Africa for such treatment. He appealed to the local committee on the ground that those expenses were incurred in the production of his income. The local committee varied the assessments and ordered the expenses to be deducted. The Commissioner of Income Tax appealed to the High Court. It was held that such expenses were not wholly and exclusively incurred in the production of income and were domestic or private expenses.

This approach is within Section 22(2) of the Income Tax Act which specifically disallows deductions of the following:

- expenditure incurred in the maintenance of the taxpayer, his family or home or for any other personal domestic purpose;[118]
- any income tax or tax of a similar nature paid on income;[119]
- expenditure or loss recoverable under an insurance or indemnity contract;[120]
- any expenditure or loss which is not wholly and exclusively incurred by him in the production of the income.[121]

In *Commissioner of Income Tax v. J.,*[122] it was held that the respondent, who was separated from his wife permanently, was not entitled to deduct from his total income the amount paid to his wife. In *Commissioner of Income Tax v. B.V.*,[123] it was held that the amount paid by the respondent to buy a farm including the growing crop of trees was not a revenue expenditure and therefore not deductible in computing his tax liability. Furthermore, in *Kenya Meat Commission v. Commissioner of Income Tax*,[124] a sum of Shs200,000 paid by the Commission to the Kenya National Fund to be used for research on the beef and mutton industry was held to be an expenditure by the Commission "wholly and exclusively" for the production of its income and therefore deductible from its chargeable income for the year. In *Withers Payne v. Commissioner of Income Tax*,[125] it was held that the amount of development levy deducted by an employer under the Development Levy Act of Tanzania, which was a form of tax, was not deductible by the employee from his salary for income tax purposes.

C. Computation of Tax Payment

1. Individual Rates

The rates of income tax for an individual are as follows:[126]

117. 1 E.A.T.C. 27 (Uganda). See also I V. C.I.T. 1 E.A.T.C. 75 (Tanganyika); *Income Tax v. M. Ltd* [1972] EA 509 (Kenya)
118. ITA S.22 (2) (a)(3)
119. ITA. S.22 (2) (d)
120. ITA S.22 (2)(c)
121. *Ibid.* ITA S.22 (1)See also *Elderkin v. Hindmarsh* [1988] S.T.C. 267
122. 1 E.A.T.C. 80 (Kenya). See also ITA S.22 (2)(l)
123. 4 E.A.T.C. (Pt I) 220 (Kenya)
124. 4 E.A.T.C. (Pt II) 199 (Kenya)
125. [1969] E.A. 464 (C.A. (T)). See also ITA, S.22 (2)(d)

Total Income or Resident Individual	Rate
a) Did not exceed Shs1,560,000/= per annum	0
b) Exceeded Shs1,560,000/= but did not exceed Shs2,820,000/=	10% of the amount exceeding Shs1,560,000/=
c) Exceeded Shs2,820,000/= but did not exceed Shs4,920,000/=	Shs126,000/= + 20% of the amount of income exceeding Shs2,820,000/=
d) Exceeded Ug.shs.4,920,000/=	Shs546,000/= + 30% of the amount by which total income exceeded Shs4,920,000/=

Total Income of Non-Resident Individual	Rate
a) Did not exceed Shs2,820,000/=	10%
b) Exceeded Shs2,820,000/= but did not exceed Shs4,920,000/=	Shs282,000/= + 20% of the amount by which the chargeable income exceeded Shs2,820,000/=
c) Exceeded Shs4,920,000/=	Shs702,000/= + 30% of the amount by which chargeable income exceeds Shs4,920,000/=

The rental income tax which is diaggregated from other income tax was set at 20 percent of 80 percent of the gross rental income per annum in excess of Shs1,560,000/=. (See ITA, ss.5, 6(2), 22 (1)(c)Schedule 3 part VI.)

The threshold was regarded[127] as too high by international standards. While Shs1,560,000/= was 5.5 times per capita GDP, the tax threshold for single individuals was 2.7 times per capita GDP in Kenya, 1.9 times per capita GDP in Zambia, 1.7 times per capita GDP in Malawi and only 0.8 times per capita GDP in Tanzania. The IMF has

126. ITA, S.6 (1) and Schedule 3 part I.

observed[128] that the high threshold, when coupled with generous exemption of employee benefits, accounts for the very low productivity of the individual income tax in Uganda. It, therefore, recommended the lowering of the threshold by 25 percent which would boost income tax receipts by at least 65 percent or alternatively retain the threshold for about four years, or until the real value of the tax threshold had been reduced by 25 percent.

The debate on the threshold both by the public and members of Parliament is ongoing.

D. Residence Rules Applicable to Individuals

The general scheme of the income tax system is to tax all income which belongs to a resident or is sourced in Uganda.[129] The term 'resident' when applied to an individual means that (1) he has a permanent home in Uganda and was present in Uganda for any period in any particular year of income under consideration, or (2) that he has no permanent home in Uganda but (a) was present in Uganda for a period(s) of an aggregate of 183 days or more in such year of income or (b) was present in such year of income and in each of the two preceding years of income for periods averaging more than 122 days in each of such year of income.[130]

Furthermore, it is provided that as long as an individual is a resident person at the time of the employment or when services were rendered, he is liable to income tax irrespective of whether such services were rendered by him or he was employed in Uganda.[131]

In *Commissioner of Income Tax v. Noorani*,[132] the respondent was assessed for income tax for the years 1962, 1963, 1964 and 1965 as a non-resident of East Africa. The respondent was born in Mombasa, Kenya. After his education abroad, he was employed and had various businesses and lived in Tanga, Tanzania, from 1932 to 1960, when he went to Europe where he bought a house in England in 1960. In 1962 he returned to East Africa on 22 December, 1962, and stayed until 14 February, 1963, when he returned to England. He returned to East Africa on 20 September, 1964, and stayed until 12 November, 1964, when again he returned to England. He came back to East Africa on 22 May, 1965, returning to England on 9 July, 1965. He also spent periods in East Africa in the years 1966 and 1967 finally returning to reside in Mombasa on 6 January, 1968. He sold his house in England. While in England, the respondent kept various properties he owned in Tanga and Mombasa, kept his investments in Tanzania and also maintained a bank account.

On appeal to the Local Committee, the Committee held that the respondent was a resident in East Africa for purposes of Section 2 of the East African Income Tax (Management) Act, 1958.[133] On further appeal, the High Court of Tanzania upheld the

---

127. IMF, *Program for Reform of Income Tax and Taxation of Mineral Resources* (1996)
128. *Ibid*
129. ITA, Ss.4, 17(2)
130. *Ibid.* Ss.9, 14
131. *Ibid* S.17 (2)(a)
132. [1969] E.A. 685 C.A. (Tanzania)

decision of the Local Committee. The Commissioner of Income Tax further appealed to the Court of Appeal, which also upheld the decision of the Local Committee.

In the course of its judgment, the Court of Appeal held that a home for purposes of the legislation was a dwelling house which for at least a portion of the year was available to the taxpayer and which was kept for the purpose of his use as a dwelling and that the home did not have to be occupied during every year for the taxpayer to have a home in the territories (country). The Court further held that a person may have two or more homes at the same time.

In *Sir George Arnautoglu v. Commissioner of Income Tax,*[134] the issues arose as to whether it was permissible, for purposes of determining residence, to aggregate periods of residence with periods of mere presence and whether "averaging" (in Section 9 ITA) meant in effect that four months' presence was required for each of the relevant years. It was held that for purposes of the East African Income Tax (Management) Act, 1958, Section 2 (1),[135] aggregating periods of residence and of presence in the territories and was permissible and that the period to be averaged was the total number of days spent in the territories over the relevant years.

133. Equivalent to ITA, S.9
134. [1967] E.A. 312 C.A. (Tanzania)
135. equivalent to ITA, S.9

4

Business Taxation

1. Introduction

The taxation of business is governed by the Income Tax Act[1] which also regulates the taxation of business entities such as companies[2] and partnerships.[3] Separate chapters will consider in more detail the taxation of corporations and related aspects and partnerships.[4] The concern of this chapter is, therefore, the taxation of business *perse.*

"Business" is defined as including "any trade, profession, vocation, or adventure in the nature of trade but does not include employment."[5] This is in line with the observation that "business" has a more extensive meaning than the word "trade."[6] In *Ransom v. Higgs,*[7] Lord Wilberforce defined "trade" thus:

> trade involves normally the exchange of goods or services, for reward not all services, since some qualify as a profession or employment or vocation, but there must be something which the trade offers by way of business...[8]

In *Smith v. Anderson,*[9] Jessel M.R. observed that "anything which occupies the time and attention and labour of a man, for purposes of profit, is business..."

It is thus evident that not every business will constitute a trade. The definition of "business" in the Partnership Act includes "every trade, occupation or profession."[10] Furthermore, in *Customs & Excise Commissioners v. British Railways Board*, the operation of a pension fund for the benefit of its employees was held to be part of the "business carried on by" the British Railways Board, even though its Statutory duty was to provide railways services.[11]

As has already been observed,[12] *Smith v. Anderson,*[13] proposed that the expression "carrying on business" implies A a repetition of acts and excludes in the case of an association for doing one particular act which is never to be repeated. That series of acts is to be a series of acts which constitutes a business." While this approach may be useful

1. Cap. 340 (hereinafter referred to as ITA)
2. ITA, ss 74-77
3. *Ibid,* ss.65-9
4. See *infra* chapters 5 and 6.
5. ITA, S.2
6. *Harris v. Amery* L.R.C.I.P.148 per Willes J.
7. [1974] 3 All E.R.94
8. For an explanation of "profession" and "vocation" see *supra*, chap.3
9. (1880) 15 Ch.D. 247 at p.258
10. Cap 114 *Laws of Uganda* (2000 ed.).s.2 See further Bakibinga, *Partnership Law in Uganda* (1992) p.9
11. [1976] 1 WLR 1036
12. *Supra* chapter 3
13. *Supra* n.9

in distinguishing between a trading and a capital transaction, it has been held that the expression "every trade, occupation or profession" (in Section 2 of the Partnership Act, Cap 114) can cover a single venture.[14]

2. Charge to Tax in Respect of a Business

A. Charge

Section 4(1) of the Income Tax Act Cap 340 charges income tax for each year of income on every person who has chargeable income. Chargeable income is the gross income of the person for the year less total deductions allowed under the Act for the year.[15] Gross income includes inter alia business income.[16]

A "person" includes "an individual, a partnership, a trust, a company, a retirement fund, a government, a political subdivision of a government, and a listed institution under the First Schedule to the Act."[17]

"Business income" refers[18] to any income derived by a person in carrying on a business and includes the following whether of a revenue or capital nature:

- The amount of any gain as determined by part VI of the Act which deals with gains and losses on disposal of assets, derived by a person on the disposal of a business asset or on the satisfaction or cancellation of a business debt whether or not the asset or debt was on revenue or capital account;[19]
- Any amount derived by a person as consideration for accepting a restriction on the person's capacity to carry on business; [20]
- The gross proceeds derived by a person from the disposal of trading stock;[21]
- Any amount included in the business income of the person under any other provision of the Act;[22]
- The value of any gifts derived by a person in the course of, or by virtue of a past, present or prospective business relationship;[23]
- Interest derived by a person in respect of trade receivables or by a person engaged in the business of banking or money lending;[24] and
- rent derived by a person whose business is wholly or mainly the holding or letting of property.[25]

14. *Re Abbenheim* (1913) 109 L.T.219. See also *Ojemen v. Okoafuda* 1977 Nig.C.L.R.192 per Uwafo J. For a case on the distinction between a trade and a capital transaction, see *Commissioner of Income Tax v. Sydney Tate* [1963] E.A.671 c.f. *Z Co. v. C.I.T.* 2 E.A.T.C.57.
15. ITA, s.15
16. *Ibid* s.17(1)(a)
17. *Ibid* s.2
18. *Ibid* s.18. Emphasis added
19. *Ibid* s.18(1)(a)
20. *Ibid* s.18(1)(b)
21. *Ibid* s. 18(1) (c)
22. *Ibid* s.18(1)(d)
23. *Ibid* s. 18(1)(e)
24. *Ibid* s.18(1)(f)
25. *Ibid* s.18(1)(g)

Furthermore, if as a result of any concession granted by, or a compromise made with, a taxpayer's creditors in the course of insolvency, the taxpayer derives again on the cancellation of a business debt, the assessed loss under Section 39 shall be reduced by such gain or benefit.[26]

B. Chargeable Income

i) General

As already mentioned, "chargeable income" refers to gross income of the person for the year less total deductions allowed under the Act for the year.[27] While this definition imports the notion of statutory deduction in order to arrive at taxable income, in business terms what is taxable are the profits of the business. Indeed the old law referred to "gains or profits" as the taxable income.[28] It is, therefore, appropriate to examine briefly what constitutes profits."

"Profits" have been judicially defined as "the difference between the price received on a sale and the cost price of what is sold."[29] Similarly, in *Gresham Life Assurance Society v. Style*,[30] Lord Hillsborough L.C. stated:

> ...profits and gains must be ascertained by ordinary principles of commercial trading, and I cannot think that the framers of the Act could be guilty of such confusion of thought as to assume that the cost of the article sold to the trader which he in turn makes his profit by selling was not to be taken into account before you arrived at what was intended to be taxable profit...

It is thus evident that profits or gains or chargeable income are computed by determining the "balance," or difference between business receipts on the one hand and certain expenditures on the other.

However, not all receipts are gains or profits for income tax purposes. Thus in *Murray v. Goodhews*,[31] a taxpayer received ex gratia payments from a brewery company following the termination by the brewery of various tenancy agreements. It was held that the payments were not trading receipts. This decision is obviously no longer good law in Uganda in view of Section 18(1)(e) of the Income Tax Act, which taxes "the value of any gifts derived by a person in the course of or by virtue of a past, present, or prospective business relationship." Furthermore, in strict income tax terms, since income tax is chargeable on income, receipts of a capital nature do not enter into the computation of profits.[32] This principle has been modified by Section 18(1)(a) of the Income Tax Act which taxes gains "derived by a person on the disposal of a business asset or on the satisfaction or cancellation of business debt, whether or not the asset or debt was on

26. *Ibid* s.18(3) read together with s.38(3)
27. *Ibid* s.15
28. Income Tax Decree No.1 of 1974, s.3(2) repealed by ITA, s.166
29. *Erichsen v. Last* (1881) 8Q.B.D.414 per Sir George Jessel, M.R.
30. [1892] A.C.309
31. [1978] 1W.L.R.499
32. *IRC v. British Salmson Aero Engines Ltd* [1938] 2 K.B.482, *Commissioner of Income Tax. Sydney Tate, supra* n.14; *Y Co. v. I.T.* 2E.A.T.C.50

revenue or capital account." Section 18(1)(a) of the ITA effectively imposes a capital gains tax on the disposal of business assets.

The general principle, however, remains that income arising from trading or business transactions is taxable.[33] In *Commissioner of Income Tax v. The L. Association,*[34] it was held that all profits going to the unincorporated association from its agency services were taxable. Furthermore, for surpluses arising from mutual transactions to escape taxation, there must be a complete identity between the contributors and participators. In *R. v. Commissioner of Income Tax,*[35] the appellant was a hotelier who was involved in various transactions involving the purchase and sale of a restaurant, photography, transport safari tours, detergents and oil business, whereby he realised a profit in some and loss in a few. He was assessed income tax on the profits of the transactions as a whole after taking into account any loss incurred on an individual transaction. He appealed on the grounds that the profits were not made in the course of a trade or business but were capital gains resulting from an appreciation of investments. It was held that while each transaction considered separately did not constitute a trade or business the transactions, considered as a whole, formed part of a general scheme of profit making and constituted a trade or business and the profits therefore were revenue and not capital receipts.

ii) Disposal of a Business Asset

General

Until the promulgation of the Income Tax Act, capital gains were not taxable. The previous law concentrated on the taxation of income of a revenue nature.

The Income Tax Act now charges tax on "the amount of any gain... derived by a person on the disposal of a business asset or on the satisfaction or cancellation of business debt, whether or not the asset or debt was on revenue or capital account."3 "Business asset," is defined as "an asset which is used or held ready for use in a business and includes any asset held for sale in a business and any asset of a partnership or company."[36] However, it is clarified that a "business asset," does not include trading stock or depreciable asset (machinery).[37]

The rationale for the taxation of capital gains is that since sales of capital confer the same economic power as gains from employment or operation of a business, equity dictates that both gains be taxed in exactly the same way.[38]

The definition of "business asset" has not been judicially considered in Uganda. However, it would arguably include payment for a release from an agreement made by a director to a company. Thus in *O'Brien v. Benson's Hosiery (Holdings) Ltd,*[39] the

---

33. *H. Co v. Commissioner of Income Tax* 1 E.A.T.C.65, *N.v.C.I.T.,* 1E.A.T.C.118, *O et al v.C.I.T.* 1E.A.T.C.124, *A.G.et al V.C.I.T* 2E.A.T.C.113; *C.I.T.v. A.M.Ltd* 2E.AT.C.164
34. 1E.A.T.C.107
35. E.A.T.C.172. See also *A.C.v.C.I.T.* 2E.A.T.C76; The Trustees of A.D. *Charitable Business Trust v. C.I.T.* 2E.A.T.C.89. *The A.E. Investment & Trust Ltd v. C.I.T.* 2E.A.T.C.99 discussed *supra* chap. 2
36. ITA, s.2
37. *Ibid* s.18(4)
38. *Report of the Royal Commission on Taxation* (Carter Commission, Canada) (1966); *Budget Speech: Chancellor of the Exchequer, Mr. James Callaghan,* April 6, 1965, Hansard H.C. Debates Vol. 710, Col 245
39. [1980] A.C.562, [1979] 3 All E.R.65 2

taxpayer company received GBP50,000 from one of its directors in furtherance of an agreement to release that director from obligations under his service contract with the company. The taxpayer company was assessed tax on the basis that its rights under the service contract were assets and that the release of those rights in return for the capital sum was a disposal of assets. It was held that the rights released by the company were assets and that the capital sum received by the company in return for their release was chargeable to tax.

Gains and Losses on Disposal of Assets

It is provided that the amount of any gain arising from the disposal of an asset is the excess of the consideration received for the disposal over the cost base of the asset at the time of disposal.[40] Conversely the loss arising from the disposal of an asset is the excess of the cost base of the asset at the time of disposal over the consideration received for the disposal.[41]

Valuation

The rules for determining the cost base of an asset are as follows:[42]

- With regard to an asset purchased, produced or constructed by the taxpayer the cost base is the amount paid or incurred by the taxpayer in respect of the asset. This includes incidental expenditures of a capital nature incurred in acquiring the asset and the market value of any consideration in kind given for the asset.[43] Alternatively, the cost base is the amount of consideration deemed to have been received by the disposer following purchase or production.[44]
- Concerning an asset acquired in a non-arms length transaction, the cost base is the market value of the asset at the date of acquisition.[45]
- In the event of disposal of part of an asset, the cost base thereof is apportioned between the part retained and the part disposed of using the market values at the time of acquisition of the asset.[46]
- Except as provided in the Act, expenditures incurred to alter or improve the asset which have not been allowed as a deduction are added to the cost[47] base of the asset.[48]
- If the acquisition of the asset by the taxpayer represents the derivation of an amount included in gross income, the cost base of the asset is the amount included in the gross income plus any amount paid by the taxpayer for the asset.[49]

40. ITA, s.50 (1)
41. *Ibid* s.50(2)
42. *Ibid* s.52
43. *Ibid* s.52(2)
44. *Ibid* s.52(4)
45. *Ibid* s. 52(5)
46. *Ibid* s.52(5)
47 *Ibid* s.52(6)
48. *Ibid* s.52(6)
49. *Ibid* s.52(7)

- Finally, where the receipt of an asset represents the derivation of an amount which is exempt from tax, the cost base thereof is the amount exempt from tax plus any amount paid by the taxpayer for the asset.[50]

It is further provided that consideration received on disposal of an asset includes the market value of any consideration received in kind.[51] Section 53(2) deals with a situation in which an asset is disposed of to an associate or in a non-arm's length transaction (other than by way of transmission of an asset to a trustee or beneficiary following the death of the taxpayer). In such a case, the disposer is treated as having received consideration equal to the greater of (1) the cost base of the asset to the disposer at the time of disposal or (2) the fair market value of the asset at the time of disposal.

In the event of disposal of two or more assets in a single transaction and unspecified consideration for each, the total consideration received is apportioned among the assets disposed of in proportion to their respective market value at the time of the transaction.[52]

Nature of Disposal

The Income Tax Act clarifies what amounts to a "disposal." This includes[53] situations in which an asset is sold, exchanged, redeemed or distributed by the taxpayer; transferred by the taxpayer by way of gift; or destroyed or lost. Disposal also includes partial disposal of an asset.[54] Furthermore, when the Commissioner is satisfied that a taxpayer has converted an asset from a taxable to a non-taxable use or has converted it from a non-taxable to a taxable use, the taxpayer is deemed to have disposed of the asset at the time of conversion for an amount equal to the market value thereof at the time and to have immediately acquired it for a cost base equal to the same value.[55] For this purpose a "taxable asset" refers to an asset the disposal of which would give rise to a gain included in the gross income of, or a loss allowed as a deduction to, a resident or non-resident taxpayer.[56]

It is further provided that a non-resident person who becomes a resident is deemed to have acquired all assets, other than taxable assets, owned by the person at the time of becoming a resident at their market value at that time.[57] This is presumably to allow them to be subject to the capital gains tax under section 18(1)(a) of ITA when disposed of. Conversely a resident person who becomes a non-resident person is deemed to have disposed of all assets, other than taxable assets, owned by the person at the time of becoming a non-resident for their market value at that time.[58] However, in case of the person who intends, in future, to reacquire status as a resident person and provides the Commissioner with sufficient security for any tax liability which would otherwise arise,

50. *Ibid* s.52(8)
51. *Ibid* s.53(1)
52. *Ibid* s.53(3)
53. *Ibid* s.51(1)
54. *Ibid* s.51(2)
55. *Ibid* s.51(3)
56. *Ibid* s.51(7)
57. *Ibid* s.51(4)
58. *Ibid* s.51(5)

the Commissioner may by notice in writing exempt the person from the application of subsection 51(5).[59]

Exemptions

It is provided that no gain or loss is considered in determining chargeable income in relation to:

- a transfer of an asset between spouses,
- a transfer of an asset between former spouses as part of a divorce settlement or bonafide separation agreement,
- an involuntary disposal of an asset to the extent to which the proceeds are re-invested in an asset of a like kind within one year of disposal, or
- the transmission of an asset to a trustee or beneficiary on the death to the taxpayer.[60]

This effectively provides an exemption from capital gains tax in respect of the transactions enumerated above. In those situations a transferee, trustee or beneficiary is deemed to have acquired the assets for a consideration equal to the cost base thereof to the transferor or deceased taxpayer at the time of disposal.[61] The effect of this is that if the transferee, trustee or beneficiary thereafter disposes of them, they would be subject to capital gains tax if they fall within Section 18(1)(a) of ITA.[60]

Finally, with respect to section 54(2)(c) relating to involuntary disposal of an asset whose proceeds are reinvested, it is provided that the cost base of the replacement asset is the cost base of the replaced asset plus the amount by which any consideration given by the taxpayer for the replaced asset exceeds the amount of proceeds received on the involuntary disposal.[62]

It should be stressed that the capital gains tax regime introduced by ITA is limited to the disposal of a business asset. This contrasts with the position in other jurisdictions where the capital gains tax regime is all embracing and covers capital sums received by way of compensation for damage or injury to assets, dissipation, depreciation or risk of depreciation thereof, under an insurance policy of risk of damage or injury to or the loss or depreciation of the assets; in return for forfeiture or surrender of rights or for refraining from exercising rights, as consideration for use or exploitation of assets.[63]

iii) Rent

Rent derived by a person whose business is wholly or mainly the holding or letting of property forms part of business income[64] and is assessable to tax under section 6(2) of ITA at a rate of 20 percent of the amount thereof in excess of the threshold of shs 1,560,000 per annum.[65]

59. *Ibid* s.51(6)
60. *Ibid* s.54(1)
61. *Ibid* s.54(2)
62. *Ibid* s.54(3)
63. Capital Gains Tax Act, 1979 (UK) ss.20(1), 21. See also *Marren v. Ingles* [1980]1 W.L.R.983; [1980] 3 All E.R.95; *Zim Properties Ltd. v. Proctor* [1985] S.T.C.90
64. ITA, s.18(1)(g)
65. *Ibid* Third Schedule, Part VI. The tax is effectively 16 percent since there is an allowable deduction of 20 percent (S.22(1)(c).

iv) Insurance

Resident Person

The chargeable income of a person for the relevant year of income arising from the carrying on of a short-term insurance business is determined by the formula A - B.[66] A represents the total income derived by a resident person for the year of income. This includes:

- amount of gross premiums, including premiums on reinsurance derived by the person during the year of income in carrying on such business in respect of insurance of any risk, other than premiums returned to the insured;
- amount of any other income derived by the person during that year in carrying on such business, including any commission or expense allowance derived from reinsurers, any income derived from investments held in connection with such business and any gains derived from the disposal of assets of the business; and
- the amount of any reserve deducted in the previous year of income at a percentage determined by the company in respect of unexpired risks referable to such a business.

B represents the total deductions allowed for the year of income in the production of income referred to in A. These include:

- the amount of claims admitted during the year of income in the carrying out of short-term insurance less any amount recovered or recoverable under any contract of re-insurance, guarantee, security or indemnity,
- the amount of agency expenses incurred during the year of income in the carrying on of such a business,
- the amount of expenditures and losses incurred by the person during the year of income in carrying on that business which are allowable as a deduction under the ITA other than expenditure or losses relating to claims and agency expenses above, and
- the amount of reserve for expired risks referable to such a business at a percentage adopted by the company at the end of the year of income.

Where a loss results from the application of the formula A - B above, that is where the deductions (B) exceed total income (A), such loss is not deducted from any other income of the person but is carried forward and deducted from the chargeable income resulting from carrying on insurance in the next year.[67]

Non-Resident Person

The chargeable income of a non-resident person for a year of income arising from carrying on of a short-term insurance business in Uganda is determined by the formula A-B.[68]

A refers to the total income derived by the person for the relevant year of income in carrying on such insurance business.

66. *Ibid* s.16(1) read together with Fourth Schedule
67. *Ibid* Fourth Schedule para 4
68. *Ibid* paragraphs 5-8

This includes:

- the amount of gross premium, including those on reinsurance received by the person during the year in respect of such business in respect of insurance of any risk in Uganda, other than premiums returned to the insured;
- amount of any other income derived from such business including any commission or expense allowance derived from reinsurance of risks accepted in Uganda, any income received from investment reserves referable to such business carried on in Uganda and any gains derived on disposal of assets of the business; and
- the amount of any reserve deducted in the previous year of income.

B represents the total deductions allowed for the year of income in the production of income referred to in A and includes the same items as those included for a resident person.[69]

Any loss is carried forward to the following year in the way indicated for a resident person.[70]

While the taxation of insurance business is considered here, it should be noted that such business is normally conducted under the framework of limited liability companies incorporated under the Companies Act.[71]

v) Presumptive Taxation of Business

The Income Tax Act, 1997, has introduced presumptive taxation in respect of a business whose gross turnover for the relevant year of income is less than Shs50,000,000 (fifty million shillings).[72] The rates of tax imposed are laid down in the Second Schedule to the Act and vary presently between Shs100,000/= and Shs450,000/= on a sliding scale covering gross turnover of between less than Shs20 million and Shs40 to 50 million per annum.

Presumptive taxation which is aimed at tapping revenue from the informal sector does not apply to business providing medical, dental, architectural, engineering, accounting, legal or other professional services, public entertainment services, public utility services or construction services.[73] The taxpayers to whom presumptive taxation applies have the option of electing, by notice in writing to the Commissioner, to be assessed normally.[74]

Where presumptive taxation applies, the tax imposed is a final tax on the business income of the taxpayer. However, no deductions in respect of expenditures or losses incurred in the production of the business income are allowed. Additionally no tax credits allowable under the ITA should be used to reduce the tax payable on the business income of the taxpayers except in relation to credit for withholding tax paid in respect of sums included in the gross turnover of the taxpayer or credit allowed for provisional tax paid in respect of sums included in the gross turnover of the taxpayer.[75]

---

69. *Ibid* para 7
70. *Ibid* para 8. See also note 66 and text thereof
71. Cap. 110 *Laws of Uganda* (2000 Edn)
72. ITA, s.5(5)
73. *Ibid* s.4(7)
74. *Ibid* s.4(5)
75. *Ibid* read together with Second Schedule and ss 111(8) and 128(3)

3. Computation of chargeable income

As already indicated, the chargeable income of a person for a year of income is the gross income of the person for the year less deductions allowed under the ITA for the year.[76] It is submitted that such deductions include exempt income under the ITA.

A. Exempt Income

The income specified in Section 21 of the Income Tax Act, Cap 340, is exempted from income tax to the extent therein indicated. This includes: the income of any organisation or person entitled to privileges under the Diplomatic Privileges Act to the extent provided in the regulations and orders made under that Act,[77] the official employment income of a person in the public service of the government of a foreign country. This is subject to the person being a non-resident or resident by virtue of performing such service and to the income being payable from the public funds of that country and being subject to tax in that country.[78]

Other exempt income are: the income of a listed institution mentioned in the First Schedule to the Act,[79] any allowance payable outside Uganda to a person working in a Uganda foreign mission,[80] the income of a local authority,[81] the income of an exempt organisation other than property income which is not used exclusively for the activities of the organisation specified in Section 2 of ITA, and business income not related to the function constituting the basis for the organisation's existence.[82] Yet other exempt income are any education grant which the Commissioner is satisfied has been made bonafide to enable or assist the recipient to study at a recognised educational or research institution;[83] any alimony or allowance received under any judicial order or written agreement of separation;[84] interest payable on treasury bills or Bank of Uganda bills;[85] the value of any property acquired by gift, bequest, devise, or inheritance that is not included in business, employment or property income;[86] capital gain that is not included in business income;[87] employment income derived by an individual to the extent provided for in a technical assistance agreement where the individual is a non-resident or a resident solely for the purpose of performing duties under the agreement and the Minister of Finance has agreed in writing with the tax provisions in the agreement;[88] any foreign source of income derived by a short-term resident of Uganda;[89] and any pension.[90]

---

76. *Ibid* S.15
77. *Ibid* s.21(1)(b)
78. *Ibid* s.21(1)(c)
79. *Ibid* s.21(1)(a)
80. *Ibid* s.21(1)(d)
81. *Ibid* s.21(1)(e)
82. *Ibid* s.21(1)(f)
83. *Ibid* s.21(1)(g)
84. *Ibid* s.21(1)(h)
85 *Ibid* s.21(1)(i)
86. *Ibid* s.21(1)(j)
87. *Ibid* s.21(1)(k)
88. *Ibid* s.21(1)(l)
89. *Ibid* s.21(1)(m)
90. *Ibid* s.21(1)(n)

Additionally, the following are exempt income: a lump sum payment made by a resident retirement fund to a member of the fund or a dependant of a member of the fund;[91] proceeds of a life insurance policy paid by a person carrying on a life insurance business;[92] and the official employment income of a person employed in the Armed Forces, Uganda Police Force, or the Uganda Prisons Service, other than a person employed in a civil capacity.[93]

B. Deductible Expenditure

1. General Rule

In order to determine the chargeable income of a person for business purposes for a particular year of income certain deductions are allowed. These are:

- all expenditures and losses, incurred by the person during the year of income in the production of income included in the gross income;
- any loss arising on disposal of business assets whether or not the asset was on revenue or capital account; and
- in the case of rental income, 20 percent of the rental income as expenditures and losses incurred by the individual in the production of such income.[94]

It is significant that the ITA had discarded the formula under the Income Tax Decree 1974 that only expenditure which was "wholly and exclusively"[95] incurred in the production of income was deductible. That expression had generated judicial debate as to its scope with the extreme position being reached that an admission of a dual purpose for incurring an expenditure would defeat a claim for the expense to be deductible.[96] With the new provision under the Income Tax Act which simply talks of "expenditures or losses ... incurred in the production of income..." it is hoped that such complications have been removed.[97]

It is nevertheless clear from Section 22(1) of the ITA that the deductible expenditure or loss must be incurred in the production of income. Thus in *Herrods (Buenos Aires) Ltd. v. Taylor Gorby,*[98] a company resident in the United Kingdom carried on business in Argentina and was liable to pay a tax there based on the share capital of the company in order to be entitled to carry on the business there. It was held that the tax was incurred to enable the company to trade and was deductible. Similarly, in *Bentley, Stokes & Lowless*

91. *Ibid* s.21(1)(p)
92 *Ibid* s.21(1)(o)
93. *Ibid* s.21(1)(q)
94. *Ibid* s.22(1)
95. Income Tax Decree, 1974,s.14(1)
96. *Bowden v. Russell* [1965] 1W.L.R.711; *Murgatroyd v. Evans Jackson* [1967] 1W.L.R.423; *Mallalieu v. Drummond* [1983] 2All E.R.1095 H.L.
97. For cases dealing with the "wholly an exclusively incurred" formula see inter alia *Strong & Co. of Romsely Ltd. v. Whitfield* [1906] A.C.448; [1906-1907]. All E.R. Rep. 953; *Mackinlay v. Arthur Young McClalland Moores & Co.* [1988]2 All E.R.I.; *Bentleys Stokes & Lowless v. Beeson* [1952] 2All E.R.82; *Commissioner of Income Tax v. D.* 1E.A.T.C.27(Uganda); *Income Tax v. Kotecha Estates* [1971] E.A.63H.C.(Uganda) *B.M.v. Commissioner of Income Tax* 3E.A.T.C.371 (Zanzibar)
98. (1964) 41.T.C.450

v. Beeson,[99] it was held that the expenses incurred by a firm of solicitors in entertaining clients to lunches at which business was discussed, were deductible. In *Mallalieu v. Drummond*,[100] it was held that a female barrister was entitled, in computing the profits of her profession, to deduct the cost of upkeep of a wardrobe of clothes of a design and colour suitable to be worn under her gown during court appearances. In *Commissioner of Income Tax v. P.Co. Et al*,[101] the company paid remuneration to four directors pursuant to a provision on its articles of association which represented a percentage of the company's profits. The company claimed the remuneration as a deduction, but it was disallowed by the Commissioner. It was held by the Court of Appeal that the whole remuneration so paid was deductible as an expense wholly and exclusively incurred in the production of the income of the company since it was a payment for services rendered.

Finally, in *Robson v. Commissioner of Income Tax*[102] it was held that a payment made by an advocate pursuant to an undertaking guaranteeing a loan made to a client was made in discharge of the liabilities and in the ordinary course of his business as an advocate. Consequently it was properly deductible under Section 14(1) of the East African Income Tax (Management) Act, 1958.[103] However, in *Liquidator Mazinde Estate Ltd v. Commissioner of Income Tax*,[104] severance allowance paid to employees upon their termination under the Severance Allowance Act, 1962, was held not to be deductible because although of a revenue nature, it was not imposed on the appellant by statute, neither was it incurred by him in the production of income since the vendor had gone into liquidation immediately after incurring the expenditure.

2. Exceptions

There are exceptions to the general rule, contained in ITA section 22(1), on expenditures which are deductible. Some of these are expenditures of a capital nature.

a) Bad Debts

A deduction is allowed for the amount of a bad debt written off in a person's accounts during the year of income.[105] However, this is conditional on the amount having been included in the person's income for the year or the debt claim being in respect of money lent in the ordinary course of business carried on by a financial institution in the production of income included in the gross income.[106] Thus in *B.O. Ltd v. Commissioner for Income Tax*,[107] the appellant, upon incorporation in 1953, took over the business of an individual who was a money lender and insurance agent. Its memorandum of association contained powers both to lend money and to acquire and hold investments of all descriptions. In 1956, it lent Shs 600,000/= on the security of a second mortgage on land at Mombasa.

99. *Supra* n.97
100. *Supra* n.96
101. 1E.A.T.C.131 (Tanganyika) C.A.
102. [1968] E.A.415(Kenya)
103. Equivalent to ITA, S.22(1)
104. [1967] E.A.734C.A. (Tanzania)
105. ITA S.24(1)
106. *Ibid* s.24(2)
107. 4 E.A.T.C.1(Pt.1) (Kenya)

The mortgagor died insolvent and the company incurred a loss of Shs539,272/=. The company claimed a deduction of the amount of the loss as a bad debt incurred in the production of income. The Commissioner disallowed the deduction on the grounds that the loss was a loss of capital. However, the Supreme Court of Kenya in allowing the taxpayer's appeal held that it was an essential part of the appellant's business to make loans and that the loss was a loss of circulating capital.

A "bad debt" is defined[108] generally as a debt claim in respect of which the person has taken all reasonable steps to pursue payment and which the person reasonably believes will not be satisfied. "Debt claim" refers[109] to a right to receive repayment of money from another person, including deposits with financial institutions, accounts receivable, promissory notes, bills of exchange and bond.

In *Income Tax v. T. Ltd,*[110] deduction of a bad debt was disallowed since no attempt had been made to recover it from the guarantors. It is, therefore, important for the taxpayer to prove that the debts are bad.[111] Where a debt in which a deduction was allowed is subsequently paid off in whole or in part, the amount received is treated as a trading receipt at the time of receipt.[112] Alternatively, where the trader decides to release the debt wholly or partly, the amount is treated as taxable income from the business.[113]

A bad debt in relation to a financial institution is defined as a debt in respect of which a loss reserve held against presently identified losses or potential losses, and which is therefore not available to meet losses which subsequently materialise, has been made.

b) Capital Deductions

As already discussed in the context of section 22(1) and (2)(b), the general rule (except as regards disposal of assets) is that capital expenditure is not deductible for purposes of ascertaining chargeable income. Only revenue expenditure is deductible for that purpose. To this general rule are exceptions. These include certain types of capital expenditure which by statute are allowable deductions for purposes of income tax. The most obvious are those laid down in sections 26 to 31 of the Income Tax Act, Cap 340.

The rationale for allowing such capital deductions is that their disallowance "would present a very unrealistic assessment of a trade's profit."[114] In this vein, it is argued that the cost of capital equipment is as much a cost of creating profits as rent or hire charges. Normal accounting principles, therefore, allow a taxpayer and his auditor to agree how the capital expenditure will be written off against business income. To impose a less haphazard system for tax purposes, parliament has identified certain categories of capital expenditure which will qualify for standard capital "allowance." The present system of allowances permits the capital expenditure (less any amount received on sale) to be deducted from trading profits by means of initial, writing down, first year or balancing allowances or a combination of these. These allowances are generally available to persons carrying on a trade, profession or vocation.

108. ITA, s.24(3)
109. *Ibid*
110. [1971] E.A.569
111. *Dinshaw v. Bombay Commission* (1934) 50T.L.R.527; *Mandavia v. C.I.T.* [1958] E.A.407
112. *Bristow v. Dickinson Ltd* [1946] K.B.321; Mandavia C.I.T. [1958] E.A.407
113. ITA, S.38(3). See also *Simpson v. Jones* (1968) 44 T.C.599
114. Mayson S and Blake, S. *Revenue Law* (14th ed., 1993, Blackstone Press) p.107

i) Industrial Buildings

Rate of Deduction

A person who incurs capital expenditure in any year of income on the construction of an industrial building and who uses the building in the production of income included in the gross income is allowed a deduction, according to the formula, for the depreciation of the building during the year of income calculated.

A x B x C/D[115]

A represents the depreciation rate applicable to the building as determined under Part III of the Sixth Schedule. The present rate is 5 percent. B refers to the capital, expenditure incurred in the construction of the building, while C represents the number of days in the relevant year of income during which the asset was used or was available for use in the production of income included in the gross income. D is the number of days in the year of income.

Partial Use of Building

When the industrial building is only partly used by the taxable person during the year of income for prescribed uses, the amount of allowable depreciation deduction is proportionately reduced.[116] In this regard, when the industrial building is only partly used during the year of income for prescribed uses and the capital expenditure incurred in the construction of that part of the building used for other uses is not more than 10 percent of the total capital expenditure incurred thereof, the building is treated as wholly used for prescribed uses.[117] Prescribed uses refers[118] to a situation in which a building is wholly or partly used or held ready for use by a person in

- manufacturing operations,
- research and development into improved or new methods of manufacture,
- mining operations,
- an approved hotel business, or
- an approved hospital.

Improvement

When the capital expenditure is incurred in making capital improvement to an industrial building in the relevant year of income, such expenditure is treated as if it was incurred in the construction of a separate building.[119]

Effect of Purchase of Building

When the industrial building is bought by a person, such person is deemed to have incurred the capital expenditure incurred by the person who constructed the building.[120]

115. ITA, s.29(1)
116. *Ibid* s.29 (2)
117. *Ibid* s.29(3)
118. *Ibid* s.29(10) read together with s.2 definition of "industrial building"
119. *Ibid* s.29(4)
120 *Ibid* s.29(5)

Furthermore, when the industrial building has been disposed of by a person during the year of income, the cost base of the building for purposes of the ITA is reduced by any deductions allowed to the person in respect of the building under Section 29 of ITA.[121] In the event of the building being bought or sold together with land, the value of the land shall be the difference between the total consideration and the value of the industrial building less deductions allowed under Section 29(7).[122]

In the event of disposal of an industrial building where there has been capital improvement, consideration thereof shall be apportioned among the separate buildings in respect of which there has been improvement as determined under Section 29(4)[123]

Limit on Deduction

An allowable deduction under Section 29 of ITA is limited to the amount which, apart from the deduction, would be the residue of expenditure at the end of the year of income.[124] "Residue of expenditure" means the capital expenditure incurred on the construction of the industrial building less any deductions allowed under Section 29 of ITA to any person, and any amounts which would have been allowed as deductions if the building was solely used for prescribed uses at all times since the construction was completed.[125]

Meaning of Capital Expenditure

It is clarified that "capital expenditure" in Section 29 of ITA does not include expenditure incurred in the acquisition of a depreciable asset installed in an industrial building[126] or expenditure incurred in the acquisition of, or of any rights in or over, any land.

The provisions of the ITA on capital deduction in respect of an industrial building have considerably simplified the law on such deductions in comparison to the repealed legislation[127] and in particular have removed complications relating to the definition of "process" in the context of a building being used for manufacturing purposes[128] and alteration of industrial premises[129] (now termed improvement under Section 29(4) of ITA).

ii) Depreciable Asset or Machinery

General

A person is allowed a deduction for the depreciation of the person's depreciable assets other than deduction for expenditure during the year of income in acquiring a depreciable asset with a cost base of less than Ug.shs.100,000/=[130].

A "depreciable asset" is defined as "any plant or machinery or any implement, utensil,

121. *Ibid* s.29(7)
122. *Ibid* s.29(8)
123. *Ibid* s.29(9)
124. *Ibid* s.29(6)
125. *Ibid* s.29(10)
126. This is catered for under ITA, s.27
127. See Income Tax Decree, 1974, Second Schedule Part I
128. For cases on the meaning of "process" see *Vibroplant v. Holland* [1962] 1All E.R.792; *Commissioner General of Income Tax v. Kiganga Estates Ltd.* 4 E.A.T.C. (Pt.II) 209 C.A. (Kenya).
129. See *B.Z. Ltd. v. Commissioner of Income Tax* 4E.A.T.C.(Pt.1) 247 (Tanzania)
130. ITA, s.27(1) read together with s.26 (2)

or similar article, which is wholly or partly used, or held read for use, by a person in the production of income included in gross income and which is likely to lose value because of wear and tear or obsolescence."[131] Depreciable assets are in turn divided into four classes, with depreciation rate applicable for each class as set out in Part I of the Sixth Schedule to ITA.[132] For computers and data handling equipment, the rate is 40 percent, while that for small vehicles with a load capacity of less than seven tonnes (construction and earth-moving equipment), the rate is 35 percent. With regard to large vehicles with loads of more than seven tonnes (specialised trucks, tractors, trailers and trailer-mounted containers, plant and machinery used in farming, manufacturing, or mining operations) the rate is 30 percent. The rate for railroad cars, locomotives, and equipment, vessels, barges tugs and similar water transportation equipment, aircraft, specialized public utility plant, equipment and machinery, office furniture, fixtures, and equipment, and any depreciable asset not included in another class is 20 percent.

Calculation of Deduction

A person's depreciable assets should be placed in separate pools for each class of asset, and the depreciation deduction for each pool should be calculated using the formula.[133]

A X B

A represents the written-down value of the pool at the end of the year of income, while B is the depreciation rate applicable to the pool. The written-down value of a pool at the end of the year of income is the total of:

- the written-down value of the pool at the end of the preceding year of income after allowing for the deduction under Section 27(3) for that year, and
- the cost base of assets added to the pool during the year of income

reduced, but not below zero, by the consideration received from the disposal of assets in the pool during the year of income.[134] If the consideration received from the disposal of any asset or assets in a pool is more than the written-down value of the pool at the end of the year of income discounting that amount, the excess is included in the business income of the person for that year.[135] However, if the written-down value of a pool at the end of the year of income after allowing for the deduction under Section 27(3) of ITA is less than shs 100,000/=, a deduction shall be allowed for the amount of that written-down value.[136] In the event of disposal of all assets in the pool before the end of the year of income, a deduction is allowed for the amount of the written-down value as at the end of that year.[137] Furthermore, the cost base of depreciable asset is added to a pool in the year of income in which the asset is placed in service.[138]

When the depreciable asset is only partly used during a year of income in the

131. *Ibid* s.2
132. *Ibid* s.27(2) and Part I Sixth Schedule
133. *Ibid* s.27(3)
134. *Ibid* s.27(4)
135. *Ibid* s.27(5)
136. *Ibid* s.27(6)
137. *Ibid* s.27(7)
138. *Ibid* s.27(9)

production of income included in the gross income, the allowable depreciation deduction under Section 27 of ITA in relation to the asset shall be proportionately reduced.[139]

The cost base of a road vehicle other than a commercial vehicle for purposes of computing the written-down value thereof is limited to Shs30,000,000/=[140]. If the cost base of the vehicle is thereby limited, the person is treated as having acquired two assets: frst, a depreciable asset being a road vehicle with a cost base equal to Shs30,000,000 and second, a business asset which is not a depreciable asset with a cost base equal to the difference between the cost base of the asset regardless of Section 27(11) termed "actual cost base" and Shs30,000,000/=.[141] In that event, if the road vehicle is disposed of, the person is treated as having disposed of each of the two assets and the consideration received therefore is apportioned between the two assets based on the ratio of the cost base of each asset as determined under Section 27(12) of ITA.[142]

To calculate the amount of any gain or loss resulting on disposal of an asset whose value is calculated by the difference between its actual cost base and Shs30,000,000/= under Sub-section 27(12)(b), the cost base is reduced by the depreciation deductions which would have been allowed to the person if the asset was a depreciable asset being a road vehicle and it was the only asset in the pool.[143]

Example in Case of Sale of Machinery

T has been in business for many years preparing accounts to 30 June each year. The balance of his capital allowances pool at 1 July 1995 was Shs10,000,000. He undertakes the following transactions in machinery and plant:

1 January 1995	Bought machinery for Shs20,000,000
1 May 1995	Sold plant for Shs9,000,000 (original cost Shs8,000,000)
1 Sept. 1995	Sold plant for Shs9,000,000 (original cost Shs11,000,000)
1 March 1996	Bought shop fittings and machinery for Shs50,000,000

First-year allowances are not available because of the timing of the purchases. T's capital allowances would be computed as follows:

139. *Ibid* s.27(10)
140. *Ibid* s.27(11) read together with Sixth Schedule, Part II
141. *Ibid* s.27(12)
142. *Ibid* s.27(13)
143. *Ibid* s.27(14)

1994/1995	**Pool (shs)**	**Allowances (shs)**
Written-down value brought forward	10,000,000	
Add new qualifying expenditure	20,000,000	
	30,000,000	
Deduct disposal value (restricted to cost)	8,000,000	
	22,000,000	
Less writing down allowance on Shs22,000,000 @ 20%	(4,400,000)	4,400,000
Written-down value carried forward	17,600,000	
1995-1996		
Written-down value brought forward	17,600,000	
Add new qualifying expenditure	50,000,000	
	67,600,000	
Deduct disposal value	9,000,000	
	58,600,000	
Less writing down allowance at Shs58,600,000 @ 20%	11,720,000	11,720,000
Written-down value added forward	46,880,000	

Meaning of Plant and Machinery

In *Yarmouth v. France*, Lindley L.J. defined "plant" to include

> whatever apparatus is used by a businessman for carrying on his business – not his stock-in-trade, which he buys or makes for sale; but all goods and chattels, fixed or movable, live or dead, which he keeps for permanent employment in his business.[144]

The expression "permanent" has been qualified as "denoting no more than some degree of durability."[145] Thus in *Hinton v. Maden & Ireland Ltd* it was held that shoemakers' lasts and knives, which have a useful life of about three years, qualified as plant.[146]

Cases also distinguish between objects used for the purposes of a business, which are plant, and objects which are merely setting in which the business is carried on, which are not plant. In *Jarrold v. John Good & Sons Ltd*, Pearson L.J. stated the following in reference to movable partitions used for dividing up the space in an office building so that the plan of the office accommodation could be varied from time to time:

> the short question in this case is whether the partitioning is part of the premises in which the business is carried on are part of the plant with which the business is carried on.[147]

Pennycuick, J., whose decision the Court of Appeal upheld, thought that the setting in which a business is carried on and the apparatus used for carrying it on were not necessarily mutually exclusive, but in this case he thought that fixtures possessing the character of movable partitions merited the title of apparatus used for carrying on business, and accordingly the partitions qualified as plant.

In this vein Ormerod L.J. thus stated:

> there may be cases ...where an asset or some article can be excluded from the definition because it is more a part of the setting than part of the apparatus for carrying on the trade. In the present case, however, the contrary is found. These partitions are required by the nature of the taxpayer's trade.

In *Bridge House (Reigate Hill) Ltd v. Hinder*,[148] restaurant owners agreed to contribute to the cost of connecting drains at the restaurant to the public sewer and claimed capital allowances in respect of the contribution. The Court of Appeal held that this was not an expenditure on the provision of machinery or plant for the purposes of the taxpayer's trade. Lord Denning, M.R., stated in this regard:

> It is very much a matter of impression. Are sewerage or drainage pipes part of the apparatus for carrying on the business? I think not. They are an essential ancillary to the house itself, just as the chimney stack. Every house large or small has to have a chimney stack to carry away smoke; and it has to have pipes to carry away effluent. None such is "plant". They are part of the setting in which the business is carried on.

---

144. (1887) 19 Q.B.D. 647. See also *A. Co. v. Commissioner of Income Tax* 1 E.A.T.C. 1 (Kenya)
145. *Rose & Co. (Wall Papers & Paints) Ltd v. Campbell* [1968] 1 All E.R. 405 per Pennycuick, J.
146. [1959] 3 All E.R. 356 H.L. See also *Rose & Co Case Ibid* where the useful life of wallpaper pattern books was put at two years.8
147. [1963] 1 All E.R. 141. See also *I.R.C. v. Barclay Curls & Co Ltd* [1969] All E.R. 732 per Lord Reid; *Cooke v. Beach Station Caravans Ltd* [1974] 3 All E.R. 159
148. (1971) 47 T.C. 182

For similar reasons, allowances have been refused in respect of a prefabricated chemistry laboratory and a gymnasium,[149] an illuminated canopy covering the service area of a petrol filling station,[150] a false ceiling in a restaurant,[151] a spectator's stand at a football ground,[152] an inflatable air dome to protect a tennis court used by a tennis coach,[153] and kennels for dogs in a quarantine.[154]

In *Benson v. Yard Arm Club Ltd,*[155] the Court of Appeal dismissed the taxpayers' capital allowances claim for capital expenditure on the purchase and conversion of a ship into a floating restaurant moored in the Thames. Templeman L.J. stated:

> The authorities disclose a distinction between premises in which business is carried on and the plant with which a business is carried on. There are borderline cases in which a structure forming part of business premises has been held to be a plant because it does not merely consist of premises providing accommodation for the business but also performs a function in the actual carrying on of business. Premises, or structures forming part of premises, which have the characteristics and perform the functions of plant, merit the claim for capital allowances. In my judgment, it follows that if a chattel, such as a ship or a hulk, only provides accommodation for a business and has the characteristic and only performs the function, of premises, the chattel does not qualify as plant for the purposes of capital allowances.

Nonetheless, in *Cole Bros Ltd v. Phillips*, a claim in respect of some electrical equipment installed in a department store was allowed on the basis that the equipment was not merely part of the setting.[156] In *I.R.C. v. Scottish–Newcastle Breweries Ltd*, a case in which the taxpayers claimed allowances in respect of electric light fittings and various categories of decor and murals in their hotels, the House of Lords held that these items constituted plant and thus qualified for allowances because part of an hotelier's function is to create an atmosphere.[157] Lord Lowry explained thus:

> Now the creation of the right atmosphere is a means to an end in the carrying on of such a trade; it is not a trade in itself or a separate part of the trade. This objective can be achieved by a combination of things, a beautiful or unusual or historic building, attractive views, gardens, shrubberies and waterfalls, ornaments, the equipment used by the staff and the glasses, china cutlery, table linen, and the tables and chairs used by the customers. Everything in this list, from the ornaments are used purely to create atmosphere. The mere fact that some ornaments are free standing on the floor or on the shelves or tables and that others are suspended from or affixed to walls or ceilings is quite beside the point. They are all part of the hotelier's plant as defined in *Yarmouth v. France.*[158]

149. *St John's School v. Ward* (1974) 49 T.C. 524
150. *Dixon v. Fitch's Garage Ltd* [1975] 3 All E.R. 455
151. *Hampton v. Fortes Autogrill Ltd* [1980] STC 80
152. *Brown v. Barnley Football & Athletic Co Ltd* [1980] 3 All E.R. 244
153. *Thomas v. Reynolds* [1987] STC 135
154. *Carr v. Sayer* [1992] STC 396
155. [1979] 2 All E.R. 336
156. [1982] 2 All E.R. 247 H.L.
157. [1982] 2 All E.R. 230
158. *supra* n.144 and text thereof

Lord Lowry distinguished this case from *Benson v. Yard Arm Club Ltd*, in which the atmosphere was created by a floating restaurant. He was of the view that in that case the ship was premises on which trade was carried on rather than a plant.[159]

An issue of controversy is whether books qualify as plant. In *Daphne v. Shaw*, a solicitor claimed a deduction in respect of wear and tear of books forming part of his law library. Rowlatt J. held that they were not plant and declined the deduction on the grounds that books were not "implements" falling within the meaning of "plant and machinery."[160] However, that case was overruled in *Munby v. Furlong* in which the English Court of Appeal allowed a deduction in respect of expenditure by a barrister on the acquisition of law reports and textbooks for the purpose of establishing a library for his practice.[161] Lord Denning, M.R., rationalised the decision thus:

> I do not think 'plant' should be confined to things which are used physically. It seems to me that in principle it extends to the intellectual Storehouse which a barrister or a solicitor or any other professional man has in the course of carrying on his profession. The difficulty has arisen because the legislature, when it extended this provision to professions, did not make clear the scope of the word 'plant' in that context. It seems to me, in the context of a profession, the provision of 'plant' should be so interpreted that a lawyer's books, his set of law reports and his textbooks are 'plant.'

iii) Repairs and Minor Capital Equipment

A person is allowed a deduction for expenditure during the year of income for the repair of property occupied or used by the person in the production of income included in gross income.[162] Furthermore, deduction is also allowed for expenditure incurred during the relevant year of income in acquiring a depreciable asset with a cost base of less than five currency points or Shs100,000/=.[163] This deduction is only permitted when the asset normally functions in its own right and is not an individual item which forms part of a set.[164]

Some judicial cases have considered situations involving capital expenditure on alterations to buildings incidental to the installation of machinery. Thus in *Bed-Odeco Ltd. v. Powlson,*[165] the taxpayers entered into various loan agreements in order to finance the construction of an oil rig, and claimed that interest and fees paid in respect of those arrangements were expenditure "on the provision of" the rig. The British House of Lords disagreed with the claim, holding that the words "on the provision of" (in Section 25 of the Income and Corporation Taxes Act 1988 of U.K.) were not wide enough to include money for the acquisition of machinery or plant. Lord Russell of Killowen stated: "In my opinion the effect of the expenditure was the provision of finance and not the provision of plant."

---

159. *Supra* n.155 and text thereof. See also *Wimpy International Ltd v. Warland Associated Restaurants* [1989] STC 273
160. (1926) 11 T.C. 256. See also *McVeigh v. Arthur Anderson & Sons Ltd* [1969] 2 All E.R. 771
161. [1977] 2 All E.R. 953 C.A. (E)
162. TA, s.26(1)
163. *Ibid* s.26(2)
164. *Ibid* s.26(3)
165. [1978] 2 All E.R.1111

However, two of the law lords indicated the permissible extent of the words "expenditure on the provision of."[166] Lord Russell thus stated:

> I do not seek to confine qualifying capital expenditure to the price paid to the supplier of the plant ... if the cost of transport from the supplier to the place of the user is directly borne by the taxpayer it would be expenditure on the provision of plant for the purpose of the taxpayer's trade. And there may well be other examples of expenditure, additional to the price paid to the supplier which would qualify on similar grounds.

Similarly Lord Wilberforce observed:

> The words 'expenditure on the provision of' focus attention on the plant and the expenditure on the plant, not limiting it necessarily to the bare purchase price, but including such items as transport and installation and in any event not extending to expenditure more remote in purpose.

Sometimes it happens that machinery or plant is purchased under a contract providing for payments in foreign currency. Currency fluctuation may render the shilling equivalent to the cost of the machinery at the time of payment significantly different. Thus in *Van Arkadie v. Sterling Coated Materials Ltd*,[167] the taxpayer company bought machinery for a price expressed in Swiss francs. The bulk of the contract price was payable in installments. As the Swiss franc appreciated against the sterling, the cost to the taxpayer company of paying the purchase price in sterling increased. It was held that the additional cost of paying the installments was expenditure on the provision of the machinery (rather than expenditure on the provision of finance as the Inland Revenue had contended), with the consequence that the company was entitled to capital allowances on the additional cost.

iv) Mining Operations

A person carrying on mining operations is allowed a deduction for any expenditure of a capital nature incurred in searching for, discovering and testing or winning access to deposits of minerals in Uganda.[168] The expression "mining operations" is defined to include "every method or process by which any mineral is won from the soil or from any substance or constituent of the soil."[169]

v) Farming

Expenditure incurred by a person in acquiring farm works is included in the person's pool for class 4 of depreciable assets in the year of income in which the expenditure is incurred and is depreciated accordingly.[170]

A deduction of 20 percent of capital expenditure incurred on the acquisition or establishment of a horticultural plant or construction of a greenhouse is allowed for a

166. Presumably equivalent to "expenditure ... in acquiring a depreciable asset" in ITA, s.26(2)
167. [1983] S.T.C. 95
168 ITA, s.36. This has considerably simplified the law in comparison with the old law: Income Tax Decree 1974, Schedule 2 paragraphs 16-21.
169. ITA, s.2
170. *Ibid* s.35(1) read together with s.28(2) and part I of Sixth Schedule discussed *supra*

person carrying on horticultural business in Uganda in the year of income so incurred and in the next four years of income in which the plant is used in the business of horticulture carried on by the person.[171] Such capital expenditure incurred in the establishment of a horticultural plan shall include expenditure incurred in draining or clearing land.[172]

"Farms works" refers to any labour quarters and other immovable buildings necessary for the proper operation of a farm, fences, dips, drains, water and electricity supply works, windbreaks, and other works necessary for farming operations but excludes farm houses or depreciable assets.[173] "Horticulture" is defined to include propagation or cultivation of seeds, bulbs, spores, or similar things; propagation or cultivation of fungi, or propagation or cultivation in environments other than soil, whether natural or artificial.

vi) Investment or Initial Allowance

A person who places an item of eligible property into service for the first time during the year of income is allowed a deduction for that year of an amount equal to (1) 75 percent of the cost base of the property at the time it is placed in service if placed in service outside Kampala, Entebbe, Namanve, Jinja and Njeru, or (2) 50 percent of the cost base of the property at the time it is place in service in those cities.[174]

The cost base of such asset is reduced by the amount of deduction allowed for purposes of determining the cost base of a depreciable asset added to a pool under Section 27(4)(b).[175]

The expression "item of eligible property" refers to plant and machinery wholly used in the production of income included in gross income but excludes goods and passenger transport vehicles, appliances of a kind ordinarily used for household purposes, or office or household furniture, fixtures and fittings.[176]

c) Other Allowable Deductions

i) Expenditure on Commencement of Business

A person who incurs expenditure in starting a business to produce income included in gross income shall be allowed a deduction of 25 percent of the amount of expenditure in the year of income in which the expenditure was incurred and in the following three years of income in which the business is carried on by that person.[177]

The issue arises as to determination of how far before the commencement of a business one can go in attributing expenditure to be connected with establishment of the business. Thus in *Birmingham and District Cattle by-Products Co. Ltd. v. I.R.C.* it was held that the construction of a factory and the purchase of machinery or plant and entering into contracts for the purchase of raw materials is not commencement of trading.[178] Once the factory is built and the machinery and plant installed, however, the

171. *Ibid* s.35(2)
172. *Ibid* s.35(3)
173. *Ibid* s.35(4). These are catered for under ss.27 and 29.
174. *Ibid* s.28(1)
175. *Ibid* s.28(2)
176. *Ibid* s.28(3). These are presumably catered for under s.27.
177. *Ibid* s.30

receipts of raw materials for manufacturing purpose is the commencement of trading. In *Cannop Coal Ltd. v. I.R.C.*, the issue arose as to when the trade of seeking coal from a subsidiary pit commenced. The taxpayers had been formed to mine coal, but had not made much money from their mining activities. Some distance from the main pit, they had exploited a subsidiary pit to provide coal for their machines. The subsidiary pit was so successful that it made more money than the main colliery. The commissioners and the High Court held that the trading started as soon as the coal was recovered from the subsidiary pit.[179]

Another issue is whether when the taxpayer engages in new activities he is setting up and commencing business. *Gordon Blair v. I.R.C.* involved brewers who were suffering losses. They decided to stop brewing and to buy beer from another brewer which they could bottle and sell as their own. This yielded profits. The Scottish Court of Session agreed with the commissioners' finding that the taxpayers had began a new trade – they had stopped brewing and started selling.[180] In *Cannon Industries v. Edwards*, Pennycuick J. agreed with the commissioners that there had been an extension of business and not a change when in spite of separate works, staff, and bank accounts the manufacturers of gas appliances began to manufacture electrical appliances.[181]

The main consideration, therefore, is whether the taxpayer gives up his original activity in favour of a new one. Thus in *Seldon v. Croom-Johnson*, it was held that a barrister who became a King's Counsel was not starting a new profession.[182] He continued to carry on the same type of business, even though the nature of his work might differ.

ii) Expenditure on Scientific Research

A person is allowed a deduction for scientific research expenditure incurred during the year of income in the course of carrying on a business from which the income is included in gross income.[183] "Scientific research" means any activities in the fields of natural or applied science for the development of human knowledge.[184] "Scientific research expenditure" in relation to a person carrying on business means the cost of scientific research undertaken for the purpose of developing the person's business, including any contribution to a scientific research institution which is used by the institution in undertaking research for the purposes of developing the person's business but does not include:

- expenditure incurred for the acquisition of a depreciable or intangible asset;
- expenditure incurred for the acquisition of land or buildings; or
- expenditure incurred for the purpose of ascertaining the existence, location, extent or quality of a natural deposit.[185]

178. (1979) 12 T.C..92
179. (1918) 12T.C.31
180. (1962) 40T.C.258
181. [1966] 1All E.R.456
182. [1932] 1K.B.759
183. ITA s.32(1)
184. *Ibid* s.32(2)

The excluded expenditures are catered for under sections 27, 29 and 36 of ITA and are so excluded in order to avoid duplication of allowable deductions.

A "scientific research institution" refers to an association, institute, college, or university which undertakes scientific research.[186]

In *Gaspect Ltd [formerly Saga Petroleum (UK)] Ltd v. Elliss (Inspector of Taxes)*, Saga had agreed with its subsidiary, Saga Ireland, under the provision of an "Illustrative agreement," to meet its subsidiary's share of the expenditure on the exploration and so on of two consortia which held licences to explore for oil in the Irish Sea. The actual operator which carried out the exploration of each consortium was Amoco and BP respectively. Saga claimed allowances under the Capital Allowances Act, 1968, S.91(1) [now Capital Allowances Act, 1990, S.137(1)] which provided that where a person "... while carrying on a trade, incurs expenditure of a capital nature and a scientific research related to that trade and directly undertaken by him on his behalf ... a deduction equal to the whole expenditure shall be allowed in taxing the trade of the relevant chargeable period." It was agreed that the exploration for oil and gas was scientific research and that Saga carried on a trade and incurred capital expenditure on the exploration, and therefore on scientific research and the expenditure related to Saga's oil trade. However, in order to qualify for the allowance, the expenditure had to be incurred "on his behalf," an expression denoting agency. It was, therefore, held that since the research was not directly undertaken by Saga, but by BP and Amoco,[187] "on behalf of" the members of the consortium, including Saga Ireland, Saga did not qualify for the allowances.

iii) Interest/Depreciation of Currency

A person is allowed a deduction for interest incurred during the year of income in respect of a debt obligation to the extent that the debt obligation has been incurred by the person in the production of income included in gross income.[188] Although the Income Tax Act is silent on this, arguably money paid as a result of the depreciation of the shilling currency and fully employed in the production of taxable income is deductible.[189]

Interest is defined to include:

- any payment, including a discount or premium, made under a debt obligation which is not a return of capital;
- any swap or other payments functionally equivalent to interest;
- any commitment, guarantee, or service fee paid in respect of a debt obligation or swap agreement; or
- a distribution by a building society.[190]

To illustrate that ordinarily interest is not deductible and that the Uganda provision is an exception to the general rule, reference is made to two English cases. In *Hafton*

185. *Ibid*
186. *Ibid*
187. [1987] 1WLR 769; [1987] S.T.C.362C.A.(E). See also *Kenya Meat Commission v. Commissioner of Income Tax* 4E.A.T.C.(PCL) 199
188. ITA, s.25
189. c.f. Income Tax Decree, 1974, s.14(3)(a)(I) as inserted by Finance Statute No.9 of 1994, s.7. See now 1TA, s.48(3).
190. ITA, s.2

Properties Ltd. v. McHugh,[191] interest had been paid gross by a United Kingdom resident borrower company to Isle of Man Bank (SIB) and the revenue assessed the taxpayer at the basic rate under Taxes Act 1970, S.54. The interest-paying company, which appealed against assessment both before the Special Commissioners and the High Court, could only succeed if SIB was (1) carrying on business in the United Kingdom and (2) that business in the United Kingdom was a bona fide banking business. It failed on both counts.

In *LysVille Ltd. & Minshaw Properties Ltd. v. Prince*[192] both appellant companies were wholly owned charitable objects. SBA had lent Minsham a substantial sum and it was agreed that, although nothing appeared in writing at the time of the loan, it was repayable on demand and bore interest at 15 percent. Minsham had made losses in two years and Lysville claimed the benefit of the group relief agreed between the two companies. The issue wás whether interest accruing on the loan was short interest and thus deductible in calculating the loss made by Minsham. Alternatively, if the interest were "yearly interest of money," was it, by virtue of entries made in books of Minsham, "paid," so constituting a deductible charge on income each year, again increasing the loss made by Minsham. The companies failed in their appeals both before the Special Commissioners and the High Court against interest being chargeable to tax. It was rationalized that interest was yearly and had to be paid under the Taxes Act 1988, s.338 (1).[193] Second, the addition of the interest to the loan account was not a real payment of interest. An actual discharge of interest was required for it to be a charge on income under Taxes Act, 1970, s.248(1).[194]

On the issue of payment arising from depreciation of the shilling, it is again significant that the statutory provision is an exception to the general rule that such payment or loss is not deductible. Thus in *Beauchamp v. F.W. Woolworth PLC*,[195] the taxpayer company traded from a number of retail outlets in the United Kingdom. In 1971 and 1972, it borrowed Swiss franc loans which were repayable after a fixed-year term. The twist in the case was that the taxpayer's intentions were to use the money to deal with a short-term cash flow problem in its trading position but the loan had to be outstanding for at least five years to comply with exchange control requirements. Owing to exchange rate changes, there was substantial loss on the repayment of the loan. The taxpayer argued that, as the money had been borrowed to meet a short-term problem connected with its trading, the loss was revenue and hence deductible. The Revenue contended that the loss was capital and hence not deductible. The House of Lords held that the purpose of the loans was to increase the company's capital funds and to further the company's trade over a five year period. The losses were therefore losses on capital and the Revenue's appeal was allowed.[196]

It has been observed that the case presents a grey area in determining whether a transaction is of a revenue or capital nature.[197] As noted above, the twist in this case

---

191. [1987] STC 16 Ch.D.(E)
192. (1990) Ch.D. (E) P.(Ed.) *Leading Cases in Business Taxation* (Longman 1991) pp 263-265
193. Following *Cairns v. MacDiarmid* [1983] STC 178
194. Applying *Paton (as Fenton's Trustee) v. IRC* 21 TC 626 H.L.
195. [1989] STC 510 H.L.
196. Applying *IRC v. Carron Co.* (1967) 45 TC 18

was that the taxpayer's intentions were to use the money to deal with a short-term cash flow problem in its trading position, but the loan had to be outstanding for five years in compliance with exchange control requirements.[198]

iv) Losses

When for any year of income, the total amount of income included in the gross income of the taxpayer is exceeded by the total amount of deductions allowed to the taxpayer, the excess, termed "assessed loss," shall be carried forward and allowed as a deduction in determining the taxpayer's chargeable income in the following year of income.[199] Similarly, "assessed farming loss," whereby total farming income is exceeded by deductions, is carried forward and allowed as a deduction in respect of the chargeable farming income of the taxpayer in the following year of income.[200] "Farming income" refers to business income derived from the carrying on of farming, while "chargeable farming income" means the total farming income of the taxpayer for a year of income reduced by any deductions allowed under the ITA for the relevant year which relates to the production of such income.[201]

However, the amount of assessed loss carried forward shall be reduced by the amount or value of any benefit to the taxpayer from a concession granted by, or a compromise made with the taxpayer's creditors by which the taxpayer's liabilities to those creditors have been extinguished or reduced and provided that such liabilities were incurred in the production of income included in the gross income.[202] Where the taxpayer has more than one class of loss the reduction arising from a concession or compromise is applied rateably to each class of loss.

A loss in an accounting period arises when in computing "profits" the allowable expenditure exceeds appropriate receipts, taking into account the changes in stock etc. If the result of the computation is a minus quantity, then there are no profits of the accounting period and there is a loss which in the circumstances, may be set against other income to reduce the amount of tax payable.[203]

The statutory provision emphasizes that losses must be connected to the business in order to be normally deductible. Thus in *Owen & Gadsdon v. Brock,*[204] the taxpayers were a firm of solicitors who wanted to retain the services of their managing clerk. To induce him to stay they had a bungalow built for him. Whilst the house was being built they bought a house for him to occupy. The house was eventually sold at a loss, which the taxpayers claimed to deduct as a trading expense. It was held that this was a capital expense and deduction thereof was not permissible. Similarly, in *Strong & Co. v. Woodfield,*[205] part of the taxpayers' hotel had collapsed and caused injury to a guest,

---

197. Rayney, P. *Supra* n.192 p.380
198. For the converse position where there is an appreciation of value. See *Pattison v. Marine Midland Ltd* [1984] A.C.362; [1984] 2 WLR 11; [1984] STC 10 H.L.
199. ITA, s.38(1) For this purpose Ugandan foreign-source income are treated separately [s.38(5)]
200. *Ibid* s.38(2)
201. *Ibid* s.38(6)
202. *Ibid* s.38(4)
203. Easson, *Cases & Materials on Revenue Law* (2nd ed. 1990) p. 259. See further *Final Report of the Royal Commission on the Taxation of Profits and Income* (Cmnd 9474) 1955 (United Kingdom) in Easson Ibid pp.259-261; *Westward Television Ltd. v Hart [1968]* 3 All E.R.91; *Butt v. Haxby* [1983] STC 239.
204. (1951) 32 TC 206. See also *C. Co Ltd.v. Commissioner of Income Tax* 1 E.A.T.C15

which they claimed to deduct. The House of Lords held this loss was not connected with or arising out of the trade (which was provision of rooms and food) and so disallowed the deduction.

However, petty thefts by employees such as cashiers in the course of trade are deductible,[206] although a misappropriation of funds by a company director is not deductible as it is not "connected with or arising out of the trade."[207] Rather it is a breach of a fiduciary duty to the company for which the director is liable to restore the loss.[208]

As mentioned, losses may be carried forward to the following year,[209] although this must still be related to the business in its existing form. Thus in *Willis v. Peeters Picture Frames Ltd,*[210] the company was taken over by a group of companies and the issue was whether the trading losses could be carried forward against profits arising after the takeover or whether carry forward should be restricted on the grounds that within the three-year period there had been both a change in ownership of the company and a major change in the nature of its trade within Income & Corporation Taxes Act 1988, s.768(1)(a). It was held that although there had been a change in the distribution of goods sold and manufactured by the company, the carry forward was permissible since that change was insignificant.

Apart from the losses which may be carried forward, it should be stressed that losses are generally deductible provided that they have been incurred in the production of income to which they relate.[211]

v) Expenditure in Training of Employees

An employer is allowed a deduction for expenditure incurred during the year of income for the training or tertiary education, not exceeding in the aggregate five years, of a citizen or permanent resident of Uganda, other than an associate of the employer, who is employed by the employer in a business, the income from which is included in gross income.[212] "Permanent resident" in this context refers to a resident individual who has been present in Uganda for a period or periods totalling five years or more.[213]

The provision in the Income Tax Act 1997 is more restrictive than the one in the repeal and law which gave discretion to the Commissioner General as to which training expenditure was deductible.[214]

vi) Medical Expenditure on Employees

The repealed law allowed deduction of medical expenditure on employees under a

205. [1906] A. C. 448 H.L. See also *B.O. Ltd v. Commissioner of Income Tax* 4 EATC (PT II) 1.
206. *Curtis v. J&G Oldfield* 91925) 94 L.J.K.B.655
207. *Bamford v. A.T.A. Advertising Ltd* [1972] 3 All E.R. 535
208. *Selangor United Rubber Estates Ltd. v. Cradock* (No.3) [1968] 2 All E.R.1073
209. ITA, S.38(1)
210. [1983] STC 453. See also *Purchase v. Tesco Stores Ltd* [1984] STC 304, *B.Q. v. Commissioner of Income Tax* 4 E.A.T.C. (Pt.I) 82
211. ITA, s.22(1)
212. *Ibid* s.33(1)
213. *Ibid* s.33 (2)
214. Income Tax Decree 1974, s.14(3)(f)

scheme with specific doctors or medical establishment to treat the employees and settle the bills directly with the doctors or medical establishment, or the employer arranged for direct treatment of the employee to an extent considered reasonable by the Commissioner General.[215] Although the ITA is silent on this aspect, arguably such expenditure could be allowed as deduction under Section 22(1) of the ITA. However, presumably the Commissioner's discretion may be exercisable in determining which medical expenditure is deductible given the possibility that such expenditure is capable of being regarded as expenditure of a domestic nature, which is not allowable as a deduction.[216]

vii) Meals, Refreshment and Entertainment Expenditure

A deduction is allowed for expenditure incurred by a person in providing meals, refreshment, or entertainment in production of income included in gross income.[217]

This is, however, only possible when the value of the meals, refreshment or entertainment is included in the employment income of the employee under Section 19(1)(b) or is excluded from employment income under Section 19(2)(d) and (e).[218] Alternatively, such deduction is permissible when the person's business includes the provision of meals, refreshment, or entertainment, and the persons to whom such items are provided have paid an arm's length consideration for them.

viii) Charitable Donations

A person is allowed a deduction for a gift during a year of income to an organization which is an amateur sporting association or a religious, charitable or educational institution of a public character.[219] The deduction allowed is the lesser of the value of the property at the time of the gift or the consideration paid by the person for the property.[220]

However, the amount of a deduction allowed shall not exceed 5 percent of the persons'chargeable income, calculated before taking into account the deduction in respect of the donation.[221]

ix) Rental Expenditures

An individual is allowed deduction in the case of rental income of 20 percent thereof as expenditure and losses incurred by the individual in the production of such income.[222]

C. Non-Deductible Expenses

215. *Ibid* s.14(3)(g). Inserted by Finance Act Cap. 182
216 ITA, s.22(2)(a)(3)(a). See also *Commissioner of Income Tax v. D.* I E.A.T.C.27(Uganda); *Murgatroyd v. Evans Jackson* [1967] 1All E.R.881 Per Plowman J.
217. ITA, S.23
218. For discussion thereof see *supra* chap.3
219. ITA, s.34(1)
220. *Ibid* s.34(2)
221. *Ibid* s.34(3)
222. *Ibid* s.22(1) (c)

1. Domestic or Private Expenses

Expenditure or loss incurred for domestic or private purposes, is not allowed as a deduction.[223] These include,[224] the cost incurred in the maintenance of the person and the person's family or residence, the costs of commuting between the person's residence and work; the cost of clothing worn to work except clothing which is not suitable for wearing outside of work and the cost of education of the person not directly relevant to the person's employment or business and the cost of education leading to a degree whether or not it is directly relevant to the person's employment.

2. Capital Expenditure

Capital expenditure is generally not deductible except in situations stipulated by the Income Tax Act Cap 340.[225]

3. Expenditure or Loss Recoverable Under Insurance or Indemnity

In line with normal taxation principles such compensation is regarded as taxable income.[226]

In *B.T.C. v. Gourley*,[227] the plaintiff was injured by the negligence of the defendant's servants and claimed damages for loss of earnings. It was estimated that, but for the accident, the plaintiff would have earned GBP37,000. Had he actually earned this sum, it would have been taxed and GBP6,000 would have been left to him. But had he been awarded damages of GBP37,000 he would have kept the whole amount, since damages for loss of earnings resulting from personal injury are not taxable. The House of Lords held that the proper measure of damages was GBP6,000, reflecting the plaintiff's actual loss. While this was a tortious action, it has been suggested, that the same principle is applicable to contractual liability.[228] The rule is premised on the reasoning that the plaintiff ought not to make a profit out of the tort or breach of contract by getting tax-free damages to compensate for loss of a benefit which would have been taxable.[229] It applies in two situations. First, the damages must be compensation for loss of taxable income or gain and not simply for loss of a capital asset. In this respect, the rule would not apply if a buyer claimed the amount by which their market value exceeded the contract price since these damages are meant to compensate him for failure to obtain a capital asset (out of which he might make a profit or loss). Second, the damages themselves must be taxable. In *Diamond v. Campbell Jones*[230] a dealer in real estate lost profits of GBP8,500 through the defendant's breach of contract to sell him a house. The argument that the damages should be reduced because of tax liability was rejected because the actual

---

223. *Ibid* s.22(2)(a)
224. *Ibid* s.22(3). See also *Commissioner of Income Tax v. D.* supra n.216; *Murgatroyd v. Evans Jackson, supra* n. 216 discussed *supra* n .4 chapter 3
225. ITA, ss.22(2)(b)(c), 26-9, 35, 36, See also *H. Co v. Commissioner of Income Tax* (hereinafter C.I.T.) 1.E.AT.C.65; *A.E. Investment Ltd. v. C.I.T.* 2E.A.T.C. Case No.31 (Kenya); *McClure V. Petre* [1988] STC 749 discussed *supra,* Chap.2
226. See also ITA, ss 38(3), 62
227. [1956] A.C.185; [1955] 3 All E.R.796. See also Bakibinga, *Law of Contract in Uganda* (1996) pp.375-376
228. Treitel, *The Law of Contract*, 9th ed.1995 Sweet & Maxwell) p.946
229. Bakibinga, *supra* note 227 pp.375-376. Emphasis supplied.
230. [1961] Ch.22; [1960] 1 All E.R.583.

damages were taxable in the dealer's hands. Similarly, in *Southern Highlands Tobacco Union Ltd. v. David McQueen,*[231] the defendant argued that tax deduction should have been made to the award of GBP10,412. The court referred to sections 3(1)(a) and 5(2)(c) of the East African Income Tax Management Act[232] which made "any amount received as compensation for termination of any contract of employment or service" chargeable to tax and decided that the damages were taxable in the hands of the plaintiff and should not be deducted before the defendant's payment of damages.[233]

In *Bwavu Mpologoma Growers Cooperative Union Ltd v. Gasston Babour,*[234] the defendants committed a copyright infringement of the plaintiff's engineering plans, whereby the plaintiff lost £2,000 profits. The Court of Appeal held that the profits would have been liable to tax, and therefore the plaintiff should not receive more than he would have done if there was no infringement. The result is that the tax, as assessed by the court – which is not particularly well equipped for the task – is deducted from the defendant's payment of damages. This deduction does not, however, go to the tax authorities. Wingham J.A. explained the operation of the Common Law rule (in *Gourley*) thus:

> In assessing such damages a court ought to award a sum approximately to the plaintiff's net loss of profits, that is to say, the net profits that he would have made after deducting the approximate tax (if any) that he would have had to pay on it, unless the damages that are being awarded will themselves be subject to taxation in the plaintiff's hands after he has received them. The later part of the rule is, of course, necessary to prevent the plaintiff from in effect being taxed twice over, once by the judge's approximate deduction and later by the tax authorities' precise taxation.

4. Income Tax Payable in Uganda or a Foreign Country

Ordinarily, income tax payable in Uganda or elsewhere is not deductible.[235] However, in keeping with Double Taxation Agreements concluded between Uganda and various countries,[236] such income tax may be allowed as a foreign tax credit in respect of foreign-source income included in the gross income of the taxpayer.[237] A tax credit is also allowable in respect of provisional tax paid[238] and tax withheld and remitted to the Uganda Revenue Authority.[239]

5. Income Carried to a Reserve Fund or Capitalised

Any income which is remitted to a reserve fund or capitalised in any way is not deductible

---

231. [1960] Ch. 490 (Tanzania)
232. Cap. 24 *Laws of the East African Community* then applicable. For the equivalent provision in Uganda see Income Tax Act Cap 340. Ss.17(1)(b) and 19(1)(d).
232. See also *Shah v. Abdulla* [1964] E.A.742
233. [1960] E.A.490; Note *Journal of African Law* 198 (1959) following the *Gourely case.* For criticisms of the *Gourely* principle see Jolowicz [1959] Camb L.J.85 Treitel, *supra* n.227; Bakibinga, *supra* n.227 pp.377-378.
235. ITA, s.22(2)(d)
236. For example, Kenya, Tanzania, South Africa, Mauritius and United Kingdom
237. ITA, ss.4(3)(a), 81(1)
238. *Ibid* ss. 4(3)(c), 111
239. *Ibid* ss.4. (3)(b), 128(3)

as it does not constitute expenditure or loss incurred in the production of income.[240]

6. Cost of Gift Not Included in Gross Income

The cost of a gift made directly or indirectly to an individual but not included in the individual's gross income is not allowed to be deducted for taxation purposes.[241]

7. Housing Allowance

An allowance given to or reimbursement or discharge of expenditure incurred by an employee in respect of the employee's housing and any expenditures incurred in respect of housing provided to an employee is not deductible for taxation purposes.[242] Since an employee's housing allowance is taxable,[243] it is difficult to appreciate why the payer of such allowance is not allowed a deduction. This may have to be reviewed by the legislature.

8. Fines or Penalties

Any fine or similar penalty paid to any government or political subdivision of a government for any breach of any law or subsidiary legislation is not deductible.[244] The rationale for this is that such payment is either personal or punitive and takes on the character of expenditure of a private nature within Section 22(3)(a) of the ITA.

9. Contribution to Retirement Fund

A contribution or similar payment made to a retirement fund either for the benefit of the person making the payment or for the benefit of any other person is not deductible.[245] The rationale for this is that such contributions are not included in an employee's income for taxation purposes.[246] The provision is therefore aimed at eliminating double taxation relief on the part of both the employer/payer and employee/payee and at implementing the recommendation of the International Monetary Fund.[247]

10. Premium on Life Insurance

A premium or similar payment made to a person carrying on a life insurance business on the life of the person making the premium or on the life of some other person is not deductible for taxation purposes.[248] The rationale for this provision is that such payment is not included in an employee's income for taxation purposes.[249] The provison implements the IMF recommendation of avoiding double taxation relief.[250] The provision could, in the context of a non-employee, be justified on the ground that a life insurance premium is

240. *Ibid* s.22(2)(e)
241. *Ibid* s.22(2)(f): NB the beneficiary is exempted from taxation S.22(1)(j)
242. *Ibid* s.22(2)(g)
243. *Ibid* s.19(1)(a)
244. *Ibid* s.22(2)(h)
245. *Ibid* s.22(2)(I)
246. *Ibid* s.19(2)(g). It is also exempt from tax: s.21(1)(o)
247. IMF, *Uganda: A Program for Reform of Income Tax and Taxation of Mining Income* (July 1996) p.60
248. ITA, s.22(2)(j)
249. ITA s.19(2)(c). Such payment to a payee is also exempt, see s.22(1) (p)

an expenditure of a domestic or private nature which is not allowable as a deduction.[251]

11. Pension

The amount of pension paid to any person is not an allowable deduction.[252] The rationale for this provision is again to avoid double taxation relief since payees of pensions are exempted from taxation.[253] The provision is based on the IMF recommendation.[254]

12. Alimony or Separation Allowance

Any alimony or allowance paid under any judicial order or written agreement of separation is not deductible for taxation purposes of the payer.[255] The rationale for this provison is again to avoid double taxation relief.[256] The payee of such alimony or allowance is exempted from taxation.[257]

Conclusion

An attempt has been made to review the provisions of the Income Tax Act, Cap 340, relating to the taxation of business in Uganda. Apart from simplifying the law, the Income Tax Act has reintroduced presumptive taxation for low-income business groups and is aimed at considering the tax base by capturing the informal sector and traders who find it difficult to prepare accounts. The Act has also introduced a limited form of capital gains tax which is restricted to the disposal of business assets. The ITA, in line with IMF recommendations, has streamlined taxation reliefs by limiting them to the beneficiaries of payments, particularly those in relation to pensions, contributions from retirement funds, payments on life insurance policies and alimony or allowance following a divorce or judicial separation of a married couple. The Act has replaced the blanket exemptions under the Investment Code with a depreciation allowance regime which is more objective and equitable to administer.

250. *Supra* n.247 and text thereof
251. ITA, s.22(2)(a),(3), *C.I.T v. D., supra* n.216
252. *Ibid* s.22(2)(K)
253. *Ibid* s.21(1)(n)
254. IMF, *supra* n.247
255. ITA, s.22(2)(l)
256. See *supra* n.247 and text thereof
257. ITA, s.21(1)(h)

5

Taxation of Companies

A. Introduction

A company is a distinct legal person. However, it is an artificial person and can only act through the agency of natural persons, that is, its owners or shareholders or its managers, normally directors. By its nature, the company poses taxation problems.[1] In this context three issues arise. First, does Parliament follow the strict legal theory and recognise the company as a truly independent entity and, therefore, tax it just like any other taxpayer? Second, does Parliament strip aside the corporate mask and look at the reality, apportion the company's profits among the true owners in proportion to their ownership, and tax the shareholders on the company's profits as well as its own. Third, does Parliament adopt a compromise solution, taxing the company's profits in one way and the distribution of those profits in another way?

In the United Kingdom, whose practice Uganda follows, the compromise position has been adopted, resulting into two systems: first, the taxation of the company's profits involving liability to corporation tax and second, taxation of the company's distributions by dividend, or otherwise, involving the payment of advance corporation tax and the use of credits. The systems are distinct but linked by the tax credit.

B. Charge to Corporation Tax

The Income Tax Act[2] charges tax for each year of income on every person (which includes a company[3]) who has chargeable income.[4] In the context of a company, chargeable income[5] includes business and property income.[6] Where the company is resident its gross income includes income derived form all geographical sources,[7] while if it is non-resident its income includes only income derived from sources in Uganda.[8]

"Company" means a body of persons corporate or unincorporate, whether created or recognised under the law in force in Uganda or elsewhere, and a unit trust, but does not include any other trust or partnership.[9]

1. See generally *Mayson on Revenue Law* (14th ed., 1993) p. 536
2. Cap. 340 *Laws of Uganda*, 2000
3. ITA, s.2
4. *Ibid* s4(1)
5. Defined ibid S.15
6. ITA, s.17(1)(a),(c), 18, 20
7. *Ibid* s.17(2)(a)
8. *Ibid.* s.17(2)(b)
9. *Ibid* s.2

C. Residence

1. Definition

Residence in relation to a company means[10] a resident company for a year of income if it:

- is incorporated or formed under the laws of Uganda,
- has its management and control exercised in Uganda at any time during the year of income, or
- undertakes the majority of its operations in Uganda during the year of income.

In *De Beers Consolidated Mines Ltd v. Howe*[11] Lord Loreburn stated in relation to the residence of a company.

> Now, it is easy to ascertain where an individual resides, but when the natural sense does not reside anywhere, some artificial test must be applied... A company cannot eat or sleep, but it can keep house and do business. We ought, therefore, to see where it really keeps house or does business. The principle in *Calcutta Jute Mills v. Nicholson* (1986) 1 T.C. 83, involved the principle that a company resides for the purposes of income tax where its real business is carried on... I regard that as a true rule, and the real business is carried on where the central management and control actually abides.[12]

However, the powers of management and control are normally vested in directors of an incorporated company.[13] The central management and control would therefore abide at the place where directors hold meetings.[14] It is notable in this respect that the powers of management and control could revert to shareholders in general meeting in four major instances: (1) where there is a deadlock on the board and directors cannot agree,[15] (2) where there is no effective quorum for the board to meet,[16] (3) where directors are disqualified from voting,[17] and (4) where there are no directors (for instance where the company is in the process of being wound up).[18]

The common law definition of "residence" is regarded as amorphous.[19] Consequently strict reliance on the statutory definition may be advisable. In the United Kingdom there is an interesting statutory definition of residence in relation to a company:

> A company which is incorporated in United Kingdom shall be regarded for purposes of the Taxes Act as resident there; accordingly, if a different place is given by any rule of law, that place shall no longer be taken into account.[20]

10. *Ibid* S.10
11. [1906] A.C. 455
12. *Ibid* p.458. See also Bakibinga, *Company Law in Uganda,* (2001) pp.21-25
13. Companies Act, Cap. 110. 1st Schedule, Table A Article 80; Bakibinga. *Ibid* pp. 191-201
14. *Calcutta Jute Mills v. Nicholson* (1876) 1 Ex.D. 428; *Egyptian Delta & Investment Co Ltd v. Todd* [1929] AC 1
15. *Barron v. Potter* [1914] 1 Ch. 895
16. *Foster v. Foster* [1916] 1 Ch. 532
17. *Grant v. United Kingdom Switchback Rlys* (1888) 40 Ch. D. 135
18. *Alexander Ward & Co. Ltd v. Samyang Navigation Co. Ltd* [1975] 2 all E.R. 424 H.L. (E)
19. Mayson *supra* n. 1. p. 535
20. Finance Act, 1988, S. 66

2. Dual Residence

The effect of the above provision is that contrary to the decision in *Unit Construction Co. Ltd v. Bullock*,[21] to the effect that a company's residence "is the actual place of management, not that place which it ought to be managed, which fixes the residence of a company," a company will under U.K. law have dual residence if, though incorporated and, therefore, resident in U.K., it operates in a country which treats management and control (or some other criterion other than incorporation) as its test of residence. However, this may be resolved by the application of the "tie breaker" clause in a double tax treaty.[22] This view is relevant in the Ugandan context given, that apart from incorporation, the test of management and control is also used, and Uganda has a double taxation convention with the United Kingdom. It is also significant that according to an earlier decision in a *Bullock* case,[23] a company could have more than one residence for tax purposes.[24]

To prevent tax avoidance arising from the concept of dual residence, a United Kingdom statute[25] provides that if the assets of a dual-resident company become no longer liable to U.K. tax (due to double taxation agreement), there will be deemed disposal of assets at that time at market value, so that unrealised gains will be charged to tax and will not escape charge. There are also limits on the availability of roll-over relief on business assets for dual resident companies.[26]

3. Change of Residence

Under the test of "central management and control" it could be possible for a company to change its residence by changing the place where its directors meet. Since residence is the test for corporate tax liability, a company incorporated in the United Kingdom could avoid taxation by having its directors meet abroad. This is dealt with in the United Kingdom by first subjecting non-resident companies to corporation tax if they trade in the United Kingdom.[27] In Uganda this is catered for under Section 17(2) of the Income Tax Act, Cap 340. A second way to prevent tax avoidance was to prevent resident companies from emigrating without the consent of the treasury,[28] although this requirement was withdrawn March 1988 and substituted with the requirement that they pay tax before they move.[29] If there is a delay in paying the tax within six months, any company within the same group or any person who within the relevant period was a controlling director of the taxpayer company or a company with control over it can be assessed for any unpaid tax.[30]

Because collection of tax from a non-resident company can be difficult, it is provided

21. [1960] A.C. 351
22. *Mayson on Revenue Law*, supra, n.1 p.539
23. *Supra* n.21
24. *Swedish Central Railway Co. Ltd v. Thompson* [1925] A.C. 495 H.L.
25. Finance Act, 1989, S. 132
26. *Ibid* s.133
27. Income and Corporation Taxes Act, 1988, S. 11 (1)
28. *Ibid* Ss 765 - 767
29. Finance Act, 1988 (U.K.), S. 130
30. Finance Act, 1989 (U.K.), S. 134

that the tax can be assessed and charged in the name of the branch or agency.[31]

D. Computation of Profits

1. General

The general principle is that a company is chargeable to corporation tax on all its profits.[32] A trust corporation is not liable to corporation tax on trust income or gains, although it will be liable to corporation tax on fees charged by it for acting as a trustee. It is also liable to corporation tax if it is a beneficiary under a trust and is such a beneficiary, if an individual would be liable to income tax.[33]

Corporation tax is charged on chargeable income.[34] The computation of profits is, therefore, made up of both gains and profits.

2. Income

Although strictly speaking companies are not liable to income tax *per se*, their income profits are computed in accordance with income tax principles.[35] Consequently, it is expected that income would be computed in accordance with Sections 15, 17, 18 and 20 of the ITA, appropriate to the source of income which accrues to the company. The company's income profits are, therefore, the aggregate income chargeable in accordance with Section S. 15, 17, 18 of the ITA.[36] Any exemptions from income tax are also available to companies charged corporation tax except where the exemption is restricted to individuals.[37]

Four aspects require special consideration.

(a) Professional Activities

A company cannot carry on a profession.[38] However, it can be assessed corporation tax in accordance with Section 18 of ITA in respect of its trade of hiring out professional services of its employees or agents.

(b) Dividends

The system inherited from the United Kingdom of corporate taxation operates by subjecting dividends and other distributions of resident companies to a separate regime.[39] However, it should be noted that the receipt of dividends and distributions of resident companies is not taken into account for purposes of corporation tax,[40] and the payment of a dividend or other distribution is not allowed as a deduction in computing that income.[41]

---

31. Taxes Management Act, 1970, Ss 78, 79, 85 (U.K.). See also ITA, S.82
32. ITA SS5(1), 17(1)(a)(c),(2)18, 20
33. *Ibid* S.71(1)
34. *Ibid* S.4 (1), 15, 17(1)(a),(c),18, 20. Part II, Third Schedule
35. See e.g. Income and Corporation Taxes Act, 1988, S. 9 (1) (U.K.)
36. discussed *supra* Chapter 4
37. ITA, Ss. 21, 22, (1) discussed *supra* Chapter 4
38. *William Epstein Son & Swainston Ltd v. IRC* [1919] 2 K.B. 731
39. See *infra*
40. ITA, S.74(1)

This achieves the separation of dividends from the charge to corporation tax and has the necessary consequence that resident companies declare their dividends out of taxed profits.

(c) Interest

A company may deduct from its income any yearly interest payable on an advance or loan borrowed or employed. In the production of income, provided that it is not an expense deductible in ascertaining taxable income under Section 16 of ITA.[42]

3. Authorised Deductions

Amounts of profit chargeable to corporation tax may only be reduced by deductions authorised by Sections 22(1), 23-38 of ITA.[43]

(a) Management Expenses

Where a company's income arises from trading activities, the expenses of managing the company are deductible under Section 23 (1) of ITA. However, if the company's income arises from investments (such as rents or dividends), the expenses of managing the investments themselves are allowable but the expense of managing the company is not. Thus in *C. Co Ltd v. Commissioner of Income Tax*,[44] it was held that the appellant company's business at all times was that of holding investments. Therefore, it was not entitled to deductions in respect of transactions of a speculative nature. In this instance the court examined the Memorandum of Association to determine the business of the company.

However, in the United Kingdom the expense of managing an investment company may be deducted in computing the total profits of a resident company.[45] An "investment company" is defined as a company whose business consists wholly or mainly in making of investments and the principal part of whose income is derived therefrom and includes a savings bank. There is no definition of "expenses of management."[46] However, the term is said to include administrative expenses, including salaries and wages, although commissions referred to will not include stock brokers' commissions on change of investments.[47]

(b) Capital Allowances

A company is entitled to the same capital allowance and is subject to the same charges as an individual in relation to capital expenditure for which relief may be claimed under the Income Tax Act.[48] The chargeable period for companies is in respect of "any year of income."

The provisions relating to capital allowances for the provision of machinery or

41. *Ibid* s. 71
42. *Ibid.* ITA, S. 25
43. Discussed *supra* Chap 4
44. 1 E.A.T.C. 15 (Kenya) discussed *supra* Chap. 4
45. ICTA (U.K.) 1988, S. 75
46. *Ibid*
47. See *Capital & National Trust Ltd v. Golder* [1949] 2 All E.R. 956; *Hoechst Finance Ltd v. Gumbrell* [1983] STC 150 C.A.
48. ITA, Ss. 26-29

plant also apply to machinery or plant provided for the management of an investment company.[49]

(c) Losses

Expenses incurred by the company in respect of a particular source of income may exceed the income from that source leading to loss in respect of source. Consequently, relief may be claimed under Section 22 (1) of the ITA.

It is suggested that[50] relief for commencement losses[51] only applies to individuals and is not available to companies. This is because the company will normally have no previous income against which a commencement loss may be set (although such a situation could arise if any existing company begins trading activities some time after its formation).

4. Allowable Charges

Allowable charges include interest on loans;[52] expenditure on the training of employees in a field relevant to the company's business;[53] medical expenses of employees where the company has a scheme for treatment of its employees, and payment is made directly to the doctors or medical establishments;[54] and donations to charitable institutions designated by the Commissioner General.[55] All these charges have been discussed in detail in the context of general taxation of business.[56]

E. Computation of Liability to Corporation Tax

1. Basis of Assessment

Corporation tax is charged for any financial year for which Parliament so determines. The tax is charged on a current-year basis by reference to the company's accounting period. "Accounting period" is defined as "the period for which such person makes up the account of its business."[57] It is, therefore, important to know what the company's accounting period is and to consider the apportionment of profits to different financial years.

(a) Accounting Period

Under the Companies Act,[58] directors of a company are required to prepare a profit-and-loss account and balance sheet by reference to the company's accounting period, which is normally a period of 12 months ending on 30 June or any other date chosen

49. *Ibid* S.27
50. Mayson, *supra* n.1 pp. 550 -551. See further, Bakibinga, *supra* n.12 pp.31-37
51. ITA, S.30
52. *Ibid* S.25
53. *Ibid* S.33
54. *Ibid* S.22 (1)
55. *Ibid* S.34
56. See *supra* Chapter 4
57. ITA, S.39 refers to the normal year of income as a period of twelve months ending on 30 June. The period may be varied following an application to the Commissioner: S.39(1), (2), (9).
58. Cap. 110

by the company and specified in a notice to the Registrar of Companies.[59] As already observed,[60] accounting period is the period for which the company makes up the accounts of its business. In this vein, the period of account must be a definite period having a beginning and an end. Normally the accounting period is the period of 12 months since the end of the previous accounting period.[61] There is normally a starting point for the first-ever accounting period (18 months after incorporation) and subsequently once at least in every year.[62]

There is also provision for cessation of trade or other income-producing activities and the time at which the company ceases altogether to be liable to corporation tax.[63]

In the event that the accounting period does not coincide with the fiscal year, for purposes of assessment, such company's year of income shall be deemed to be the fiscal year in which such company's accounting year ends.[64] Such accounting year can only be changed with the approval of the Commissioner General.[65]

(b) Full Amount of Current Profits

Corporation tax is assessed and charged for any accounting period on the full amount of gains or profits arising in the period.[66]

(c) Apportionment

Corporation tax is charged by reference to the profits of an accounting period which falls within the financial year for which the tax is charged (1 July-30 June). If a company makes up its accounts to any date other than 30 June, each accounting period will fall into two different financial years. The profits for each accounting period will then have to be apportioned on a time basis to determine how much of the profits fell within a particular financial year and fall to be charged at the rate of corporation tax appropriate for that year.[67]

Example

C Ltd makes up its accounts to 31 December. For the accounting period ending December 1993, its profits are Shs20,000,000. Its liability to corporation tax will be computed as follows:

Period from January 1993 to June 1993

These six months fall within the financial year 1992/1993 and the profits for this period of tax are 6/12 of Shs20,000,000/= = Shs10,000,000/=.
Corporation tax on these profits will be Shs10,000,000/= @ 35 percent (rate for 1992/93

59. *Ibid.* Ss 148, 155, 157. See also Bakibinga, *supra* n.12, pp. 236 - 239
60. See *supra* n. 57 and text thereof
61. ITA, S. 39(1)
62. Companies Act, Cap.110, S. 148. See ITA, S.39(1), (2)
63. ITD, S. 27
64. ITA, S.39(6)
65. *Ibid* ITA, S. 39(2)
66. *Ibid* ITA Ss 15, 17(1) (a) (c), 19, 20
67. *Ibid* S. 111 (2)

Fiscal Year) = Shs3,500,000/=.

Period from 1 July 1993 to 31 December 1993

The six months fall within the Financial Year 1993/1994 and the profits for this period are 6/12 of Shs20,000,000/= = Shs10,000,000/=.

Corporation tax on these profits will be Shs10,000,000 @ 30 percent (rate for 1993/1994) = Shs3,000,000/=.

TOTAL corporation tax for this accounting period is 1 January to June 1993 Shs3,500,000/=

+ 1 July to 31 December 1993 Shs3,000,000/=

Shs6,500,000/=

2. Rate of Corporation Tax

The rate of corporation tax is 30 percent for companies.[68]

3. Payment

The corporation tax is payable within 45 days from the date of service of notice of such assessment.[69] However, when the return is required to be submitted under Section 96, the date is the date of submission of the return.[70]

Where a provisional assessment is made on a company pursuant to Section 112, the tax charged is payable in two equal installments as follows:

> On or before the last day of the sixth and twelfth months of the year of income in respect of the taxpayer's liability for income tax for that year.[71]

For this purpose the amount of each Instalment of provisional tax is calculated according to the formula 50% x (A-B)

A represents the estimated tax payable by the provisional taxpayer for the year of income, while *B* is the amount of any tax withheld under the ITA before the due date for payment during the year of income which would be included in the gross income of the taxpayer for that year.[72]

The due date for payment of an Instalment of provisional tax may be extended and installments varied upon application to the Commissioner.[73] Since the installment is a debt due to the government, it may be recovered in accordance with provisions of ITA relating to collection and recovery of provisional tax.[74] Finally, each installment of provisional tax is credited against the income tax assessed to the provisional taxpayer for the relevant year of income.[75] When such credit exceeds the income tax assessed for the year, the excess shall be refunded to the taxpayer.[76]

4. Change in Control of Companies

68. ITA, S.7, Third Schedule Part II
69. ITA, S.103(1) (b)
70. *Ibid* S. 103 (1) (a)
71. *Ibid* S.111(2) (a)
72. *Ibid* S.111(3)
73. *Ibid* S.111(6)
74. *Ibid* S.111(7) read together with S.104
75. *Ibid* S.111(8)
76. *Ibid* S.111 (9) read together with S.113

When, during a year of income, there is a change of 50 percent or more in the underlying ownership of a company in comparison with its ownership the previous year, the company is not allowed to deduct an assessed loss[77] in the year of income or in subsequent years with two exceptions. The company can deduct on an assessed loss if the loss is (1) exhausted within two years of the change or (2) for a period of two years after the change the company

- continues to carry on the same business and
- does not engage in any new business or investment the primary purpose of which or the beneficial owners thereof is to utilise the assessed loss so as to reduce the tax payable on the income arising from the new business or investment.[78]

The effect of this provision is that an assessed loss will be deductible for purposes of taxation where there has been a minimum change of ownership of 50 percent if the company continues to carry on the same business or does not engage in other business with the aim of reducing the tax liability using the assessed loss. This is in line with the basic principle under the ITA that deductions should be related to production of the relevant income.[79]

5. Roll-over Relief in Relation to Transfer of Business Assets

a) Transfer

If a resident person (transferor) transfers a business asset, with or without any liability not in excess of the cost base of the asset, to a resident company other than an exempt organisation (transferee) in exchange for a share in the transferee and the transferor has a 50 percent or greater interest in the voting power of the transferee immediately after the transfer:

- the transfer is not treated as a disposal of the asset by the transferor but is treated as the acquisition by the transferee of a business asset;
- the transferee's cost base for the asset is equal to the transferor's cost base for the asset at the time of the transfer; and
- the cost base of a share received by the transferor in exchange for the asset is equal to the cost base of the asset transferred, less any liability assumed by the transferor in respect of the asset.[80]

The relief is applicable to probable liability for capital gains tax in respect of disposal of a business asset under Section 18(1)(a) and Part VI of the ITA.[81]

b) Liquidation

77. See ITA, S.38 (1)
78. *Ibid* S75
79. *Ibid* SS.22(1), 39(1)
80. *Ibid* S.77(1)
81. Discussed *supra* chapter 4

If as part of the liquidation of a resident company a business asset is transferred to a shareholder being a resident other than an exempt organisation[82] (transferee company) and immediately before the transfer the transferee held 50 percent or greater interest in the voting power of the liquidated company:

- the transfer is not treated as a disposal of the assets by the liquidated company but instead is treated as the acquisition of a business asset by the transferee company,
- the transferee's cost base for the asset is equal to the liquidated company's cost base for the asset at the time of transfer,
- the transfer of the asset is not a dividend, and
- no gain or loss is taken into account on the cancellation of the transferee's shares in the liquidated company.[83]

Similar to a transfer (above), the relief is given to possible liability for capital gains tax in respect of a disposal of a business asset under Section 18(1)(a) and Part VI of the ITA.[84]

c) Reorganisation of Company

In the event of a resident company or group of companies being re-organised without any significant change in the underlying ownership or control of the company or group, the Commissioner is empowered to permit any affected company to treat the re-organisation as not giving rise to the disposal of any business asset or the realisation of any business debt as may be applicable. The Commissioner may also determine the cost base of any business asset held or business debt undertaken by the company after reorganisation to reflect the fact that no disposal or realisation is treated as having occurred.[85]

F. Dividends and Distributions

1. Preliminary

The rules for computation of a company's profits prohibit the deduction of the company's dividends and other distributions to its share and security holders both as an expense[86] and as a charge on income. These distributions must, therefore, be made after the company has paid corporation tax. The taxation of dividends is, therefore, dealt with by a distinct system from the taxation of a company's profits.

The logical way to tax dividends and distributions is to say that the company has paid its corporation tax, made its distributions and ought therefore to drop out of the picture, leaving shareholders to pay tax on their receipts. Although this is logical, it involves the risk that the Uganda Revenue Authority (URA) might be too late to collect the tax on

82. Defined in ITA, S.2 as an institution, company or irrevocable trust which is an amateur sporting association, religious, charitable or educational institution of a public character, trade union or employers' association or employees' association legally registered or an association set up to promote farming, mining, tourism, manufacturing or commerce and industry in Uganda; exempted from tax by the Commissioner and none of whose income or assets confers or may confer a private benefit or any person.
83. ITA, S.77(2)
84. See *supra* n.81
85. ITA, S.77(3). For rationale thereof see *supra* n.81 and 84 and text thereof.
86. See e.g. Income and Corporation Taxes Act, 1988, S. 337 (2) (a) (U.K.)

distributions, the shareholders having spent the receipts pending assessment to tax.[87] The practice is to collect tax at source. The source in this instance is the company. When it makes a distribution it is liable to make payment to URA equal to the relevant tax rate on the gross amount of the dividend. This payment is known as "advance corporation tax" because the company, having itself become liable to pay corporation tax on all profits including the distributions, is allowed to set the advance corporation tax against the final liability to corporation tax.

Since the object of the system is to collect tax on behalf of the recipients, the amount of the tax paid by the company confers a tax credit to shareholders. Advance Corporation Tax is, therefore, the key to the whole system of corporate taxation. The effect is that it links the taxation of the company's profits with the taxation of dividends and distributions by acting as a tax credit for the company itself. It links the company to payment of tax on behalf of its shareholders by treating Advance Corporation Tax as a tax credit for shareholders. This is otherwise known as the "imputation system," because Advance Corporation Tax is imputed to its shareholders. This system is, however, restricted to qualifying distributions.

2. Distributions

(a) Shares

(i) Charge

A share is a bundle of rights and liabilities to the company which issued that share.[88] One of the rights is the right to dividend or distribution in respect of the share. Company law rules governing declaration of dividends are complicated and tied to a desire by the legislature to ensure that the company's capital is maintained for the benefit of the creditors.[89]

For corporation tax purposes, a dividend paid by a resident company shall be deemed to be income of the year of income in which it is payable.[90] With regard to a company in the process of liquidation, any profits earned before or during the winding up which are distributed in any form – that is, by cash or otherwise in excess of the nominal value of the share redeemed, cancelled or subject to liquidation – are deemed to be payment of a dividend.[91] However, a dividend received by a company which controls, directly or indirectly, less than 25 percent of the voting power of the paying company is exempted from tax.[92]

The discussion which follows applies to legal positions before the promulgation of the Income Tax Act, 1997. In contrast to the repealed Income Tax Decree, 1974, the Income Tax Act contains no provisions on deemed distributions.

87. ITA, S.118 (1) read together with S.111(8)
88. See generally, Bakibinga, *Company Law in Uganda* Chapters 8 and 9, pp. 154-156
89. *Lee v. Neuchatel Asphalte* (1889) 41 Ch. D.1.; *Foster v. New Trinidad Lake Asphalt Co.* [1901] 1 Ch. 208
90. ITA, Ss. 2 (definition of dividend), 20 (1)(a)
91. *Ibid.* Ss.2 (b) (definition of dividend), 20 (1) (a)
92. *Ibid.* ITA, S. 74 (2)

(ii) Deemed Distributions

Ordinarily, dividends must be distributed within 12 months after the end of the relevant accounting period. Where this is not done and the company retains the profits, the Commissioner General may treat such profits as having been distributed as dividends within the said required period.[93] This is called a deemed distribution of dividends. For this purpose, the Commissioner General may adjust the charge to tax on the company relative to the liability of any shareholder,[94] which would entitle the company to recover the relevant tax attributable to the shareholder from the shareholder.[95] Where the profits are subsequently distributed, the proportionate share in the adjustment of any shareholder is excluded in computing the total income of the shareholders.[96]

The deeming of dividend requirements does not apply to a private company which is a subsidiary of a public company or to a company which is substantially controlled by government.[97]

A private company, may, before making a distribution, inquire from the Commissioner General whether he intends to apply the deemed dividend rule.[98]

Where the deemed distribution is applied as between holding and subsidiary companies, the dividend deemed to have been received by the holding company shall be deemed to be part of the income of that company that is available for distribution to its shareholders.[99] The application of the deemed dividend rule may be seen from the following decisions.

In *G v. Commissioner of Income Tax*[100] the appellant was a shareholder in a private company, which did not declare any dividends in respect of its total income for the years 1943 and 1944. The Commissioner served the relevant notice deeming 60 percent of the total income of the company for those years to have been distributed as dividends. The appellant was assessed income tax for the years of assessment, 1945 and 1946, in respect of the portions of the dividends deemed to have been distributed relevant to his shareholding. He appealed to the Local Committee, which varied the assessment to 25 percent and 40 percent, respectively, for the relevant years. On further appeal by the Commissioner to the High Court, the court restored the Commissioner's assessment, which was also upheld by Court of Appeal in dismissing the appellant's appeal.

In *Commissioner of Income Tax v. U*,[101] the respondent, a director of a company in which he held about 75 percent of the shares, challenged the application of the deeming of dividend rule under Section 21 of Ordinance No. 8 of 1940 on the ground that the company was a company in which the public was substantially interested.[102] The Privy Council and the Court of Appeal for Eastern Africa reversed the High Court by holding

---

93. Income Tax Decree 1974 S. 23 (1) For construction, see *Jafferali Mohamedali Alibhai v. Commissioner, Income Tax* 3E.A.T.C. 328
94. *Ibid.* S. 23 (2)
95. *Ibid.* S. 23 (2) Proviso (a)
96. *Ibid.* S. 23 (2) Proviso (b)
97. *Ibid.* S. 23 (3)
98. *Ibid.* S. 23 (4)
99. *Ibid.* S. 23 (5)
100. 1 E.A.T.C. 43 C.A. (Tanganyika)
101. 2 E.A.T.C. (Pt I & II) 1 P.C. (Uganda). See also *B. U. v. Commissioner of Income Tax* 4 E.A.T.C. (Pt I) 210
102. Presumably within the equivalent of S. 23 (3) of ITD, 1974

that the company, by having shareholders other than the respondent and his brother who had a controlling interest therein, was one in which the public was substantially interested and was therefore exempted from the application of the deeming of dividend rule.

In *A.N. v. Commissioner of Income Tax,*[103] the appellant's wife was a shareholder to which Section 22 of the East African Income Tax (Management) Act 1952[104] applied. The Commissioner made an order whose effect was to deem 100 percent of the total income of the company being deemed to have been distributed as dividends. The appellant was then assessed income tax on the proportionate share of the deemed distribution attributable to his wife. He appealed to both the Local Committee and the Supreme Court on the ground that the money standing to the credit of shareholders in their current accounts and utilised by the company was loan capital of the company and, therefore, the 100 percent deemed distribution order was improper. Both the Local Committee and the Supreme Court rejected the appeal and confirmed the assessment. They held that the sums in question were not loan capital within Section 22 of the East African Income Tax (Management) Act, 1952.

Furthermore, in *Sir George Arnautoglu v. Commissioner of Income Tax,*[105] in 1953, the appellant entered into an agreement with C that he would sell 40,000 shares in Arnautoglu Estates Limited to C (Pty) Limited, the purchase price of £40,000 to be paid within one year and until then the shares to be held cum dividend by a bank for transfer to the purchaser upon payment. The transfer of the shares to the bank was duly registered on 29 June, 1953. On 22 March, 1954, a dividend of £1,500 was declared in respect of the shares, and on 7 May of that year C informed the appellant that C (Pty) Limited was unable to pay the purchase price. Thereafter the legal ownership of the shares reverted to the appellant.

In June 1953, the Commissioner issued an order to Arnautoglu Estates Limited under Section 22 of the East African Income Tax (Management) Act 1952,[106] to the effect that the sum of Shs3,386,532 of the undistributed profits of the company for the period ending December 1952 was deemed to have been distributed to the shareholders of the company on 30 June, 1953. The amount deemed to have been distributed in respect of the shares held in the name of the bank was £23,705, and the appellant was assessed tax on this sum for the year of income 1953. The assessment was raised on the appellant irrespective of the shares' registration in the name of the bank in exercise of a power under Section 22 (1) of the Act. The appellant's appeals to the Local Committee, High Court and Court of Appeal were rejected. The Court of Appeal held that the bank held the shares in the capacity of a trustee within Section 22 (1) of the Act and that it held the shares and actual dividend on behalf of the appellant and no beneficial interest became at any time vested in the intended purchaser.

In *Houry v. Commissioner of Income Tax,*[107] the appellant had transferred shares in a company to his two sons who were "children" within the meaning of Section 24 (a) of the

103. 2 E.A.T.C. (Pt I & II) 167 (Uganda)
104. equivalent to ITD, 1974, S. 23
105. 3 E.A.T.C. 473; [1964] E.A. 132 C.A. (Tanganyika). See also *T.M. Bell v. C.I.T.* [1960] E.A. 224
106. equivalent to ITD, 1974, S. 23
107. [1958] E.A. 350

East African Income Tax (Management) Act, 1952. The Commissioner made an order under Section 22 (1) of that Act[108] deeming a portion of the undistributed income of the company to have been distributed as dividends among the shareholders. The appellant conceded that this was proper. However he brought a further appeal to determine whether the notional income arising from an order under Section 22 (1)[109] of the Act was, or was to be treated as "income paid to or for the benefit of a child of the settler" under Section 24 of the Act.[110] In this regard, it was contended that "paid" meant "paid in cash." It was held that the plain meaning of the section is that notional income arising in consequence of an order made under [S. 23 (1) ITD] is to be treated for all purposes of the Act [Decree] as income actually paid to the shareholder, and, therefore, for purposes of Section 24 such notional income must be treated as income actually paid.

The case of *H v. Commissioner of Income Tax*[111] is relevant to the application of Section 7 (1) (c) in a case where a company is in the process of voluntary liquidation and the deeming rule under Section 23 ITD. In that case the Commissioner on 17 April 1956 ordered that under Section 22 of the East African Income Tax (Management) Act, 1952,[112] 60 percent of the undistributed profits of a company were to be deemed to have been distributed among the shareholders as at July 31, 1953, and the taxpayer was accordingly assessed for the year of income, 1953. He appealed to the Local Committee which allowed the appeal and indicated that the dividends should have been deemed to be distributed on July 21, 1954. A fresh assessment was accordingly issued in respect of the year of income 1954, from which the appellant unsuccessfully appealed to the committee. The company had on July 21, 1954, passed a special resolution to wind up as a member's voluntary winding-up. In applying the relevant legislation to the facts, the court found that the relevant period in which the company's accounts should have been made up where the company was being wound up was August 1, 1953, to July 21, 1954, and the penultimate period was from August 1, 1952, to July 31, 1953. The company had declared no dividend for the penultimate period. The taxpayer argued that the date of the deemed distribution of income for the year ending July 31, 1953, should be the date of the Commissioner's first order from which he successfully appealed to the Committee or alternatively July 31, 1953, and in any event not a date in 1954. The Commissioner contended that such a date was discretionary on him, and in any case the Committee had indicated a date in 1954.

It was held that the apparent omission of any express reference to the date on which the deemed distribution is to be made in the case of the penultimate period would not under the Act be meaningless, since the provisions of Section 22 (1) as modified by Section 22 (8) of the E.A. Income Tax (Management) Act can reasonably be construed as making the date that of the Commissioner's order. Accordingly, the assessment was wrong, and the income from the deemed distribution should have been assessed to the year of income 1956.[113]

---

108. equivalent to ITD, 1974, S. 23
109. *Ibid*
110. Equivalent to ITD, 1974, S. 24
111. [1958] E.A. 303 (Uganda). See also *Commissioner of Stamps, Straits Settlements v. Oei Tjong Swan* [1933] A.C. 37
112. equivalent to ITD, 1974, S. 23 (Uganda)
113. See further *Cape Brandy Syndicate v. IRC* [1921] 1 K.B. 64

In *Voi Sisal Estates Ltd v. Hassan Kassim Lakha,*[114] the respondent company sued the appellant a former shareholder, for the refund of income tax paid by the respondent company in respect of the appellant following service upon the company of a notice under Section 22 of the E.A. Income Tax (Management) Act, 1952.[115] The claim had arisen out of an agreement made in 1952 between the company and two main groups of shareholders to divide the assets of the company between certain continuing and departing shareholders who would transfer their shares to the continuing shareholders. The appellant was one of the departing shareholders.

Clause 9 of the agreement stipulated that the liability for income tax and other taxes on profits accrued due up to June 30, 1952, should be the joint responsibility of both groups and their members in proportion to their shareholding. Clause 19 provided that both groups should pay their respective shares of income tax or any other tax assessed and indicated when the same should become due and payable. In 1953, the shares were transferred by the departing members to the continuing shareholders, but the income tax for 1952 was not finalised until 1958. As no profits for 1952 were distributed to the shareholders, the Commissioner, in exercise of Section 22[116] ordered that 60 percent of the total income of the company for the accounting period ending June 30, 1952, should be deemed to have been distributed among the shareholders as at December 30, 1952.

The appellant's share was assessed at Shs33,267/= and under Section 22 (4) of the E.A. Income Tax (Management) Act, he elected that the tax should be paid by the company. The High Court held that the appellant was obliged to reimburse the company with the tax paid under the agreement.

The appellant appealed to the Court of Appeal, which allowed the appeal and held that the tax payable on dividends deemed to have been distributed is payable on the income of the shareholder and that it does not matter who pays the tax, whether it be the shareholder or the company. Additionally, the court held that clauses 9 and 19 of the agreement related to tax upon the profits of the company and had no application to any tax which the company, by reason of the provisions of Section 22, had been called upon to pay in respect of the income of the shareholder. Finally, the court held that the appellant was not liable to reimburse the company the amount of the tax paid by the company under Section 22.

(iii) Taxation of Dividend

Finally on the issue of taxation of dividend, the case of *Commissioner of Income Tax v. Holdings Ltd*[117] is illustrative. In that case the respondent company deducted all its income received from dividends from resident companies from its chargeable income. The Commissioner contended that this was incorrect, and that only the net income from such dividends (i.e. after deduction of expenses) should have been deducted. The High Court having rejected the Commissioner's appeal, he appealed to the Court of Appeal. In dismissing the appeal, the court held that Section 58 (c) of the E.A. Income Tax (Management) Act, 1958, (then applicable) meant that the entire dividend received from

114. [1964] E.A. 532 (H.C. Uganda); [1965] E.A. 387 C.A.
115. equivalent to ITD, 1974, S. 23
116. *Ibid*
117. [1972] E.A. 128

resident companies should be deducted from the chargeable income and not the net dividend income after deducting expenses.

(iv) Returns

A resident company which pays any dividend is required to furnish a return of income within four months of the end of the relevant year of income.[118]

(v) Permissible Retention of Profits

Under the deeming of dividend rule,[119] the company may be permitted to retain profits up to 60 percent of income from ordinary activities and NIL for all investment income.[120]

Example

	Ordinary Income	Investment Income	Total
Income	6,000,000	1,500,000	7,500,000
Company Tax	1,800,000		1,800,000
After Tax	4,200,000	1,500,000	5,700,000
Retentions (60%)	2,530,000	--	2,520,000
	1,680,000	1,500,000	5,180,000

If the company had distributed less than Shs3,180,000/=, the difference is a shortfall which is deemed to have been distributed and is assessed on the company, which may claim from shareholders, at corporate rate of tax.

(b) Securities

If the company issues debentures or redeemable preference shares to any of its shareholders and receives no payment therefore, such issue is deemed to be payment of a dividend on the shares held by such shareholders equal to the nominal value or redeemable value, whichever is greater of such debentures or redeemable preference shares.[121] Alternatively, if debentures or redeemable preference shares are issued at a sum less than par or redeemable value provided that the discount exceeds 5 percent of par, the dividend is equal to the difference between the issue price and the higher of par or redeemable value.[122]

118. ITA, S.92(1)
119. ITD S.23
120. Simiyu, *Taxation* (Nairobi, 1992) pp 111-112
121. ITA, S.2w(i)(A) (definition of dividend)
122. *Ibid* S.2w(i)(B)

Example

Shs

Par Value	1,000/=
Redeemable Value	1,200/=
Issue Price	900/=

The dividend is equal to Shs1,200 - 900/= = Shs300/=.

(c) Withholding Tax

Dividend income is normally received net of withholding tax at the rate of 15 percent of the gross, and the tax so withheld is a final tax.[123]

d) Scope of a Dividend

As already pointed out,[124] the Income Tax Act 1997 does not contain provisions on deemed distributions. However, the definition of a dividend[125] describes situations which are regarded as giving rise to a dividend, such as when a company issues debenture or redeemable preference shares to a shareholder. If the shareholder provides no consideration, the taxable value of the dividend is the greater of an amount equal to the nominal or redeemable value of the debentures or shares. If issue is made for a lesser consideration than the true value, the amount equal to the excess is taken into account for taxation purpose. A dividend also includes a distribution upon redemption or cancellation of a share or made in the course of liquidation in excess of the nominal value of the share redeemed, cancelled or subject to liquidation. A dividend comprises, in the case of partial return of capital by a company, any payment made in excess of the amount by which the nominal value of the shares is reduced. In the case of a reconstruction of a company, a dividend covers any payment made in respect of the shares in the company in excess of the nominal value of the shares before the reconstruction. Finally, a dividend includes any loan, payment for an asset or services, the value of any asset or services provided or the value of any debt obligation released by a company to, or in favour of, a shareholder to the extent to which the transaction is, in substance, a distribution of profits.

The definition of dividend, therefore, tries to capture disguised distributions by a company to its shareholders for purposes of taxation.

e) Dividend Stripping

When a company takes part in a transaction involving dividend stripping and receives a dividend from a resident company in the transaction, the receiving company is required to include the dividend in its gross income to the extent to which the Commissioner considers necessary to offset any decrease in the value of shares in respect of which the dividend has been paid or in the value of any other property caused by the payment of a

123. *Ibid* S.118(1) Schedule 3 , Part V
124. See discussion on deemed distributions.
125. ITA, S.2

dividend.[126] In that situation, the Commissioner may reduce the amount of any deduction arising relative to the decrease in value of the shares or other property.[127]

Dividend stripping is defined[128] to include the following arrangements:

i) A target company has accumulated or current-year profits or both represented by cash or other readily realisable assets.

ii) Another company (acquiring company) acquires the shares in the target company for an amount which reflects the profits of the target company.

iii) The disposal of the shares in the target company gives rise to a tax-free capital gain to the shareholders in the target company.[129]

iv) Following acquisition of shares in the target company by the acquiring company, the former pays a dividend to the latter, which under S.74(2) would be exempt from tax in the hands of the target company.

v) Following declaration of dividend, the acquiring company sells the shares at a loss.

The Income Tax Decree, 1974 did not contain provision on dividend stripping.

G. Unit Trusts

1. Nature

A unit trust is defined as a unit trust registered or required to be registered as Parliament may by law prescribe.[130] Another definition is that a unit trust is "any arrangement made for the purpose, or having the effect, of providing for persons having funds available for investment, facilities for the participation by them, as beneficiaries under a trust, in profits or income arising from the acquisition, holding, management or disposal of any property whatsoever."[131] The definition of "securities" includes units under a unit trust scheme.[132]

Essentially, then the unit trust is an investment scheme by which persons pool their subscriptions under a trust deed.[133] The scheme involves a managing company and a trustee or trustees – usually another company or bank. The practice is normally for the managing company to acquire securities such as shares or debentures which have been quoted on the stock exchange and to transfer them to trustees who become the sole custodians thereof. The securities are in turn divided into units and offered to the public for investment after quotation on the stock exchange. The investors become beneficiaries under the trust deed and are entitled to securities in proportion to their holdings. The unit trust may be fixed, that is, with securities to be held strictly defined, or it may be flexible or managed. In the latter case, the managing company has wide powers and discretion to invest, subject to the provisions of the trust deed. The unit trust has the advantage of enabling people with small investments to spread the risk over a wide area.

---

126. *Ibid* S.76(2)
127. *Ibid* S.76(2)
128. *Ibid* S.76(3)
129. This may happen in the context of transfer envisaged under S.77 (discussed *supra*).
130. ITA, S.2
131. Exchange Control Act Cap. 171 (*Laws of Uganda* 2000 ed.), S. 46
132 *Ibid*
133. Gower's *Principles of Company Law* (4th ed. 1979 Stevens) pp. 266-272. See also Bakibinga, *Company Law in Uganda* (Professional Books Publishers, Kampala, 1993) p. 28

2. Charge to Tax

In contrast to the repealed law,[134] there are no detailed provisions in ITA, Cap 340, for taxing unit trusts. However, since a company is defined to include a unit trust, it is assumed that the rules applicable to a company also apply to a unit trust.

H. Members' Clubs and Trade Associations

1. Definition

A members' club is defined[135] as a club or similar institution, all the assets of which are owned by or held in trust for the members thereof. A member, relative to a club, is a person, who, while a member, is entitled to an interest in all the assets of such club in the event of liquidation. In relation to a trade association, a member is a person who is entitled to vote at a general meeting of that trade association.

2. Liability to Tax

A body of persons which carries on a members' club is deemed to be carrying on a business, and the gross receipts on revenue account (including entrance fee and subscriptions) shall be deemed to be income from a business.[136] Clubs and associations are taxed at the corporate rate of 30 percent.[137]

J. Rate of Tax

The corporate rate is 30 percent for all companies.[138]

---

134. ITD, 1974, S.19
135. ITA,. 60 (4). See further Bakibinga, supra n. 133 pp. 25-26. See also *Commissioner of Income Tax v. Law Society of Kenya* [1967] E.A. 669
136. *Ibid* S.60(2)
137. *Ibid* S.7 Schedule 3 part II
138. *Ibid*

6

Taxation of Partnerships

A. Nature of Partnership

1. Existence

A partnership is an association of persons (partners) formed for the purpose of carrying out a commercial objective. It is defined as the "relation which subsists between persons carrying on a business in common with a view of profit."[1]

The relationship is normally created by a deed of partnership. However, a deed will not create a partnership if it does not in fact exist.[2] In *Saywell v. Pope,*[3] Slade J. explained:

> I take it to be clear law that when persons enter into a written partnership agreement and state therein that they are to be partners as from the date prior to the date of execution of the agreement, or, as in the present case, that the partnership commenced on a date prior to the date of such execution, such a statement cannot in law operate retrospectively.

Similarly, in *Sterios Thomopoulos & Anors v. John Mandilas*,[4] it was indicated that a partnership can arise firstly from a mere agreement to agree which is subsequently implemented by all parties as shown by their conduct. The mode of dealing adopted by the partners may be evidence of formation and original terms of the partnership if such terms are not set forth in any document. It is evident from this that a partnership can arise informally or can be implied from the conduct of the parties. In *Ojemen v. Okoafuda*,[5] Uwaifo J. stated:

> The formation and terms of a partnership may be evidenced by partnership articles under seal, by an agreement signed by the partners, by an unsigned document drafted by one partner and adopted and acted (upon) by the others and even by an informal document initialled by the partners and intended only to form instructions for a formal document. Furthermore, a partnership may be established by parol evidence and this may be so even when articles of partnership are in existence.[6]

The existence of a partnership is a factual question. Thus in *Emorut v. Ojakol*,[7] it was held that the act of opening a bank account preparatory to the conclusion of a partnership did not amount to the creation of a partnership. The registration of the firm depended on the plaintiff meeting his obligation to pay the necessary contribution, which he failed

1. Partnership Act Cap. 114 (*Laws of Uganda* 2000 ed.), S. 2 (1). See also ITA, S.2
2. *Dickenson v. Gross* (1927) 11 TC 614; See also ITA, S.65(2)
3. [1979] STC 324
4. (1946) W.A.C.A. 269 (Nigeria)
5. 1977 NCLR 192 (High Court of Bendel State, Nigeria)
6. *Ibid.* pp 197-8. See also Bakibinga, *Partnership Law in Uganda* (1992) pp. 5-6
7. [1984] HCB 62

to do. In this regard it is important to stress, in line with the statutory definition of a partnership,[8] that a partnership depends on the existence of a business. In *Henshaw v. Roberts*[9] the court stated:

> ..... the existence of a partnership depends on the carrying on of business in partnership and not on the agreement to form a partnership.... if the parties have begun to carry on business (though prematurely) they will be regarded as partners.[10]

In *Bank of the North v. Dabare*,[11] Jones SPJ. observed that[12]

> The question of whether a partnership exists is one of mixed law and fact. The law is contained in Ss. 1 and 2 of the Partnership Act 1890 of the United Kingdom.[13] The facts are the common business activities of the parties as proved by their words and actions including if one exists, a written partnership agreement.

In *Arthur Corrie Lewin & Ors v. D.N. Neylan*,[14] it was held that the conduct of the parties could lead to the inference that a partnership exists.

The existence of a partnership is critical in establishing the tax liability or otherwise of the partners. Thus in *E v. Commissioner of Income Tax*,[15] before June 1942, the appellant carried on business as E & Co. In June 1942 he decided to admit three of his daughters and an infant son as partners. On 23 November 1942, a partnership deed was executed, whereby the partnership was stated to have commenced on 1 June, 1942. E and the children were each entitled to one-fifth share of the partnership profits. The partnership deed also provided that the appellant should have the sole exclusive management and control of the partnership business to the exclusion of the other partners and that other children of the appellant might be admitted to the partnership on such conditions as he might decide. Neither the three daughters nor the son contributed property, labour or skill to the partnership.

In November 1942, a deed of covenant was executed whereby each of the three daughters in consideration of being taken into partnership covenanted to pay one-sixth of her share of the partnership profits to her mother and another one-sixth of her share of partnership profits to each of two other infant daughters of the appellant.

In December 1942, a notice of change in the registered particulars was, under the Registration of Business Names Ordinance, given. Accounts for 1942 credited the profits of the business among the appellant, his wife and children in accordance with the partnership deed and deed of covenant. The effect was that in the books of the partnership the appellant was credited with only one-fifth of the profits.

The appellant was assessed on the whole of the profits of E & Co for 1942. He appealed to the local committee on the ground that he should be assessed only on his share of the profits of the partnership. The local committee confirmed the assessment and

8. *Supra* n.1 and text thereof
9. 1967 (1) ALR Comm 5. See also *W. v. Commissioner of Income Tax* 1969 (1) ALR Comm. 91 (Malawi)
10. *Ibid* pp. 11 - 12
11. 1976 NCLR 448 (Nigeria)
12. *Ibid* p. 451 Emphasis supplied.
13. equivalent to Partnership Act, Cap. 114, Ss 2 and 3
14. (1934) 1 E.A.C.A. 5
15. 1 E.A.T.C. 30 (Tanganyika). See also *CD & Co. v. Commissioner of Income Tax* 4 E.A.T.C. (Pt II) 15 (Kenya)

that the appellant had produced insufficient evidence to allow the appeal. It considered that appellant was in fact the proprietor of E & Co. and that members of his family were not partners for purposes of assessment of income tax. He appealed to the High Court, which dismissed the appeal and held that there was no evidence that a partnership existed before the execution of the deed, that no real partnership existed under the partnership deed, and that the proprietor was the sole proprietor of the business.

E v. Commissioner of Income Tax was distinguished in *M v. Income Tax,*[16] where the appellant owned an industrial property and needed money, which was borrowed from another company, to complete the buildings. In 1965 the appellants took in their six sons as further partners in the firm. There was no evidence that the sons brought in any property to the partnership. There were no provisions excluding the new partners from control or management[17] or operation of bank accounts or providing for future diminution of their shares. It was held that the sons were full partners and entitled to be treated as such.

2. Membership of the Partnership

(a) General

A second requirement for taxation purposes is to determine the membership of the partnership before it can be assessed. This is because income tax is not assessed on the partnership but on the partners' profits. It is, therefore, necessary to know who is a partner on whose profits income tax should be assessed.[18] In *I.R.C. v. Lebus' Executors,*[19] the widow of a deceased partner was entitled under his will to receive a share of the partnership profits for the rest of her life. The share due remained largely unpaid. It was held that she was not a partner and the share did not form part of her income unless and until paid to the executors for her benefit. Lord Greene MR explained thus:

> It is said that, where partners carry on business and make profits, they are assessable to income tax in respect of those profits, whether they take them out of the business and divide them or whether they do not... The fact that the profits are not released and paid over in cash to the partner has nothing to do with it from the income tax point of view. From the income tax point of view, they have made profits are taxable... But there is a difference in the world between the two cases, because Mrs Lebus is not a partner, and the assets of the partnership do not belong to her ... a person who is only entitled to payment by the partners of a share of the profits has not proprietary interest in anything whatsoever unless and until it is paid over...[20]

16. [1971] E.A. 338 (Kenya High Court). See also *E.C. & Co v. Commissioner of Income Tax Ibid*
17. See Partnership Act Cap. 114, S.27(e) which gives partners a right to participate in management, a right was excluded in *E v. CIT* 1 EATC 30
18. See *E v. Commissioner of Income Tax Ibid*
19. [1946] All E.R. 476 C.A. (E)
20. See also Partnership Act Cap 114 3(c) and *Cox v. Hickman* (1860) 8 HL 268 *A.A. Aaal v. Mohammed* [1932-40] S.L.R.426 (Sudan)

(b) Salaried Partner

The position of a salaried partner may be problematic. The problem is to determine whether such a person is in fact a partner liable as such whose reward is described as a salary, or is simply an employee of the partnership for some reason (presumably of prestige) as a partner. It is significant that, subject to any agreement express or implied, to the contrary, a partner is not entitled to remuneration for acting in the partnership business.[21] His reward would be a division of the partnership profits. Alternatively, Section 4 (3) (c) (ii) of the Partnership Act may be applicable. It provides that

> A contract for the remuneration of a servant or agent of a person engaged in a business by a share of the profits of a business does not itself make the servant or agent a partner in the business or liable as such.

A salaried partner could, therefore, be accurately described either as a partner rewarded by salary or as a salaried employee described as a partner. Thus in *Stekel v. Elice* Megarry J observed that:

> it is impossible to say that as a matter of law a salaried partner is or is not necessarily a partner in the true sense... What must be done, I think, is to look at the substance of the relationship between the parties; and there is ample authority for saying that the question whether or not there is a partnership depends on what the true relationship is and not any mere label attached to that relationship.[22]

It is possible to conclude that in any situation the existence of a partnership is a question of mixed law and fact depending on the parties' intentions.[23]

B. Taxation

1. Charge

Although in law a partnership is inseparable from its members,[24] it is assessed for income tax in the firm name. A joint return of income is required to be made by the "precedent partner."[25] The income of a partnership is normally computed in accordance with the ordinary principles applicable to individuals[26] and must then be allocated among the partners. Thus Section 67(1) of the Income Tax Act, Cap 340, provides that the gross income of a resident partner for a year of income includes the partner's share of partnership income. That of a non-resident partner includes the partner's share of partnership income attributable to sources in Uganda. In each case a partner is allowed a deduction for the partner's share of the partnership loss for the year – a share equal to the partner's percentage interest in the partnership income as agreed or where there is no such formula, the loss is shared equally.[27] Partnership income is its gross income less

21. Partnership Act *Ibid,* S. 27 (f)
22. [1973] 1 All E.R. 465
23. *Mayson on Revenue Law* (14th ed. 1993) p. 615. See also *Bank of the North v. Dabare, supra* n.12
24. Bakibinga, *Partnership Law in Uganda* (1992) pp1, 14 - 18
25. See e.g. Taxes Management Act, 1970, S. 9 (U.K.); ITA.S.65(3),(4)
26. See *supra* Chapter 3; ITA, S.65(1)
27. ITA, S.67(2),(3),(4),(6),(7)

the total amount of deductions allowed under the Act for expenditure or losses, other than an assessed loss under Section 38, incurred by the partnership in the production of that income.[28]

Example[29]

LINE	FIRM	X	Y	Z
1 Profits to December 31, 1995, adjusted	10,000,000			
2. Less interest on capital and salary	1,500,000			
3.	8,500,000	1,770,000	3,540,000	3,540,000
4. Add interest on capital	450,000	nil	200,000	250,000
5. Add salary	700,000 10,000,000	nil 1,770,000	400,000 4,140,000	300,000 4,090,000

Notes

1. The Shs10 million are the profits of the basis period adjusted for tax purposes, less capital allowances.[30] All debits in the partnership accounts for partners, share of profits, partner's salaries and interest on capital will have been added back and are thus included in the Shs10 million. This is because these items are not expenses which are deductible in computing profits.[31] The salary paid to a "salaried partner" (as with interest on capital contributed) is an allocation of profit, not an expense in earning profit.[32]
2. This is the total figure of interest on capital and salary.
3. Each partner has allocated to him a share of Shs8,850,000/= corresponding to the share of profits to which he is entitled in the year 1996-1997.[33]
4. It is usual for a partner to receive interest on any capital contributed by him. Each partner is credited with the full amount due to him in the current year, for this is

28. *Ibid* S,66(1)
29. See *Pinson on Revenue Law* (16th ed. Sweet & Maxwell) pp. 259 - 260. See also M. T. Abdulrazaq, "Taxation of Partnership Income," *Review of Business & Property Law* (Lagos) Vol. 2, No. 8, pp. 44 -46
30 ITA, Ss.26-9
31. *Ibid.* S. 22(2)
32. Expenditure in earning profits is distinguishable from the application of profits after they have been earned. See *Vallambrosa Rubber Co. Ltd v. Farmer* (1910) STC 529. The payment of income tax is an application of profits after they have been earned. It is not an expense in earning profits: *Ashton Gas Co. v. A-G* [1906] A.C. 10 H.L. See also Pinson, *supra* n. 29, p. 51 and S. 22(2) ITA
33. *Gaunt v. IRC* (1913) 7 T.C. 219

not an annual payment. If there is other income (e.g., fees for appointments held by the partners for which the partners are accountable to the partnership), it must be brought into account and apportioned between the partners in their profit-ratio.

5. The salary credited to each partner is the salary to which he is entitled in the current year 1996/1997.
6. The partnership income apportioned to each partner is included in his computed income. The profits of each partner (including interest on partnership capital) are treated as earned income, unless the partner is a sleeping partner or is not an individual. Interest on capital loaned to the partnership is investment income (i.e., income other than earned income).

It should be noted that the partner's share includes any salary or commission payable to him and any interest on capital contributed by him.[34]

The income arrived at above is called the "computed income" of the partnership. It is not, however, assessed on the partnership or, collectively, on the partners. The partners are individually assessed, as though they were trading individually.[35] In *Harrison v. Wills Bros,*[36] Lord Denning MR (as he then was) explained the rules of liability of a partnership to tax thus:

> The partnership firm is not an entity for taxing purposes or any other purposes. Its name is simply a convenient way of describing the persons who constitute the firm. The provision on joint assessment shows that it is a joint liability imposed on those who were partners during the year of assessment, that is, during the year when the profits were made which are being taxed. The provision that the assessment is to be made "in the partnership name" is a machinery by which those persons are designated who were partners during the year the profits were made. They are still to be designated by that name even after the partnership is dissolved. When one of the partners (who were jointly chargeable) dies, the survivors become chargeable. In any such case, of course, when a surviving partner is made liable, he may be able to obtain a contribution from the estate of the deceased partner. But that is not the concern of the Revenue. The Revenue must make the assessment in the partnership name and impose liability on the survivor, and not on the executor of the deceased partner.

2. Losses

When a firm suffers a loss, the loss is apportioned between the partners in the same way that profits are apportioned.[37] Each partner deals separately with his share[38] of the loss against his income of the same or the following or by carrying the loss forward against his future share of the partnership profits.[39] Each partner may claim relief in respect of the share apportioned to him,[40] as he thinks fit.

---

34. *Lewis v. IRC* (1933) 18 T.C. 174
35. ITA S. 67
36. [1966] Ch. 619. See also *A.A. of Nigeria v. Registrar of Business Names* 1968 (2) ALR Comm 342, 344 per Adedipe J. and Bakibinga, *supra* n. 24, pp 14 - 17
37. This will be equally if there is no contrary agreement: Partnership Act Cap. 114 S. 28 (1); ITA, S.67(7)
38. ITA, S.67(6)(7)
39. ITA S.67(3) read together with S.38
40. Ss.22(1) 38(1)

In *S.F. Hassan v. Commissioner of Income Tax*,[41] the appellant was in practice as an advocate and this constituted the major source of his income. He was also interested in partnership with his brother in a safari firm in which his activities were of a minor nature. The partnership agreement provided that his brother would receive a salary of £900 per annum, and the profits were to be divided: two-thirds to the appellant and one-third to the brother. In 1951, the partnership incurred a loss of £427, or £428 before charging the brother's salary, or £1,328 if the salary were taken into account. The appellant claimed to deduct from his gross income – under the equivalent of ITA, S. 22 (1) – the sum of £886 being two-thirds of £1,328. The Commissioner allowed the deduction of £427 only and was upheld by the Local Committee and confirmed by the Supreme Court. On appeal to the Court of Appeal for East Africa, it was argued that the appellant's brother's salary should be a deductible expense in ascertaining the appellant's profit or loss from the partnership business. In dismissing the appeal, the Court of Appeal held that the "income" f the partnership was a loss of £427 and with regard to the partnership agreement, the appellant was correctly allowed to deduct the whole of £427 and not merely two-thirds of it.

In *A.H. v. Commissioner of Income Tax,*[42] it was held that the salary paid to a partner is not an expense wholly and exclusively incurred in the production of the partnership income and that the partnership loss or profit is to be ascertained without deduction of any salary paid to a partner. It was also held that a partner's loss cannot exceed the amount of the partnership loss.[43]

3. Change in Partnership

For purposes of assessing a partnership which has changed its composition or persons carrying on a trade, profession or vocation in partnership, for income tax purposes, at the date of the change, it is deemed that the business has been discontinued and a new one set up or commenced. However, if at least one person who was a partner immediately before the change continues to be so immediately before or immediately after the change and all the partners immediately before and after the change elect for continuance, then it shall be so deemed. Nevertheless if there is no election, a discontinued business will be assessed according to the closing-year rules, while the new business will be assessed either according to the usual opening rules or with reference to special opening rules of the year.

It is often difficult to determine when a trade or business has ceased or recommenced.[44] However, the following propositions may be advanced:

(a) If a person takes over the whole of a trade as a going concern, he succeeds to that trade, even if he already has a trade of the same nature and the newly acquired trade is merged with it.[45]

---

41 [1957] E.A.793

42. 2 EATC 124(Kenya)

43. Easson, *Cases and Materials on Revenue Law* (2nd ed. 1990) p.416. For application of rules to capital gains tax, see ITA, Ss.68, 69.

44. *Ibid* See also ITA, Ss 65(4), 68(5).

45. *Merchiston Steamship Co Ltd v. Turner* (1910) STC 520; *Kirk & Randall Ltd v. Dunn* (1924) 8 STC 663; H&G *Kineinas Ltd v. Cook* (1933) 18 T.C. 116

(b) If a person merely takes over the assets of a trade with no intention of taking over the business as a going concern, there is no succession.[46]

4. Rate of Tax

The rates of tax applicable to individuals are imposed with regard to the taxation of partners.[47]

46. *Bell v. National Provincial Bank* [1904] 1 K.B. 149; *Briton Ferry Skel Co Ltd v. Barry* [1940] 1 KB 463; *I & C. v. Watson & Philip Ltd* [1984];STC 184 *Laycock v. Freeman, Hardy & Willis* [1939] 2 K.B. 1
47. *Watson v. Lothian* (1902) 4 TC 441; *Reynolds, Sons & Co Ltd. v. Ogston* (1930) 15 T.C. 501
48. ITA, S.6 and Schedule 3, Part I. See also *supra* Chap. 3.

7

Investment Tax Regime

A. Introduction

This chapter reviews provisions of the Investment Code[1] and Income Tax Act, Cap 340, which provide tax incentives for investment in Uganda and double taxation agreements between Uganda and other countries with which conventions in that area have been concluded.

While it has become a practice among developing countries to provide tax incentives in order to attract investment and capital inflows,[2] controversy centres around whether such tax incentives are desirable for developing countries given their narrow tax base. In this vein it is contended that a stable political and economic environment, including economic liberalisation policies allowing for free unregulated trade and the speedy repatriation of profits for investors, is more important than tax incentives which in the main are irrelevant.[3] On the other hand, it is argued that the shortfall in revenue is a short-term phenomenon which is outweighed by increased yields in revenue in the long term resulting from increased investment and economic activity arising from enhanced investment. These conflicting perspectives are now of academic interest in Uganda since the introduction of the depreciation tax regime.[4]

B. The Investment Code

1. Objectives and Exemptions

The Investment Code is aimed at protecting and attracting investments both local and foreign. However, not every investor is entitled to the tax exemptions. It is only those investors who qualify as "investors" within the meaning of the Code and also satisfy the conditions therein.

An investor in a business qualifies for incentives if he satisfies three or more of the following objectives:[5]

1. generation of new earnings or savings of foreign exchange through exports, resources-based import substitution, or service activities;
2. utilisation of local materials, supplies and services;

1. Cap. 92 *Laws of Uganda*, 2000
2 See e.g. Investment Law No. 230 of 1989 of Egypt and Investment Act, 1993, of Zambia
3. See generally Fetaa and Bakibinga, "The Relationship between Taxation Regimes and Investment Policies in Africa – The Uganda Case." Paper delivered at the 8th General Assembly of the Association of African Tax Administrators and 9th Technical Workshop, Cairo 2-5 December 1996, pp. 2-3, 7-8.
4. Income Tax Act Cap. 340, ss.26-30. This is in line with IMF recommendations: *Uganda: A Program for Reform of Income Tax* (1996), pp.27-30. These provisions have been discussed supra Chap.4
5. Investment Code, Ss 12, 22 (1)

3. creation of employment opportunities in Uganda;
4. introduction of advanced technology or upgrading of indigenous technology;
5. contribution to locally or regionally balanced economic development;
6. any other objectives which the Uganda Investment Authority may consider relevant to achieving the objects of the Code.

Additionally an investor in a business enterprise will qualify for incentives if as a foreign investor he makes capital investments or equivalent in capital goods worth at least US$300,000, or as a Ugandan citizen he makes an investment valued at least at US$50,000.[6]

Domestic investors intending to benefit from the incentives under the Code must apply to the Uganda Investment Authority (UIA) for a certificate of incentives.[7] A foreign investor is not required to apply separately for such a certificate if his application for an investment licence contains the relevant information relating to the incentives.[8]

The exemptions from income and corporation tax for periods ranging from three to six years in the code[9] have been repealed[10] subject to transitional application to existing incentives.[11]

C. Double Taxation

1. Nature and Purpose of Double Taxation Agreements

Double taxation agreements have an unusual dual nature. First, they are international agreements entered into between governments for the allocation of fiscal jurisdiction. Second, they become part of the tax law of each contracting state, whether by direct incorporation into the domestic law or by direct enactment into that law.[12]

From the perspective of the two governments concerned, the treaty is an agreement to limit the exercise of the taxing jurisdiction of each state. The restrictions on exercising tax jurisdiction are, therefore, seen as a form of bargain, based upon the reciprocal flows of investment and return on investment between the two states. This is all the more pertinent when double taxation is understood as a situation in which states, in the exercise of their sovereignty, tax all income arising in the state, no matter to whom it belongs, and all income of residents, no matter where it arises.[13] This has the effect of taxing foreign income twice: first in the state where the income arises, and second where the person entitled to such income resides.[14]

The conclusion of a double taxation treaty is, therefore, part of an overall policy of

6 *Ibid.* S. 22
7. *Ibid.* S. 23 (1)
8. *Ibid.* S. 23 (2)
9. *Ibid* s.24
10. Income Tax Act Cap 340 s.163, Seventh Schedule
11. *Ibid* s.166(21)-(25)
12. Baker P., *Double Taxation Agreements and International Law* (*A Manual on OECD Model Double Taxation Convention* 1977) (Sweet & Maxwell, London, 1991) p.5, para 2-01; ITA, S.88 (1),(2)
13. ITA, S.17 (2), 79
14. Easson, *Cases & Materials on Revenue Law* (Sweet & Maxwell, London, 1991) p.315

each state to encourage foreign investment or to assist the state's investors to participate in overseas trade and development without undue financial hardship arising from double taxation.[15]

From the perspective of the taxpayer, the treaty is generally seen as a description of the tax system he will face if he invests in, or works in, or moves temporarily to another state. The treaty does not generally describe the actual system facing the taxpayer, but instead the ultimate limits to which the tax system may extend. It describes the permissible boundaries of the tax system, not the actual system itself. Where one contracting state does not currently take up its full taxing rights under a treaty, the treaty does at least serve as a guarantee to the foreign investor that future taxation cannot go beyond the level fixed by the treaty, unless the treaty is first abrogated or amended.

For double taxation to apply, it must relate to the same type of tax affecting the same person and over the same period.[16] Consequently, corporate taxation involving the company and shareholders is not regarded as double taxation,[17] since two entities are being taxed separately.

A number of models of double taxation conventions have been formulated over the past 50 years.[18] First was the League of Nations-sponsored model which was signed in Mexico in 1943 and in London in 1946. Second was the United Nations model under Resolution No. 1541 of the UN Social and Economic Council, and adopted in 1979. This model was updated in 1995. Third is the Organisation for Economic Co-operation and Development (OECD) model of 1963, which was revised in 1977. Fourth is the United States and German model, which largely caters to the interests of those two countries.[19] Fifth is the Arab League's Economic Unity Council model, which affects 11 countries.[20] This model caters largely to Arab interests and was concluded in 1996. It modifies the UN and OECD models to suit Arab conditions. Presumably a sixth model based on African conditions will emerge under the auspices of the Association of African Tax Administrators. It should be stressed that the models are mere guides as to the double taxation agreements to be concluded between the affected states.[21]

2. The Position of Double Taxation in Uganda

Presently, Uganda has two double taxation conventions. One with the United Kingdom which was concluded in 1992 and the second with the Republic of South Africa, the text of which was initialled in December 1995 but is yet to be ratified. Uganda is in the process of negotiating double taxation agreements with its immediate neighbours – Kenya, Mauritius and Tanzania – and all other major trading partners.[22] An earlier double taxation agreement with Zambia in 1975 lapsed.

15. Baker, *supra* n.28, p.5, para 2-01. See also Khalifa, "International Tax Agreements and Their Role in Encouraging Foreign Investment." Paper delivered at the 9th Technical Workshop of the Association of African Tax Administrators, Cairo, 2 - 5 December 1996, pp.4 6-8
16 Khalifa *Ibid* pp. 7 - 9
17 *Ibid* pp. 6-7
18 *Ibid.* pp. 15 - 19
19 See also Baker, *supra* n. 28
20 Egypt, Iraq, Jordan, Libya, Mauritania, Palestine, Somalia, Sudan, Syria, United Arab Emirates and Yemen
21 Khalifa, *supra* n. 15, p. 18
22. Fetaa & Bakibinga, *supra* n. 3 p.6

a) Legal Effect of Double Taxation Agreements

Section 88(1)(2) of the Income Tax Act, 1997, provides that an international agreement entered into between the Government of Uganda and the government of a foreign country(ies) shall have effect as if such agreement was contained in the Act and agreement prevails over the Act in the case of any inconsistency.[23]

Where Uganda is a party to a double taxation agreement, credit is given for foreign tax already paid on income payable to residents. Consequently, foreign tax payable in respect of income is allowed as a credit against tax chargeable in respect of such income.[24] The effect of this is that total chargeable income is less by the amount of the tax credit.[25] The tax chargeable in respect of a person seeking to enjoy the credit relief is the amount before allowance of the credit, payable in respect of total income and increased by inclusion of such income in the taxpayer's total income. The effect is that income before the credit allowance is deducted. However, foreign tax payable is reduced or allowed as a credit against the tax that was charged. The credit allowed, however, should not exceed the amount of tax chargeable upon the income in respect of which the credit is to be allowed or upon each part of such income as the case may be.[26]

b) Double Taxation Agreement: Uganda and United Kingdom

i) Preliminary

The double taxation treaty between Uganda and the United Kingdom is titled a "convention ... for the avoidance of double taxation and the prevention of fiscal evasion with respect to taxes on income and capital gains." Herein can be found the purpose of the convention. The convention is based on the OECD/UN model.[27] The purpose inherent in the title to the convention is in line with the UN view that the purpose of double taxation agreements is to remove impediments to the flow of trade and investment by the elimination of international double taxation.[28] Substantially, however, the purposes of a double taxation agreement include the following:

i) elimination of double taxation in order to prevent the discouragement of international trade,
ii) provision for co-operation between tax administrations in order to combat tax evasion,
iii) provision of certainty as to the tax regime faced by investors and traders so as to prevent discouragement of international trade, and
iv) elimination of discriminatory taxation.[29]

As a result of the above objectives, the treaty reduces the level of source-country taxation, thereby increasing residence-country tax revenue in countries which relieve

23. See also Khalifa, *supra* n. 15 p. 14 for the Egyptian position.
24. ITA, S. 81
25. *Ibid.* S. 81 (3). See also Khalifa, *supra* n. 15, p. 23
26. ITA, S.81(2)
27. IMF, *supra* n. 4, pp. 46 - 47
28. *Manual for the Negotiation of Bilateral Tax Treaties in Developed and Developing Countries* (New York, 1979) (Doc. : ST/ESA/94) p.1
29. Baker, *supra* n. 12, p 10, para 2-09

double taxation through the credit method, as is the case with Uganda.[30] Furthermore, while the treaty may not fully succeed in combating fiscal evasion, its main advantage is the provision of reciprocal information exchange, thereby opening channels for co-operation.[31] For the taxpayer, the treaty provides guidance and limited guarantee to the investor of the tax treatment that he will receive in a foreign territory.[32]

ii) Scope and Definition

Pursuant to the above objectives and principles of double taxation (relief), the treaty between Uganda and the United Kingdom indicates that the convention is applicable to persons who are residents of one or both of the contracting states.[33] In the United Kingdom, the Convention covers income tax, corporation tax and capital gains tax, while in Uganda it covers income tax, including that charged on corporations.[34] There follows an article defining terms such as "United Kingdom," "Uganda," "national," "contracting state," "person," "company," "enterprise of a contracting state," and "international traffic."[35] Terms not otherwise defined bear the meaning attributable thereto under the relevant tax laws of the contacting state.[36]

iii) Domicile and Permanent Establishment

Under the convention, the expression "resident of a contracting state" means a person who under the law of that state is liable to tax therein by reason of residence, domicile, place of management or any other criterion of a similar nature.[37] When a person could be a resident of both contracting states, he is deemed to be a resident of the state in which he has permanent home available to him.[38] When he has a home in both states, he is deemed to be resident in the state with which his personal and economic relations are closer (centre of vital interests).[39]

If the state in which he has his centre of vital interests cannot be determined or if he has no permanent home available to him in either state, he shall be deemed to be resident of that state in which he has a habitual abode.[40]

If he has a habitual abode in both states or in neither of the states, he is deemed to be a resident of the state of which he is a national.

If he is a national of both states or neither of them, the competent authorities (Commissioners of Inland Revenue in the United Kingdom or the Minister of Finance in Uganda) shall settle the issue by mutual agreement.

---

30. ITA, S.81
31. Baker, *supra* n. 12, para 2-10. See also Article 26 of the Uganda-United Kingdom. Treaty
32. *Ibid.* para 2-11
33.. Article 1
34. Article 2
35. Article 3 (1)
36. Article 3 (2)
37. Article 4 (1) read together with ITA, S. 9 defining residence; considered *supra* Chapters 3 and 4
38. Article 4 (2)
39. For an illustration, see *Commissioner-General of Income Tax v. Noorani* [1969] E.A. 685, considered *supra* Chapter 3.
40. *Ibid*

If a company is a resident of both contracting states, it shall be deemed to be a resident of the state in which its place of effective management is situated.[41]

The term "permanent establishment" is defined as a fixed place of business through which the business of an enterprise is wholly or partly carried on.[42] It includes:

- a place of management;
- a branch;
- an office;
- a factory;
- a workshop;
- premises used as a sales outlet or for receiving or soliciting orders;
- a warehouse in relation to a person providing storage facilities for others;
- a mine, an oil gas well, a quarry or any other place of extraction of natural resources; and
- an installation or structure used for the exploration or exploitation of natural resources.

A building site or construction or installation project constitutes a permanent establishment only if it lasts more than 183 days.[43] Article 5 (4) of the Double Taxation Treaty contains the exclusionary list of items which do not constitute a permanent establishment; while Article 5 (5), (6), (7) deal with the significance of agency in constituting a permanent establishment.

iv) Business Profits

Article 7 of the Treaty deals with the taxation of business profits. It has a two-pronged approach. First, where an enterprise of a contracting state carries on business in the other state, but has no permanent establishment there, the profits of the enterprise may not be taxed in that other state. Second, where an enterprise has a permanent establishment in the other state, that other state may only tax so much of the profits as are attributed to that permanent establishment. In the first situation, in order to rely on the exemption from tax, it is necessary to first prove that there is an enterprise of a contracting state and then prove the absence of a permanent establishment. In the second scenario, the main concern is with the method of attributing income in that permanent establishment. The attribution of profits applies to both contracting states, that is, the state of the enterprise and the state in which the permanent establishment is situated. The basic rule for apportionment of profits is that these are profits which the permanent establishment might be expected to make if it was a distinct and separate enterprise engaged in the same or similar activities.[44] Expenses incurred for the purposes of the establishment are allowable deductions in calculating the taxable profits of the permanent establishment.[45]

41. Article 4 (3). See also *De Beers Consolidated Mines Ltd v. Howe* [1960] EA. 455; *Unit Construction Co Ltd. v. Bullock* [1960] A.C. 351 H.L. distinguishing *Swedish Central Railway Co. Ltd v. Thomson* [1925] A.C. 495; discussed *supra* Chapter 4
42. Article 5 (1), (2)
43. Article 5 (3) read together with definition of residence in S. 9 ITA. Discussed *supra* Chapters 3 and 4
44. Article 7 (2)
45. Article 7 (3)

The determination of profits attributable to a permanent establishment can be made by apportioning of the total profits of the enterprise as is customary.[46] Where a permanent establishment also carries out purchasing activities for the enterprise, no profits are to be attributed by reason of the mere purchase of goods or merchandise for the enterprise.[47]

v) Shipping and Air Transport

Profits from the operation of ships or aircraft in international traffic are taxable only in the contracting state in which the place of effective management of the enterprise is situated.[48] Where this is located aboard a ship, it shall be deemed to be situated in the contracting state in which the home of the harbour of the ship is situated, and if there is no such home harbour, in the contracting state of which the operator of the ship is resident.[49] Article 8 also applies to profits derived from participation in a pool, a joint business or an international operating agency,[50] as is the case with operations involving airline tickets.

i) Associated Enterprises

The double taxation treaty provides that profits made by one enterprise from dealings with an associated enterprise may be increased to the level they would have been had the enterprises been independent and dealing at arm's length.[51] In such a situation, a corresponding adjustment is made if as a result, the same profits would be taxable in both states.[52] Article 9 is concerned with the issue of transfer pricing, although its exact purpose is unclear.[53] In this vein the main issue is whether Article 9 (1) itself authorises states to make adjustments on an arm's length basis or whether it merely permits contracting states to enact and apply separate domestic legislation allowing for arm's length adjustment. The purpose of Article 9 (1) is conceived[54] as

- limiting the methods which may be used for adjusting profits between associated enterprises,
- providing an anchor for the international solution to transfer pricing issues, and
- providing a legal basis for the operation of Article 9 (2).

vii) Dividends

Dividends derived from a company which is a resident of a contracting state by a resident of the other contracting state may be taxed in the other state of residence of their recipient or the state of source.[55] However, if the recipient is the beneficial owner of the dividends, there is a ceiling to the level of tax permitted. In these instances, the state of residence of the recipient grants relief from double taxation under Article 23 via the credit method.[56]

46. Article 7 (4)
47. Article 7 (5)
48. Article 8 (1). See also cases cited at note 41 *supra.* See also ITA, S.86.
49 Article 8 (2)
50. Article 8 (3)
51. Article 9 (1)
52. Article 9 (2)
53. Baker, *supra* n. 12, p. 151
54. Ibid pp. 151-152. For a fuller discussion, see paras 13-03 and 13-04.
55. Article 10 (1), (2). See also ITA, S.83(3),(4).

The dividend rate is set at a maximum of 15 percent. However, the double taxation treaty with South Africa sets the maximum rate on dividends at 5 percent for dividends paid abroad if the beneficial owner is a company which holds at least 25 percent of the company paying the dividends.[57]

"Dividends" are defined[58] as income from shares or other rights not being debt claims, participating in profits, as well as income from other corporate rights assimilated to income from shares by the taxation law of the state of which the company making the distribution is a resident.

The requirement in respect of "beneficial ownership" of the shares is aimed at preventing treaty-shopping.[59] "Beneficial owner" is described as a term of art under English law and excludes a legal owner who is a trustee for another.[60] However, it appears that the term is not meant to be employed in the treaty in this technical and limited sense. The problem of definition is compounded by the fact that the term is not recognised in the law of most civil countries which apply the OECD double taxation model.[61] In this regard the Dutch Parliament confirmed that it would not regard as a beneficial owner a person who was contractually bound to pay to a third party most of the dividends, interest or royalties received by him.[62]

Finally on dividends, limitations contained in Article 10 do not apply where the shareholding is effectively connected with a permanent establishment or fixed base of the beneficial owner of the dividends.[63] In addition, a contracting state is precluded from taxing dividends paid by a company resident in the other state merely because the profits or income underlying the dividends arose in the first state.[64] Taxation of dividends is precluded where the payer or payee is a resident of that state. This is aimed at the so-called "secondary withholding taxes" whereby a company is required to withhold tax on paying dividends because the underlying profits derive from the state imposing the tax. The Article also prevents the imposition of tax on the undistributed profits of a company which is a resident of the other contracting state.[65]

(viii) Interest

The state of residence of the person to whom interest is paid may tax the interest, in which case double taxation is relieved by the credit method under Article 23.[66] However, where taxation is in the state of source, this is limited to a maximum of 15 percent of the gross amount of the interest.[67] The limitation on source-country taxation only applies

56. Article 10 (4) read together with Articles 7, 15 and 23 (2)
57. IMF, *supra* n. 4, p. 45. This is in line with the OECD Model Article 10.
58. Article 10 (3). See also ITA, S.2
59. Baker, *supra* n. 12, pp 165 - 166, paras 14-04, 14-05
60. Baker, *Ibid,* p. 165. See also generally Bakibinga, *Law of Trusts in Nigeria* (1989)
61. Killius J. "The Concept of Beneficial Ownership of Items of Income under German Tax Treaties" *Intertax* 340 (1989)
62. Quoted in K Van Raad, "The Netherlands Model of Income Tax Treaty," *Intertax* 241, 245 (1988)
63. Article 10 (4)
64. Article 10 (5)
65. Baker, *supra* n. 12 p. 168. See also OECD Commentary paras 32-34
66. Article 11 (1). See also ITA, s.83(5)
67. Article 11 (2), S.118 ITA

if the recipient is a beneficial owner of the interest.[68] Again the aim is to prevent treaty shopping.[69]

"Interest" is defined as income from debt-claims of every kind – whether or not secured by mortgage, and whether or not carrying a right to participate in the debtor's profits – and in particular income from government securities and income from bonds or debentures.[70] It does not include any item which is treated as a distribution under Article 10 of the Convention.

It is further provided that where interest is "effectively connected" to a permanent establishment or a fixed base (for independent personal services), the interest should be dealt with under Articles 7 and 15 and not Article 11.[71] The effect is that the permanent establishment is assimilated to the status of a resident of the state of the payer.[72]

Since the effect of Article 11 is to fix a maximum level of tax in the country of source, Article 11 (6) provides rules for determining the country of source. Generally, this is the contacting state of which the payer is resident. However, where the indebtedness on which the interest is paid is connected with a permanent establishment or fixed base in a contracting state and is borne by that permanent establishment or fixed base, the interest is deemed to arise in the state where the permanent establishment or fixed base is situated (whether the payer is a resident of a contracting state or not). The exemption only applies "where the economic link between the loan and the permanent establishment [or fixed base] is sufficiently clear cut."[73]

Article 11 (7) contains an anti-avoidance, arm's-length rule, where by virtue of the "special relationship" between the payer and payee of interest, the amount of interest exceeds that which would be payable between parties at arm's length. In such a situation, Article 11 is only applicable to such amount as would have been paid between unrelated parties. The term "special relationship," though not defined in the convention, is explained to cover relationships by blood, marriages and any other community of interests.[74] The concept of persons enjoying a "special relationship" thus appears to be wider than the concept of associated enterprises under Article 9.

(ix) Royalties

Article 12 relating to royalties is similar in many respects to Article 11 on interest.[75] There is no provision for deeming royalties to arise in one or other of the other contracting state [equivalent to Article 11 (6)].

"Royalties" are defined[76] as payments of any kind received as consideration for the use, or the right to use, of any copyright of literary, artistic or scientific work (including

68. Article 11 (3)
69. Baker, *supra* n. 12, p. 184, para 15-01
70. Article 11 (4). See also OECD commentary, paragraphs 18 and 19, the latter of which indicates that the definition is exhaustive without recourse to domestic law meanings. For the definition in ITA, see S.2.
71. Article 11 (5)
72. Baker, *supra* n. 12, p. 186
73. OECD Model Commentary, para 25
74. OECD Convention Model Commentary para 32 in Baker, *supra* n. 12, p. 198, para 15 - 22. See also ITA, S.3(2)(a)
75. Discussed above
76. Article 12 (3). See also OECD *Model Convention Commentary,* paras 9, 11, 13, 14. See also ITA, S.2.

cinematograph films and films or tapes for radio or television broadcasting), any patent, trademark, design or model, plan, secret formula or process or the use of or the right to use industrial, commercial or scientific equipment.

Royalties effectively connected to a permanent establishment or fixed base are governed by Articles 7 and 15 and not Article 12. The effect is that royalties are then taxable in the state where the permanent establishment or fixed base is situated.[77]

Provisions on royalties rising from a special relationship between a payer and payee are similar in effect to those in relation to interest.[78]

x) Technical Fees

Article 13 of the Convention deals with the treatment of technical fees and is in substance similar to Article 11 relating to interest, apart from the definition of "technical fees."[79]

"Technical fees" are defined as payments of any kind to any person other than an employee of the payer in consideration for any services of a technical, managerial or consultancy nature.[80]

xi) Income from Immovable Property

Income from immovable property may be taxed in the state where the property is situated,[81] although the state of residence of the taxpayer may also tax the income, in which case relief from double taxation under Article 23 would apply. Income from immovable property includes income from forestry or agriculture and income from the direct use, letting or use in any other form of immovable property.[82] The article also applies to income from immovable property of an enterprise or property used for the performance of independent personal services[83] (property of a fixed base).

The expression "immovable property" is not defined but reference is made to its meaning under the domestic law of the contracting state in which the property is situated. The term must, however, include in all cases certain property rights.[84]

The term "income" from immovable property is also not defined, but would presumably by virtue of Article 3 (2) have the meaning attributed to it by the domestic law relating to income tax of the relevant contracting states.[85]

---

77. Article 12 (4)
78. Article 12 (5) and (6) compare with Articles 11 (5) and (7) considered supra to which the discussion there is relevant.
79. See discussion on interest *supra*. See also ITA, s.83(1).
80. Article 13 (3). See also *Hindusthan Electrographites Ltd v. Inspecting Assistant Commissioner of Income Tax* [1982] Tax L.R. 1828 (Madhya Pradesh High Court, India) in Baker, *supra* n. 12, pp. 203 - 204. See also ITA, S.86(4).
81. Article 6 (1)
82. Article 6 (1), (3)
83. Article 6 (4)
84. Article 6 (2). For difficulties of determining "immovable property," see Baker, *supra* n. 12, pp 112-114, paras 10-02 - 10-04 reviewing concepts in Germany, Sweden and United Kingdom.
85. Baker, *ibid.* p. 114. See also Income and Corporation Taxes Act, 1988, S. 776 (U.K.). ITA, Ss.5,6(2), 22(1) (C), 8,114.

(xii) Non-Discrimination

Article 24 of the Double Taxation Convention prohibits discriminatory taxation against residents of another contracting state. Residents of a contracting state are not to be subjected to any taxation which is either more burdensome than that imposed on residents of the other contracting state in the same circumstances. Furthermore, where an enterprise of one contracting state has a permanent establishment in the other contracting state, taxation is not to be less favourably levied on that permanent establishment than is levied on enterprises of the first state carrying on the same activities.

(c) Adverse Effects of a Double Taxation Treaty

A major disadvantage of double taxation agreements occurs when an agreement is between unequal trading partners. Between developed or developing countries the agreements are likely to be more or less equivalent in their revenue effects. However, between developed and developing countries, capital flows tend to be one way from the developed countries to developing countries. As a result, the reductions in tax by the country where the investment occurs may not be reciprocal in effect under the agreements. Consequently, developing countries should constantly balance the need for tax revenue and the desire to attract foreign investment.[86]

D. Taxation of Expatriates

Prior to the promulgation of the Income Tax Act, Cap 340, there was concern[87] about considerable exemptions extended to expatriates.[88] The expatriates fell into four categories: tax residents versus non-residents, those who work for non-profit "NGOs," workers of governments versus those who work for private entities and those who work for profit companies. Given international practice, it would be difficult to scrap most of the exemptions. Therefore it was recommended that Uganda should restrict these exemptions or only impose tax on Uganda-source income of residents from those sources.[89]

These recommendations have been largely implemented by the Income Tax Act, Cap 340.[90] An attempt is made to highlight some of these.

1. Source of Income

a) Goods/Transportation

Income derived from the sale of goods manufactured, grown or mined by the seller in Uganda or from a purchase agreement made in Uganda, is taxable.[91] Similarly, income arising from transportation business, regardless of where the vehicle, ship, or aircraft operates, is taxable.[92]

86. Fetaa & Bakibinga, *supra* n.3, pp. 6-7; IMF, *supra* n. 4, pp 45-46
87. IMF, *supra* n.4 pp.48-51
88. Income Tax Decree, Schedule 1 Items 20,23,24,27,28,34,36
89. IMF, *supra* p.51
90. Part IX
91. *Ibid* s.79(a)
92. *Ibid* s.79(b)

b) Employment

Furthermore, income from any employment exercised or services rendered in Uganda or under a contract with the Government of Uganda, regardless of where the employment is exercised or services rendered, is taxable.[93] The income of a resident pilot, driver or member of a crew of any vehicle, ship, aircraft, wherever such are operated, is chargeable to tax.[94]

c) Property

Additionally, income derived from rental of immovable property located in Uganda and from the disposal of an interest in immovable property located in Uganda or from the disposal of a share in a company the property of which consists directly or indirectly principally of an interest(s) in such property where the interest of share is a business asset is chargeable to tax.[95] Similarly, income derived from the disposal of movable property other than goods under an agreement made in Uganda for the sale of the property whenever the property is to be delivered is taxable.[96]

The income included in the business income of a taxpayer from the disposal of a depreciable asset in Uganda and that arising from recovery of an expenditure loss or bad debt is taxable.[97]

d) Royalties

The earnings from a royalty arising from the use of, or right to use, in Uganda of intellectual property, motion picture film, video or audio material, sound recording or advertising matter connected with a motion picture film or video or audio material or any intangible movable property is taxable.[98] Royalties from imparting of or undertaking to impart, any scientific, technical, industrial or commercial knowledge or information for use in Uganda as well as royalties from the use of or right to use or receive in Uganda any video or audio material transmitted by satellite, cable, optic fibre or similar technology for use in connection with television or radio broadcasting are taxable.[99] Additionally, royalties arising in connection with the above or from total or partial forbearance in Uganda with respect to the above activities or from the disposal of industrial or intellectual property used in Uganda are chargeable to tax.[100]

e) Interest and Dividend

The income from interest is taxable when (1) the debt obligation generating the interest is secured by immovable property located or movable property used in Uganda, (2) the payer is a resident person, or (3) the borrowing relates to a business carried on in Uganda.[101] Similarly, a dividend or director's fee paid by a resident company is taxable.[102]

93. *Ibid* s.79(c), (d)
94. *Ibid* S.79(e)
95. *Ibid* s.79(f)(g)
96. *Ibid* S.79(h)
97. *Ibid* S.79(I) read together with Ss.27(5) and 62
98. *Ibid.* S.79(j) (i)
99. *Ibid* S.79(i)(ii),(iii)
100. *Ibid* S.79(j)(iv),(v),(vi)
101. *Ibid* S.79(k)
102. *Ibid* S.79(l)

f) Pension and Annuity

Income from a pension or annuity which is paid by the Government of Uganda or by a resident person or one which is paid in respect of an employment exercised or services rendered in Uganda is taxable.[103] In view of the constitutional exemption of pensions from taxation,[104] this provision may be unconstitutional. Income derived from a contribution to a retirement fund made by a tax-exempt employer in respect of an employee whose employment is exercised in Uganda is taxable.[105] This provision removes doubts about the taxability of expatriates or persons working for tax-exempt bodies such as NGOs and institutions listed in the First Schedule to the Income Tax Act.[106]

g) Natural Resource

The income from a natural resource payment in respect of a natural resource taken from Uganda is chargeable to tax[107] in relation to a business debt which has arisen in the course of carrying on a business in Uganda is chargeable to tax.[108]

i) Management Charge

Income from a management charge paid by a resident person is taxable.[109]

j) Income Taxable in Uganda Under International Agreement

The income which is taxable under an international agreement is taxable.[110]

k) Miscellaneous

The income attributable to any other activity which occurs in Uganda, including an activity conducted through a branch in Uganda, is taxable.[111]

2. Foreign-Source Employment

Foreign-source employment income derived by a resident individual is exempted from tax if the individual has paid foreign income tax in respect of the income.[112] For this purpose a resident individual is treated as having paid foreign income tax on foreign-source employment income if tax has been withheld and paid to the revenue authority of the foreign country by the employer of the individual.[113]

103. *Ibid,* s.79(m)
104. Constitution of Uganda, 1995, Article 254(2)
105. ITA, S.79(p)
106. This is also applicable to employment income generally. See *supra* notes 93 to 94.
107. ITA, S.79(n)
108. *Ibid,* S.79(0)
109. *Ibid* S.79(q)
110. *Ibid* S.79(r). For an example see Double Taxation Conventions, discussed *supra.*
111. ITA, S.79(S)
112. *Ibid.* S.80(1). This is in line with provisions of Double Taxation Conventions. Discussed. *supra*
113. *Ibid.* S.80(2)

3. Taxation of Branch Profits

a) General

In contrast to the repealed law,[114] which laid emphasis on residence-based taxation, the ITA singles out the taxation of branch profits of a non-resident company carrying out business in Uganda through a branch.[115] Arguably, this is consistent with the taxation of the profits of a permanent establishment within the context of a double taxation treaty.[116]

b) Computation

Tax is imposed on every non-resident company carrying on business in Uganda through a branch which has repatriated income for the relevant year of income.[117]

The tax payable is calculated by applying a rate of 15 percent[118] and is computed according to this formula: A+(B-C)-D.[119]

A is the total cost base of assets and net liabilities of the branch at the commencement of the year of income. *B* is the net profit of the branch for the year of income calculated in accordance with generally accepted accounting principles. *C* is the Uganda tax payable on the chargeable income, while *D* is the total cost base of assets and net liabilities of the branch at the end of the year of income. For this purpose the repatriated income of a branch is taken to be the total cost base of assets at the commencement of the next year of income.[120] Furthermore, the tax imposed is in addition to any tax imposed under the ITA on the chargeable income of the branch.

4. International Payments

a) General

Every non-resident person is taxed on any dividend, interest, royalty, natural resource payment or management charge derived from sources in Uganda.[121] The tax is calculated at the rate of 15 percent of the gross amount of such income.[121(a)]

b) Dividends

Only dividends paid out of profits sourced in Uganda are taxable.[122] Where the non-resident company has profits sourced both within and outside Uganda, it is treated as having paid a dividend out of profits sourced in Uganda first.[123]

---

114. Income Tax Decree 1974
115. ITA, S.82(1)
116. See e.g. Double Taxation Convention between Uganda and the United Kingdom, Article 7
117. *Supra* n.115
118. ITA S.82(2); part IV of Third Schedule
119. *Ibid* s.82(3). See also the UK-Uganda Double Taxation Convention, *supra* n.116, Article 7(4)
120. *Ibid* S.82(4)
121. *Ibid* S.83(1). See also the United Kingdom-Uganda Double Taxation Convention, Articles 10, 11, 12, 13.
121 (a) Ibid S.83(2); Third Schedule, Part IV
122. *Ibid* s.83(3)
123. *Ibid* s.83(4)

c) Interest

An investment incentive is evident from the provision that interest paid by a resident company in respect of debentures is exempt form tax in three instances: (1) when debentures were issued by the company outside Uganda for the purpose of raising a loan outside Uganda, (2) when the debentures were issued for the purpose of raising funds for use by the company in a business carried on in Uganda, and (3) when the interest is paid outside Uganda.

5. Payments to Non-Resident Public Entertainers or Athletes

a) General

Every non-resident entertainer or athlete, theatrical, musical, or other group of non-resident entertainer or sports person who derives income from any performance in Uganda must pay tax on that income. The tax is imposed on any group irrespective of whether or not the performance is conducted for the joint account of all or some members of the group.[124] For this purpose every member of the group is jointly and severally liable for payment of the tax and shall remit the tax due before leaving Uganda.[125] In practice the promoter of the entertainment or sports activity is required to withhold the tax and remit it to the Commissioner.[126]

b) Computation

The tax is imposed at a rate of 15 percent on the gross amount of remuneration derived by a non-resident public entertainer or sports person or receipts derived by the theatrical, musical or other group of non-resident public entertainers or sports persons.[127]

6. Payments to Non-Resident Contractors or Professionals

a) General

Every non-resident person who derives income under a Uganda source services contract is taxable.[128] However this does not apply to royalties or management charges covered under section 83 of ITA.[129]

A "Ugandan-source services contract" means[130] a contract, other than an employment contract, the principal purpose of which is the performance of services which gives rise to income sourced in Uganda. Any goods supplied are only incidental to that purpose.

124. *Ibid* s.84(3)
125. *Ibid* s.84(4)
126. *Ibid* ss.84(4) read together with s.87(1)(c)
127. *Ibid* s.84(2)
128. *Ibid* s.85(1)
129. *Ibid* s.85(3)
130. *Ibid* s.85(4)

b. Computation

The tax is computed at the rate of 15 percent on the gross amount of the payment under the Uganda-sourced services contract.[131]

7. Income of Non-Residents Arising from Shipping, Air-Transport or Telecommunications in Uganda

a) General

Every non-resident person carrying on the business of ship operator, charterer, or air transport operator who derives income from the carriage of passengers who embark, or ship cargo or mail which is embarked in Uganda is taxable.[132] This, however, does not apply to income so derived arising from transhipment of passengers, cargo or mail.[133]

b) Telecommunications

A non-resident person who carries on the business of transmitting messages by cable, radio, optical fibre or satellite communication and derives income from the transmission of messages by apparatus established in Uganda, irrespective of whether such messages originated in Uganda is chargeable to tax at 5 percent of the gross amount so derived in respect of the transmission.[134]

c) Computation of Tax on Shipping and Air Transportation

The tax is charged at 2 percent on the gross amount derived by a non-resident person from shipping and air transportation operations.[135]

d) General Provision on Taxation of International Payments, Entertainers and Sports Person, Payments to Non-Resident Contractors and Professional and Shipping and Air Transportation

The tax imposed on international payments, non-resident entertainers and sports persons, payments to non-resident contractors and professionals and in respect of the income of non-residents operating shipping and air transportation business is a final tax on such income.[136] Additionally, such income is segregated from the gross income of the affected non-resident person, and no deduction is allowed for expenditures or losses incurred by such a person in producing the income.[137]

The liability to tax of a non-resident person is satisfied if the tax payable is withheld by a withholding agent and remitted to the Commissioner.[138]

131. *Ibid* s.85(1); Third Schedule, Part IV
132. *Ibid* s.86 (1)
133. *Ibid* s.86(3)
134. *Ibid* S.86(4)
135. *Ibid* s.86(2); Third Schedule Part VII
136. *Ibid* s.87(1)
137. *Ibid* s.87(1)(a),(b)
138. *Ibid* s.87(1)(c) read together with ss.115, 120, 123

E. Thin Capitalisation

Thin capitalization occurs when multinational companies decide to fund their subsidiaries with the minimum amount of equity capital and the maximum amount of debt capital. The main advantage of debt capital financing, in contrast to equity capital financing, is that interest on the debt is paid out of the pre-profit income. This is an allowable expense to the business[139] and usually attracts low or no withholding tax.[140]

In view of this the International Monetary Fund recommended[141] that in order to limit tax avoidance through excessive debt/equity ratios, a thin capitalization provision to define excess interest with a view of limiting deduction thereof should be promulgated. The IMF proposed a maximum debt/equity ratio for tax purposes at either 3:1 or 2:1 with excess interest being treated as a dividend. This recommendation has been implemented by the Income Tax Act, Cap 340, which provides that where a foreign controlled resident company which is not a financial institution has a foreign debt-to-foreign equity ratio in excess of 2 to 1 at any time during the year of income, a deduction is disallowed for the interest paid by the company during that year on that part of the debt which exceeds the 2 to 1 ratio.[142]

139. ITA, S.25
140. See *ibid* s.83(1), (2),(5)
141. Contrast *ibid* 83(2), relating to dividend with s.83(5)
142. ITA, s.89(1)

8

Taxation of Trust Incoome

A. Nature of Trust

Trust income refers to income from trusts. This in turn poses the question "What is a trust?" A trust has been described as strictly referring to

> "the duty or the aggregate accumulation of obligations that rest upon a person described as a trustee. The responsibilities are in relation to property held by him, or under his control. That property he will be compelled by court in its equitable jurisdiction to administer in the manner lawfully prescribed by the trust instrument, or where there be no specific provision written or oral, or to the extent that such provision is invalid or lacking, in accordance with equitable principles."[1]

Alternatively, a trust is described as a relationship which is recognised by equity.[2] It arises where property is vested in a person or persons known as trustees. Those trustees are under a duty to hold the property for the benefit of other persons known as *cestuis que trust* or beneficiaries.

The interests of the beneficiaries are normally described in the trust instrument creating the trust. However, these may be implied or imposed by law. The beneficiary's interest is proprietary in the sense that it can be bought or sold, given away or disposed of by will. It ceases to exist when the legal estate in the property passes to a bona fide purchaser for the value of the legal estate without notice of the trust.[3]

The subject matter of the trust must be some form of property, which normally takes the form of legal ownership of land or invested funds. Nevertheless, it may be any sort of property such as land, money, chattels, equitable interests and choses in action.[4]

B. Trust Income

Trust income is what the beneficiary receives. Trust income is distinguishable from estate income since an estate in the course of administration differs from a trust.

In the case of income from a trust, a beneficiary who is entitled to the income of the trust of a particular year of assessment, or to a share of such income other than by way of annuity or annual payment, is liable to tax on such income, or his share of it, whether he receives it in that year or not, subject to deduction for expenses properly incurred

1. Stroud's Judicial Dictionary (5th ed. Sweet & Maxwell, London, 1986) p. 2696 quoting *Re: Scott* (1943) S.A.S.R. 193 per Mayo J. See also ITA, s.2
2. Keeton, *Law of Trusts* (10th ed.) p.5 For definitional problems, see pp. 4-6 thereof. See also Bakibinga, *Company Law in Uganda* (1993) pp. 181-182 in relation to the fiduciary powers of directors when compared to trustees.
3. *Pilcher v. Rawlins* (1872) L.R. 7 Ch. App. 259. See also generally Bakibinga, *Law of Trusts in Nigeria* [Ilorin, Nigeria (1989)] Chapter 2
4. Bakibinga, *Ibid.* p. 18

and paid by the trustees out of the trust income.[5] However, for this principle to apply, the beneficiary must be entitled to the income as, and when, it arises; if such income is retained by the trustee and the title of the beneficiary to it is liable to be divested on some later event, it is not the income of the beneficiary, but only of the trustee.[6] This would normally occur in connection with the income of an infant which is accumulated by trustees during his minority. If the infant has an absolute right to the income and it is not paid to him only because he cannot give a good receipt, then the income is treated as his. If, however, the infant's right to the income depends upon a contingency (e.g. attaining his majority) and if that contingency does not occur, the income passes to others, then it is not his income.[7] Although this situation normally arises mainly in connection with infants, it is of general application and in deciding whether a beneficiary is, or is not, entitled to the income. When it arises, a useful test to apply is whether his personal representatives would be entitled to it if he died immediately after the income arose. Income which is not accumulated but is extended under a discretionary power for the maintenance of an infant, is treated as the income of the infant,[8] unless it is deemed to be the income of the settlor.

In *B.H. v. Commissioner of Income Tax*,[9] the appellant was entitled to a life interest in her deceased husband's estate. After her death, his estate was to be divided among their children. In 1954 and 1956, the appellant, in accordance with the wish and intentions of the deceased, divided the income among herself and her children equally. In 1959, a deed for family arrangement was executed to give effect to this trust, and the estate investments were then transferred to trustees for this purpose. The appellant claimed that the deed was of a retrospective effect and that the assessments for the years 1955 to 1957 should be amended accordingly. It was held that as the accounts for the years 1954 to 1957 did not demonstrate a trust in favour of the children by virtue of which they received any income of their own in those years, and as the deed of arrangement did not recite any parol declaration of trust in 1954, the appellant had not discharged the onus upon herself of satisfying the Court that she had divested herself of part of the income in favour of the children in those years.

For a beneficiary to be taxable, he must be a beneficiary entitled to income under the general law, subject to any special terms of the trust. If for instance, a trust makes a profit of a particular nature which, by the terms of the trust, is added to capital, that profit will not be attributed to it; any income tax charged on it, in the absence of any special provision in the trust, will be charged to capital. Consequently, two tests must be applied. First has such income, as defined by the Income Tax Act, been received by the trust? Second, what part, if any, of that income is attributed to a beneficiary as income under the terms of the trust, otherwise than as an annual payment out of the trust income?[10]

---

5. *Baker v. Archer-Shee* [1927] A.C. 844; ITD, S. 11 (2)
6. *Stanley v. IRC* (1944) 26 T.C. 12 [1944] K.B. 255
7. *Whiteman & Wheatcroft on Income Tax* (2nd ed.) p. 176, para 17-04
8. *Drummond v. Collins* [1915] A.C. 1011 H.L. (E).
9. 3 E.A.T.C. (Pt I & II) 192 (Uganda)
10. *Whiteman & Wheatcroft on Income Tax*, supra n.7 para 17-04. See also the *Trustees of the A.D. Charitable Business Trust v. Commissioner of Income Tax* 2 E.A.T.C. (Pt.1&II) 89

In contrast with an estate in the course of administration, a residuary benefit is not regarded as taxable income of an estate in the course of administration. A share of residue does not belong to the beneficiary until it is ascertained either in whole or part by transfer or assent to him or by appropriation. It is, therefore, important to ascertain when an estate ceases to be administered and residue is ascertained.

With specific legacies, an assent by personal representatives, although two years after death, has been held to relate back to the date of death, so that income of shares specifically bequeathed become income of the beneficiary from the date of death.[11]

A pecuniary legacy belongs to the legatee for taxation purposes from the time of payment, but any interest due and paid to him for a period since the death will be chargeable to tax in the normal way.

Additionally, an annuitant is in a special position: tax is chargeable by deduction from his annuity and, accordingly as it is paid out of taxed income or not, the year of assessment in which it is treated as having the income will be determined. If, however, owing to insufficiency of assets he becomes entitled to a part of the estate, in lieu of annuity, he is treated as a residuary beneficiary, and payments made to him before insufficiency was ascertained are treated as having been paid on his account of his residuary share.[12]

2. Statutory Position

The current statutory position as to what constitutes trust income is contained in the Income Tax Act, Cap 340, which provides[13] that chargeable trust income relative to a year of income means the gross income of the trust (other than amounts attributable to beneficiaries or legatees) for that year is calculated as if the trust is a resident taxpayer, less the total amount of deductions allowed under the ITA for expenditures or losses incurred by the trust in deriving that income.

C. Taxation of Trust Income

1. Preliminary

Trust income may be received either by the trustees/personal representatives or the beneficiary. Consequently, any of them may be adjudged liable to income tax in respect of the income of the trust property, depending on certain conditions which deem either of them liable.

2. Assessment to Income Tax of Trustees/Personal Representatives

a) Charge

Generally, all income received by the trustees (or by the personal representatives, in the case of the deceased's estate) is assessed in their hands. This arose from the principle that legally income of the trust or from trust property is deemed to be income of the trustee. This concept has been slightly modified by the ITA which stipulates[14] that save in

11. *Ibid* para 17-05
12. *Ibid.* p. 176
13. ITA, S.70

relation to a settlor trust or qualified beneficiary trust, the income of a trust is taxed either to the trustee or to the beneficiaries of the trust. In addition, a trustee of an incapacitated person's trust is liable for tax on the chargeable trust income of the trust.[15]

For a trustee/personal representative to be liable to tax, he must have received such income in his capacity as a trustee/personal representative. Thus in *Williams v. Singer*,[16] trustees resident in the United Kingdom held shares in a foreign company on behalf of a beneficiary resident and domiciled abroad. The dividends were paid to the beneficiary and were never received in that country. Viscount Cave observed

> .... the fact is that if the Income Tax Acts are examined, it will be found that the person charged with tax is neither the trustee nor the beneficiary as such, but the person in actual receipt and control of the income which it is sought to reach. The object of the Acts is to secure for the state a proportion of the profits chargeable and this end is attained (speaking generally) by simple and effective expedient of taxing the profits where they are found. If the beneficiary receives and controls them, he is liable to be assessed upon them. If the trustee receives and controls them, he is primarily so liable.[17]

It was, therefore held that the trustees could not be assessed upon income which had not come into their hands. Section 4 (1) of the ITA imposes income tax on the personal income of a taxpayer. The effect of this is that a person cannot be liable to tax by proxy or on behalf of another person. Income tax is borne personally. However, Section 71 (1) of the ITA is an exception to that rule in that a trustee who receives income from trust property is liable to income tax upon such income on behalf of others, and he is so assessed in that capacity.[18]

(b) Rate and Computation of Tax

(i) Rate

Income assessed in the hands of a trustee bears the corporation tax rate[19] which is 30 percent.[20] Where such tax has already been deducted at source, the trustees cannot be assessed upon it because this would amount to double taxation. Exceptionally a trustee would not be assessed to income tax in two instances. First, where the trust income is paid directly to the beneficiary without passing through his hands.[21] Second, a trustee, may have a good answer to a particular assessment as regards some share or part of the income assessed, on the ground that such a share or part of it arises or accrues beneficially to a *cestui que* trust or in whose hands it is not liable to income tax.[22]

In *E.C. Boucher v. Income Tax Commissioner*,[23] in 1953 and 1955, the appellant

---

14. *Ibid* S.71(1)
15. *Ibid.* S.71(6)
16. [1921] A.C.65
17. Emphasis supplied.
18. *Williams v. Singer*, supra n. 16; E.C. *Boucher v. CIT* [1965] EA 576 C.A. (Kenya)
19. ITA, S. 8, Part III, Third Schedule
20. *Ibid*
21 *Williams v. Singer, supra* n.16
22. *Reid's Trustees v. IRC* (1929) 14 TC 512 at p. 525 per Lord Clyde

settled shares in a Kenya Company on discretionary trusts in favour of his infant children by deeds executed in the United Kingdom. The settlor, the trustees and the beneficiaries were at all relevant times resident in the United Kingdom. The dividends accruing to the trust from these shares from 1957 to 1960 were deemed by the respondent to be the income of the appellant as a settlor under Section 24 of the E.A. Income Tax (Management) Acts, 1952 and 1958,[24] and he was assessed accordingly. On appeal, the Supreme Court of Kenya upheld the assessments. On further appeal the appellant contended firstly that Sections 11, 24 and 75 of the 1958 Act were irreconcilable and nullified any charge to tax. Second, the appellant contended that the trustees of the settlement were "individuals" within para 6 (2) of the Double Taxation Relief (Kenya-UK) Arrangements Notice 1952, so that the income the appellant was deemed to have received under Section 24 qualified for double taxation relief. Third, the appellant contended that the income caught by Section 24 was income of the beneficiaries under the U.K. settlement and not the income of the trustees from the Kenya shares, with the result that it was not chargeable to tax because it had not accrued in the [East African] territories. The Court of Appeal held that the interaction between Sections, 11, 24 and 75 produces no uncertainty as to who should be taxed and at what rate. Section 11 amplifies Section 3 and provides that generally in the case of trusts the income thereof is first deemed to be the income of the trustee which is liable to tax at the standard rate.[25] When part of the trust income so chargeable is paid to or for the benefit of a beneficiary, then as a result of Section 11 (2), such income, grossed in the way specified, is assessed on the beneficiary at his individual rate.[26] Section 75 merely provides the machinery for an infant beneficiary to be assessed at the individual rate in the name of the trustee. Furthermore, the Court of Appeal held that there is no conflict between Section 11 (1) which deals with the assessment of a trustee for income received in trust and Section 24 which deals with the assessability of a settlor for income paid to or for the benefit of a beneficiary. Additionally, the Court held that "individual" in its normal sense and as used in the East African Income Tax (Management) Act and the Double Taxation Relief (Kenya-UK) Arrangements Notice does not include the holder of an office such as a trustee.

It should be noted that the ITA charges trust income in respect of a trustee at a uniform rate of 30 percent except where the trust relates to an estate of a deceased resident individual or an incapacitated person where the individual rate is chargeable.[27] Income from a retirement fund is also chargeable at the trust rate.[28] Where a trust has two or more trustees, they are jointly and severally liable.[29]

(ii) Computation

23. *Supra* n.18
24. equivalent to ITA, S. 71(5)
25. Under ITA, S.8 (1)
26. [S.8(I)] apart from situations in which the trustees are in charge of an incapacitated person's trust or the estate of a resident individual [S.8(2),(3)].
27. *Ibid*
28. *Ibid* S.8(4)
29. ITA, S.71(7)

A trustee cannot claim any deduction, against income so taxed, for expenses incurred by him in relation to the trust. Thus in *Aikin v. Macdonould's Trustees C.E.* (Scotland),[30] the trustees in Scotland received remittances of income from trust properties abroad and distributed the net income, after deducting the expenses of management, among the beneficiaries. It was held that the trustees were assessable upon the full amount of income received by them, without deduction of expenses. The Lord President Robertson thus observed:

> It seems to me that all the authorised deductions and charges occur at an earlier stage than that at which these expenses have been incurred. When the net sum was placed in the hands of the trustees, it has passed through all the vicissitudes which entitled anyone to make deductions. It had come home, and was in their hands for them to apply to their uses.

3. Assessment to Income Tax of a Beneficiary

Income of the beneficiary liable to tax is the amount received as income in any year of income by a person beneficially entitled thereto from any trustee in his capacity as such, or paid out of income by the trustee on behalf of such person.[31] However, amounts received from a trustee in the form of an annuity or which have borne tax are excluded from taxation.[32] The assumption that the amounts received by a beneficiary have already borne tax is based on the general rule that income received by the trustees is assessed or charged in their hands.[33]

For a beneficiary to be liable to income tax, he must (1) have received income or (2) during the course of administering an estate been entitled to receive income.[34] Consider *Drummond v. Collins.*[35] Income received from a foreign discretionary trust formed part of the total income of a person resident in the United Kingdom for the purpose of income tax and surtax. It was argued that these allowances, which were sent from America, were not "income" of the children, because they were voluntary payments by the trustees. Earl Loreburn stated:

> I do no assent to the proposition that a voluntary payment can never be charged, but it is enough to say that these were not voluntary payments in any relevant sense. They were payments made in fulfilment of a testamentary disposition for the benefit of the children in the exercise of a discretion conferred by the will. They were the children's income in fact.

Where trustees apply trust income for the benefit of a beneficiary rather than paying him in cash, the beneficiary is assessable on the value of the benefit received.[36] Where the income is retained by the trustee and the interest of the beneficiary to it is liable

---

30. (1894) 3 T.C. 306
31. ITA, Ss. 72(1), (2),73(1)
32. *Ibid* S. 71 (8)
33. *Williams v. Singer*, supra n.16; *Reid's Trustees v IRC supra* n.22
34. Easson, *Cases and Materials on Revenue Law* (2nd ed. 1990), p. 392. See also ITA, S.72(2),(3) which indicates that the discretion by a trustee to vest trust income in the beneficiary should be exercised within the second month after the relevant year of income.
35. [1915] A.C. 1011
36. *Lord Tollemach v. IRC* (1926) 11 TC 277; *IRC v. Miller* [1930] AC 222

to be divested on some later event, it is not income of the beneficiary, but only of the trustee. Consequently, the beneficiary is not liable to tax thereon. In *Stanley v. IRC,*[37] the appellant was a life tenant of a trust fund, the income of which, apart from certain payments for the maintenance of the appellant, was accumulated during his minority. The Revenue claimed to assess the appellant to surtax on the accumulated income. It was held, by virtue of Section 31 (2) of the Trustee Act 1925,[38] that the income could not be said to be the income of the appellant during the year in question. Lord Greene, MR observed:

> The infant does not during infancy enjoy the surplus income. It is not his in any real sense. The title to it is held in suspense to wait the event, and if he dies under twenty one,[39] his interest in it (whether or not it be only described as a vested interest) is destroyed. He is in fact for all practical purposes in precisely the same position as if his interest in surplus income was contingent. If he attains 21, he takes the accumulations; if he dies under 21, he does not.

Furthermore, where property is settled upon discretionary trusts for the benefit of a number of possible objects, but during the relevant period there is in fact only one person with the discretion, such a beneficiary cannot be said to be entitled to income from such fund. In this vein in *Cornwell v. Barry,*[40] Harman J. stated:

> The question at issue can be stated tersely: Was the income of this fund in the years in question the infant's income? If it was, he is entitled, through his Trustee, to get the usual personal relief against the tax suffered. If, however, it could not be said to be his income, he is not a person who can get that relief! Consequently, though it may well be and I think is the fact that Michael being in existence had got a vested interest in this money, it was an interest which was liable to be divested if another object of the trust came into existence during the eight years. It is not until the end of this time that you could say: The class is closed; the object is achieved; and the money, if there be any unapplied, vests absolutely in any of the persons who were objects of the trust and whether then dead or then living matters not.[41]

Where a beneficiary is absolutely entitled, accumulated income forms part of his total income and is assessable to tax.[42] However, if the income is accumulated during the minority of the infant, it is not his income. Where the accumulations are later paid to him, they come as capital and are not assessable to tax.[43]

Income in the hands of the trustees may be received as capital by the beneficiary. Equally payments from the capital fund may be received as income, and assessed as such, in the hands of the beneficiary. Thus in *Brodie's Trustees v IRC,*[44] the trustees of the will

37. [1944] K.B. 255; [1944] 1 All E.R. 230
38. Equivalent to Trustees Act Cap. 164, S. 32 (2) (Uganda)
39. The majority age in Uganda is 18: Contract Act, Cap 73, S. 3 (2)
40. (1955) 36 T.C. 268 Ch.D (E)
41. Emphasis supplied.
42. *IRC v. Hamilton-Russel's Executors* [1943] 1 All E.R. 474
43. *IRC v. Blackwell* [1924] 2 K.B. 351 [1926] 1 K.B. 389 c.f. *Gascoigne v. IRC* [1927] 1 K.B. 594

held property on trust to pay income to the testator's widow for life with a provision that if, in any year the income did not amount to £4,000, the trustees were to raise and pay her out of capital. The income was in fact below £4,000 in certain years, and the trustees duly raised sums out of capital in augmentation of the income. It was held that the sum so raised out of capital was taxable as income in the hands of the widow.

D. Income of the Settlor - the Anti-Avoidance Provisions

1. Methods of Avoidance

The manner of taxing the income of trusts and of beneficiaries suggests two methods of reducing the impact of taxation:[45]

1. Transfer income of the trust from a higher-rate taxpayer to a basic-rate taxpayer. For example, a wealthy grandfather could transfer income-bearing assets to trustees for the benefit of his grandchildren.[46] Instead of paying income tax at the individual rates or at the source of his assets, the grandfather puts assets on a trust rate of 25 percent in the United Kingdom and 30 percent in Uganda.[47] Tax is avoided by splitting income among the members of the settlor's own family, to whom he already might be responsible — in particular, the children — thereby reducing tax liability while retaining disposable wealth within the family unit.
2. Ensure that the income of the trust belongs to no individual (i.e., the settlor has completely divested himself of any interest in the trust, but no beneficiary is entitled absolutely to all or any part of the income, e.g., as in a discretionary trust).[48] The trustees will then be taxed on the trust income at the basic rate/corporation rate (for both Uganda and the United Kingdom) and at the additional rate (for the United Kingdom). The trustees might accumulate the post-tax income and later extract it in the form of capital distributions to the beneficiaries, or they may distribute the income to those beneficiaries who pay income tax at the basic/individual rate,[49] in which case no further tax will be due for the beneficiary.

Avoidance is attractive in this case. It can be achieved by disposing of income in a manner that allows a lower rate to be paid, or by providing for its accumulation, while power to enjoy the income can be retained by parting with it for a limited period by (1) revoking the settlement, (2) reserving a beneficiary interest, or (3) continuing to derive a benefit in some other manner.[50] In this case, the settlor uses the trusts to reduce tax, and the rate paid is much reduced when a settlor is a beneficiary.[51]

2. Anti-Avoidance Provisions

44. (1933) 17 T.C. 432. See also *Cunard's Trustees v. IRC* [1946] 1 All E.R. 159 and *Stevenson v. Winshart* [1987] 2 All E.R. 428
45. In the British context
46. *Easson, Cases and Materials on Revenue Law* (2nd ed. 1990) pp 400-401
47. ITA, S.8(1). In Uganda the reduction can be achieved by transferring the trust income to an incapacitated person or to the estate of a deceased person [(ITA, S.8(2), (3)].
48. Easson, *supra* n. 46, pp 400-401
49. Contrast with trust tax rate of 30 percent (S.8(1) except in relation to the estates of deceased or incapacitated persons. See n.47 above.
50. Easson, *supra* n. 48
51. This is no longer possible in Uganda. See *supra* n.49.

However, the taxing acts, including the ITA, contain provisions aimed at preventing this type of avoidance. For income tax purposes, these provisions deem the income under certain types of settlement to be the income of the settlor. Thus a settlor or a qualified beneficiary trust is not treated as an entity separate from the settlor or qualified beneficiary, and the income of such trust is taxed on the settlor or qualified beneficiary. Furthermore, the property owned by the trust is deemed to be owned by the settlor or qualified beneficiary.[52]

A "settlor trust" is defined as a trust in relation to a whole or part of which the settlor has the power to revoke or alter so as to acquire a beneficial entitlement in the corpus (body) or income of the trust, or a reversionary interest in the corpus or income of the trust.[53]

A "qualified beneficiary trust" means a trust in relation to which a person, other than the settlor, has a solely exercisable power to vest the corpus or income of the trust in himself or a trust whose sole beneficiary is an individual or an individual's estate or appointees. A qualified beneficiary trust does not include a trust whose beneficiary is an incapacitated person.[54]

The effect of these provisions is to prevent arrangements, outlined above, for using the trust device to avoid tax.

The following discussion reviews cases which have tried to deal with the problem. In *E.C. Boucher v. Income Tax Commissioner*,[55] the court held that there was no conflict between Section 11 (1), which deals with the assessability of a trustee for income received in trust, and Section 24, which deals with the assessability of a settlor for income paid to or for the benefit of a beneficiary. Furthermore, the court held that Section 11 (2) is a general provision that yields to the special provision of Section 24; this is an expedient to prevent tax avoidance and is an exception to the general rule that the income of a person should be assessed on that person. Finally, the court held that the dividends on the Kenya shares accrued as income of the settlement on which the trustees could be assessed at the standard rate; to the extent that it was thereafter paid to or for the benefit of the children and was deemed under Section 24 to be income of the settlor, such income was not chargeable to tax under Section 3 because it was derived from the settlement whose locus was outside the territories (East Africa).[56]

In *W B. v. Commissioner of Income Tax*,[57] the appellant, who was a director of certain companies, had three children, each of whom in 1951 was a minor. At different times between 1945 and 1951 each of the children had acquired from the appellant or his wife shares in companies of which the appellant was a director. It was alleged that the purchase price for the shares was obtained by money lent to the children by the parents under an arrangement whereby the dividends on the shares were received by the parents in repayment of the loans. The shares were acquired at their nominal value, and bonus

52. ITA, S.71(5)
53. *Ibid* s.70
54. *Ibid*
55. [1965] E.A. 576, for facts see supra p. 122.
56. *Ibid* p. 580 applying *Archer Shee v. Baker* 11 T.C. 749 and *Commissioner of Income Tax v. P. Co Ltd* 1 E.A.T.C. 131 C.A. (Tanganyika). See also *F v. Commissioner of Income Tax* 1 E.A.T.C. 36 (Uganda)
57. 2 E.A.T.C. 32 (Uganda). See also *F v. Commissioner of Income Tax Ibid*

shares were issued to the children as a result of their shareholdings. In 1951 the children obtained dividend income from the shares originally acquired and the bonus shares. The Commissioner of Income Tax treated the dividend income of the children as the income of the appellant. The appellant appealed to the High Court on the ground that the purchase of the shares by the appellant's three children were not settlements within Section 24 of the East African Income Tax (Management) Act, 1956.[58]

The court held that the dividends on the shares were income originating from the appellant as the appellant directly or indirectly provided the funds for the purchase of the shares.[59] Second, the court held that whenever a father provides funds, whether by way of gift or of loan, so as to enable his infant children to acquire shares, there is prima facie evidence that the transaction is a settlement within the meaning of the Section [70 of ITA]. Third, the court held that the appellant had failed to discharge the onus on him of proving that the shares were transferred for adequate consideration. Finally, the court held that the transfers of the shares to the appellant's children were not genuine commercial transactions and that the transactions were settlements within the meaning of the Section [71 of ITA].

In *Kanjee Naranjee v. Income Tax Commissioner*,[60] the appellant made a settlement to make provision for his existing and future grandsons. The appellant and his wife were trustees of the settlement, and the property settled by the settlement consisted of shares in two companies. The operative clauses of the settlement provided that in no circumstances was the settlor to retain or become entitled to any beneficial interest under the settlement and that the settlement "shall be absolutely irrevocable in all circumstances." Additionally, clause 10 thereof provided *inter alia* that the trustees might invest the trust monies with any firm or company regardless of the trustee(s) having any interest in such firm or company.

In respect of the "year of income 1958" the appellant was personally assessed on the whole of the dividends received by the appellant and his wife as trustees of the settlement on the ground that such income had arisen "under a revocable settlement" within the meaning of Section 25 (2) of the Income Tax (Management) Act, 1958.[61]

The appellant appealed against the assessment. In dismissing the appeal, the judge held that the settlement was a revocable settlement by virtue of the terms of Section 25 (4) (b)[62] of the Act, because according to the meaning and effect of Clause 10 of the settlement, the appellant was "able to have access by borrowing or otherwise" to the income or assets of the settlement. The judge construed the words, "is able to have access by borrowing or otherwise" to mean that there was no lawful bar to be found in or under the settlement to the passing of any of the settlement income to the appellant and concluded that the appellant was able to have access by borrowing or otherwise to the income or assets of the settlement because the trustees could have lent the trust monies to the appellant as a member of a firm had he in fact been such a member. The decision of the judge was affirmed by the Court of Appeal for East Africa. The appellant appealed

58. equivalent to ITA, S.71(5)
59. See *Ibid.* S.70 (definition of settlor) read together with S.71(5)
60. 4 E.A.T.C. (Pt 1) 19; [1964] E.A. 257 P.C. (Tanganyika)
61. equivalent to ITA, S. 70 (definition of settlor trust)
62. See *ibid*

to the Privy Council.

The Privy Council held, firstly, that during the year of income 1958, the appellant was a trustee of the settlement and, therefore, it was incompetent for trustees of the settlement to lend him personally any of the trust monies or income or to allow him to have access thereto in other than his capacity as trustee. Secondly, the Council held that there was no evidence that the appellant was a partner in a firm which was within the category of those with "the ability to have access" to the trust property, and even if the appellant had been a partner in such a firm, it would have been to the firm as such that the possible lending would have been made and the access given. Third, the Council held that the words "is able to have access by borrowing or otherwise" in Section 25 (4) (b)[63] of the East Africa Income Tax (Management) Act, 1958, in relation to a settlor in a settlement, presuppose that the settlor, if he falls into the contemplated category, as an individual some existing characteristic, some positive ability, and it is not enough to say that there must be in the settlement some bar or disqualification to his having access to any of the trust property. Fourth, the Council held that the "access" which a settlor must be able to have for a settlement to be treated as revocable within the meaning of Section 25 must clearly be "access" otherwise than in his capacity as a trustee. Finally, the Council held that that in respect of the tax year 1958, the appellant was not a person who could properly be described as "under the terms of the settlement ... able to have access" to any part of the trust property or its income.

3. Ineffective Disposition under a Trust

In the case of an ineffective disposition, there is a resulting trust in favour of the settlor with the result that the income under the disposition will be his in any event. Thus in *Vandervell v. IRC,*[64] Mr Vandervell, having formed a wish to give £150,000 to fund a chair at the Royal College of Surgeons and having consulted his experts, decided by September 1958, to make over to the college the 100,000 "A" shares in his manufacturing company, Vandervell Products Ltd. In November 1958, he proposed to the college (and it accepted) the proposal that the college should grant an option to resell the shares to the Company Vandervell Trustees Ltd for £5,000. It was explained in a letter of November 19, 1958, that Mr Vandervell had decided to make £150,000 available to the college and that £145,000 (gross) would be paid by way of dividend on the shares in Vandervell Products Ltd; the balance of £5,000 would be paid when the option should be exercised. The transaction was completed by transfer of the shares and the grant of the option on or about November 25, 1958.

The issue arose as to whether the grant of the option prevented Mr Vandervell from having divested himself absolutely of the shares. Lord Wilberforce thus observed:

> The conclusion, on the facts found, is simply that the option was vested in the trustee company as a trustee on trusts, not defined at the time, possibly to be defined later. But the equitable, or beneficial interest, cannot remain in the air: the consequence in law must be that it remains in the settlor.

---

63. *Ibid*

64. [1967] 2 A.C. 291. See also Bakibinga, *Law of Trusts in Nigeria* (1989) pp 36, 124, 232 and generally Chapter 7 on resulting trusts. See further *Re: Vandervell's Trusts* (No. 2) [1973] 3 W.L.R. 744. See now ITA, S.70 (definition of settlor trust).

9

Tax Avoidance

A. Nature of Tax Avoidance

Tax avoidance entails techniques by which the lawyer and an accountant can arrange a client's affairs to achieve a reduction in the amount of tax that he would otherwise have to pay.[1] This is significant in that the tax burden may be so great as to constitute one of the major costs of production. Consequently, increasingly enterprising and productive tax avoidance schemes are conceived by intelligent tax planning.

Tax avoidance is distinguishable from tax evasion. While tax avoidance is lawful, tax evasion is illegal. Tax evasion is said to denote:

> All those activities which are responsible for a person not paying the tax that the existing law charges upon his income. *Ex hypothesi* he is in the wrong, though his wrong doing may range from the making of a deliberately fraudulent return to mere failure to make his return or to pay his tax at the proper time.[2]

In contrast, tax avoidance means

> some act by which a person arranges his affairs that he is liable to pay less tax than he would have paid but for the arrangement. Consequently, the situation which he brings about is one in which he is legally in the right, except so far as some rule may be introduced that puts him in the wrong.[3]

Recognition of the taxpayer's right to seek to avoid tax by lawful means – e.g., to reduce, minimize, nullify or simply defer a liability to tax — can be found in judicial statements. Thus in *IRC v. Duke of Westminster*,[4] Lord Tomlin stated "Every man is entitled, if he can, to order his affairs so as that the tax attaching under the appropriate acts is less than it would otherwise be."[5]

The critical question, therefore, in any case related to purported avoidance is whether the taxpayer, by his or her actions, has succeeded in avoiding tax which would otherwise be payable – e.g., by falling outside the provisions imposing liability to tax by securing entitlement to an exemption or relief or by circumventing the provisions of anti-avoidance legislation.[6] Alternatively, the issue is whether the arrangement of the taxpayer's affairs is fiscally effective. This is resolved by determining the legal result of the step or steps taken by the taxpayer insofar as it or they affect tax. This is a determination which is

1. *Pinson on Revenue* Law p.686
2. *Final Report of the Royal Commission on the Taxation of Profits and Income* (Cmnd 9474). para 1016 (1955) (U.K.)
3. *Ibid*
4. [1936] AC 1; [1935] All E.R. Rep. 59
5. *Ibid* [1936] AC 19
6. Easson, Cases and Materials on Revenue Law (2nd Ed, 1990) p.45

reached in accordance with the principles pertinent to the resolution of any revenue case. In the words of Lord Oliver of Aylmerton:

> In the ultimate analysis, most, if not all, revenue cases depend upon a point of statutory construction, the question in each case being whether a particular transaction or particular combination of circumstances does or does not fall within a particular formula described by the taxing statute as one which attracts fiscal liability. As part of that process it is, of course, necessary for the courts to identify that which is the relevant transaction or combination before construing and applying to it the statutory formula.[7]

B. Judicial Approach to Tax Avoidance

At the outset, it should be stressed that tax avoidance is not an outright creature of the statute, but of case law and principles to be found in judicial statements.

1. Basic Principles

Before a taxing statute can be applied in relation to any given transaction, the revenue authority or the courts must first ascertain the effect of the transaction – that is, the rights and obligations created by the transaction must be determined according to the general principles of law.[8]

The starting point is the decision in *IRC v. Duke of Westminster*.[9] In that case, the Duke of Westminster executed a series of deeds in which he covenanted to pay certain of his employees weekly sums for a period of seven years or for the joint lives of the parties. The covenantees continued in their employment and continued to receive such sums as, together with the payments under the covenants, made up the amount of their wages before the deeds were executed. The employees could have left their employment and still enforced the covenants. However, there was an "understanding" that an employee would not sue for full remuneration so long as he continued to receive the covenant sums.

The Crown (government) contended that the payments were, in reality remuneration for services and could not be deducted from the Duke's income for surtax purposes since the employees were not employed in any business by the Duke. The Duke contended that they were deductible for surtax purposes. In his rationalisation of the House of Lord's decision, Lord Atkin stated:

> ...the deeds were brought into existence as a device by which the respondent might avoid some of the burden of surtax. I do not use the word device in any sinister sense, for it has to be recognised that the subject, whether poor and humble or wealthy and noble, has the legal right so to dispose of his capital and income as to attract upon himself the least amount of tax. The only function of a court of law is to determine the legal result of his disposition in so far as they affect tax

7. *Craven v. White; IRC v. Bowater Property Developments Ltd & Bayliss B. Gregory* [1988] 3 W.L.R. 423, at p. 453; [1988] 3 All E.R. 495. See also Abdulrazaq M.T., "New Trends in Nigerian Law of Company Taxation" in Yerokun & Bakibinga (eds), *Law and Social Justice in Nigeria* (1988) pp. 245 - 247.
8. Easson, *supra* n.6, p. 46
9. *Supra* n.4 See also *Snook v. London & West Riding Investments Ltd* [1967] 2 Q.B. 786; Monroe, H.H. "Fiscal Finesse: Tax Avoidance & the Duke of Westminster" [1982] *British Tax Review* 200, 205

In the same vein, Lord Tomlin postulated:

> Every man is entitled if he can to order his affairs so as that the tax attaching under the appropriate Acts is less than it otherwise would be. If he succeeds in ordering them as to secure this result, then, however unappreciative the Commissioner of Inland Revenue or his fellow taxpayers may be of his ingenuity, he cannot be compelled to pay an increased tax.

With regard to the contention that the Court should look at the "substance" of the transaction, the Court reasoned that "it is necessary, apart from the substance of the transaction to look at the effect of the legal effect of the bargain which the parties have entered into." In this vein, Lord Tomlin observed that:

> .... the substance is that which results from the legal rights and obligations of the parties ascertained upon ordinary legal principles.
>
> .... the conclusion must be that each annuitant is entitled to an annuity which as between himself and the payer is liable to deduction of income tax by the payer and which the payer is entitled to treat as a deduction from his total income for surtax purposes.

Concerning the deeds used, the House of Lords concluded that they were *bona fide* and were given their proper legal operation.

It added:

> They cannot be ignored or treated as operating in some different way because as a result less duty is payable than would have been the case if some other arrangement (called for the purpose of the appellant's argument "substance") had been made.

The reasoning in the *Duke of Westminster* case was extended in *IRC v. Mallaby-Deeley*.[10] In that case, payments made to a publishing firm under a seven-year covenant – payments that replaced a previous obligation to pay a lump sum to finance the publishing of a literary work – were held to be of a capital nature. This finding was based on the precise character of the transaction. In order to determine the effect of the relevant deed, the Court held that apart from the legal position (ascertainable from the deed) it is necessary to examine the true legal transaction by looking at all relevant documents, including an undertaking in the form of letter affecting the deed.

2. Changes in the Doctrine of Tax Avoidance

It is significant that in the *Duke of Westminster* case, there was one transaction, namely the grant of an annuity, and the issue was whether the annuity could be treated as a salary or wages. With time, however, there developed integrated transactions, which initially involve a series of tax-saving procedures designed to show no signs of change of ownership and thereby facilitating the evasion of tax. This new development demonstrates the limitations of the Westminster doctrine in that if each of the series of tax-saving procedures was to be considered independent of the other(s), the taxpayer would not be

10. [1938] 4 All E.R. 818 C.A. (E). See also *Littlewoods Mail Order Stores Ltd v. IRC* [1969] 1 WLR 124q; *IRC v. Church Commissioners of England* [1977] A.C.329 on admission of extrinsic evidence to determine the nature or character of a transaction.

found liable to tax. Thus in *Floor v. Davis,*[11] the taxpayer wished to dispose of shares in a company to an American company (KDI). A direct sale to KDI would have given rise to liability to capital gains tax. The taxpayer sought to avoid that liability by a scheme which involved *inter alia* the incorporation of another company, FNW, to which the taxpayer transferred the shares in consideration of the issue of shares by FNW to KDI. FNW was later placed in liquidation and its assets distributed. The Crown argued that there was a disposal for capital gains tax purposes of the shares by the taxpayer to KDI directly. The Court of Appeal held (Eveleigh L.J. dissenting) that the transaction did not attract capital gains tax on the taxpayer.

In reply to the argument that FNW company was a mere conduit through which the transfer of shares was effected, Sir John Pennycuick thus stated:

> this contention disregards the legal effect of what were admittedly genuine transactions and really seeks to resurrect the conception of substance which was buried by the House of Lords in *IRC v. Duke of Westminster* ...in my judgment it is impossible, upon the plain legal effect of (the transactions by which the shares were exchanged and sold) to maintain that the taxpayers and sons-in-law sold their shares in IDM to anyone other than FNW or that KDI purchased those shares from anyone other than FNW. That is not a disposal by the taxpayer and the sons-in-law to KDI.

In his dissenting judgment, Eveleigh L.J. felt that the transfer of shares to FNW was "only part of a larger transaction" and the Court had to determine whether that transaction was a "disposal" to KDI. He added that in this case the Court was not required to consider each step taken in isolation.

> It is a question of whether or not the shares were disposed of to KDI by the taxpayer. I believe they were. Furthermore, they were in reality at the disposal of the original shareholders until the moment they reached the hand of KDI, although the legal ownership was in FNW. This, in my view, shows that there were no signs of change of ownership and as such the true character of this transaction is that it was an integrated transaction to be regarded as a whole for tax purposes.

Eveleigh L.J. distinguished the Westminster case on the ground that it only dealt with a single transaction, while *Floor v. Davis* dealt with an integrated transaction. Eveleigh L.J.'s approach influenced later modifications of the Westminster doctrine.

3. The Redefinition or New Approach

As time passed, the techniques of tax avoidance progressed and were technically improved. The effect was the development of composite transactions.

Thus in *W.T. Ramsay Ltd v. IRC* and in *Eilbeck v. Rawling,*[12] W.T. Ramsay Ltd, a farming company, appealed against the decision of the lower courts to impose tax on transactions in which it was involved. In its accounting period ending 31 May 1973, it made a "chargeable gain" for the purposes of corporation tax by a lease- back transaction.

11. [1978] 2 All E.R. 1079. See also *IRC v. Plummer* [1980] AC 896; *Chinn v. Collins*; *Chinn v. Hochstrasser* [1981] AC 533; Millett, P.J., "A New Approach to Tax Avoidance Schemes," (1982) *Law Quarterly Review* 209, 229
12. [1982] AC 300; [1981] 1 All E.R. 865. The facts are taken from the judgment of Lord Wilberforce.

It desired to counteract this gain, so as to avoid tax, by establishing an allowable loss. The method chosen was to buy from a company specialising in such matters a ready-made scheme. The result was creation of a neutral situation from two assets, one of which would decrease in value for the benefit of the other. The decreasing asset would be sold, yielding a gain which the company hoped would be exempt from tax. In the lower courts, the issue was whether the gain was exempt from tax. The Court of Appeal decided that it was not. On appeal, the House of Lords affirmed the Court of Appeal decision, but the Crown fundamentally attacked the whole scheme and contended that it should simply be disregarded as artificial and fiscally ineffective.[13]

In *Eilbeck v. Rawling*,[14] the scheme was different in character from that in *Ramsay*, but also one designed to create a loss allowable for purposes of capital gains tax together with a non-taxable gain. The Court of Appeal decided against the taxpayer after considering the particular aspect of the scheme. The Crown once more advanced a fundamental argument against the scheme as a whole.

In the course of judgment, the House of Lords considered the following principles:

a) A person's liability to taxation only arises from statutory provision.
b) A person is entitled to arrange his affairs in such a way as to minimise his tax liability. The fact that the motive for a transaction may be to avoid tax does not invalidate it unless a particular enactment so provides. It must be considered according to its legal effect.[15]
c) It is for the finding commissioners to find whether a document or a transaction is genuine or a sham. To say that a document or transaction is genuine means that in law it is what it professed to be, and it does not mean anything more than that.[16]
d) Given that a document or a transaction is genuine, the Court cannot go behind it to some supposed underlying substance.[17] However, the document or transaction can be examined in the context of other relevant circumstances or series or combination of transactions.[18]

The House of Lords then observed that the *Westminster* case doctrine on the issue of substance had been limited by the dissenting judgment of Eveleigh L.J. in *Floor v. Davis*[19] and *IRC v. Plummer*[20] claimed by the Revenue to be "circular" in the sense that its aim and effect was to pass a capital sum through the various hands back to its starting point. In this vein Lord Wilberforce observed:

> The scheme, consists as do others which have come to the notice of the Courts, of a number of steps to be carried out, documents to be executed, payments to be made, according to a timetable, in each case rapid... In each case two assets appear, like particles in a gas chamber with opposite charges, one which is used to create the loss,

13. Emphasis supplied.
14. *supra* n.12
15. See the *Westminister* case supra and *Floor v. Davis, supra* n.11
16. *Ibid.*
17. *Ibid.*
18. *IRC v. Mallaby-Deeley*, supra n.10; *IRC v. Plummer, supra* n. 11
19. *supra* n.11
20. *supra* n.11

> the other gives rise to an equivalent gain which prevents the taxpayer from supporting any real loss, and which gain is intended not to be taxable. Like the particles, these assets have a very short life. Having served their purpose they cancel each other out and disappear.

Lord Wilberforce concluded:

> At the end of the series of operations, the taxpayer's financial position is precisely as it was in the beginning, except that he had paid a fee and certain expenses to the promoter of the scheme.

In a similar vein, Lord Fraser thus stated:

> The essential feature of both schemes (*Ramsay* and *Rawlings*) was that, when they were completely carried out, they did not result in any actual loss to the taxpayer.

To this could be added that there was no third person whose tax position was affected by the operations. They were "off-the-peg" tax avoidance schemes with no enduring legal consequences.

While respecting the Westminster doctrine, the House of Lords developed a new approach, that is, that a Court could consider the scheme as a whole and was not confined to a step-by-step examination, as the majority in the Court of Appeal did in *Floor v. Davis*.[21]

IRC v. Burmah Oil Co Ltd[22] involved a scheme to "manufacture" an allowable loss. But this "scheme" evolved within a group of companies and was not bought off the peg from a "tax house," as was the case in *Ramsay* and *Rawling*. Lord Fraser (with whom the other law lords concurred) formulated the issue thus:

> The question ... is whether the present scheme, when completely carried out, did or did not result in a loss such as the legislation is dealing with, which I may say for short, a real loss.[23]

It was held that it did not.

The principle to be gathered from both the *Ramsay* and *Burmah Oil* cases is that there is no legal principle which compels the court to examine separately each step in a series of operations which are planned in advance and are intended, when embarked upon, to proceed to completion. The Court is not confined to a single-step approach. On the contrary, it is entitled to look at the operations as a whole and the purpose of the legislation as a whole in deciding the tax consequences of the transactions. Thus in relation to a multi-stage schemes designed to create losses, the Court is entitled to ask whether, looking at the steps as a whole, the loss which is said to result to the taxpayer is the kind of loss which is an "allowable loss" for capital gains tax purposes. The cases (particularly the *Westminster* case) do not decide that the Court should disregard or ignore the steps in a composite transaction. It must have regard to all steps as a whole.

21. *Supra* n. 11. See also *IRC v. Plummer, supra* n.11; *Chinn v. Hochstrasser*, supra n.10. See further Tiley, J. "Tax Avoidance – A Change in the Rules," [1982] *Cambridge Law Journal*, 50.
22. [1982] T.R. 535; [1983] T.C. 200
23. *Ibid.* [1982] STC 30 at p. 38

This approach does not introduce a new principle. It applies to new and sophisticated legal devices the undoubted power and duty of the Courts to determine their nature in law and relate them to existing legislation.[24]

Lord Diplock in the *Burmah Oil* case thus observed that the *Ramsay* case marked:

> A significant change in approach adopted by this House in its judicial role to a pre-ordained series of transactions (whether or not they include the achievement of a legitimate commercial end) into which there are inserted steps that have no commercial purpose apart from the avoidance of a liability to tax which in the absence of those particular steps would have been payable.[25]

The *Duke of Westminster* case was distinguished on the ground that it was about a simple transaction entered into between two real persons (natural). However, recent tax-avoidance schemes involved inter-connected transactions between artificial persons, limited companies, without minds of their own but directed by a single mastermind. In *Ramsay*, the mastermind was the deviser and vendor of the tax-avoidance scheme. In *Burmah*, it was Burmah, the parent company of wholly owned subsidiary companies between which the pre-ordained series of transactions took place.[26]

The new approach was further elucidated in *Furniss v. Dawson*.[27] In that case, the taxpayers wanted to sell some shares to Wood Bastow Holdings Ltd for £152,000. Such a sale would have given liability to capital gains tax. A plan was devised by virtue of which the taxpayers sought *inter alia* to defer liability to capital gains tax. Under the plan, the taxpayer transferred the shares to a newly incorporated company, Greenjacket Investments Ltd, in exchange for the issue to the taxpayers of shares in the company. Greenjacket Investments Ltd then sold the shares it had acquired from the taxpayers to Wood Bastow Holdings Ltd for £152,000. The Crown (Revenue) argued that there was a disposal for capital gains tax purposes of the shares by the taxpayers to Wood Bastow Holdings Ltd.

Vinelott J. at first instance held that the principle in the *Ramsay* and *Burmah* cases did not apply, and a transaction cannot be regarded as fiscally a nullity if it has enduring legal consequences.[28] He identified "enduring legal consequences" as

i) the fact that Greenjacket owned beneficially the proceeds of sale of the shares in the operating companies, which were brought into Greenjacket's accounts and upon the income of which Greenjacket was liable to tax; and
ii) the fact that Wood Bastow's rights under the second sale agreement were rights against Greenjacket, whereas it would have had no such rights if the sale had been by the Dawsons to Wood Bastow.

The case went to the House of Lords, where Lord Brightman explained the new approach to anti-tax avoidance, thus:

24. per Lord Wilberforce in the *Ramsay* case
25. *Supra* n.23, at p.33
26. See further Millett, *supra* n. 11; Monroe [1982] B.T.R. 200; Goldberg, [1982] B.T.R. 13; Kerridge, R., "Fitzwilliam C.T.T. and the New Approach" (1994) *Law Quarterly Review* 217-221
27. [1984] A.C. 474; [1984] 1 All E.R. 530 H.L. (E). See also Beattie, C.N. "*Furniss v. Dawson*" [1984] B.T.R. 109; Millett, P. "Artificial Tax Avoidance: The English and American Approach," [1986] B.T.R. 322.
28. See also *Floor v. Davis*, *supra* n. 11 Emphasis supplied.

> In a pre-planned tax-saving scheme, no distinction is to be drawn for fiscal purposes because none exists in reality, between (i) a series of steps which are followed through by virtue of an arrangement which falls short of a binding contract and (ii) a like series of steps which are followed through because the participants are contractually bound to take each step seriatim... The formulation by Lord Diplock in *Burmah Oil* expresses the limitations of the *Ramsay* principle. First there must be pre-ordained series of transactions, or, one single composite transaction. This composite transaction may, or may not include the achievement of a legitimate commercial (i.e business) end. The composite transaction does in the instant case; it achieved a sale of the shares in the operating companies by the Dawsons to Wood Bastow. It did not in *Ramsay*. Second, there must be steps inserted which have no commercial (business) purpose apart from the avoidance of liability to tax - not "no business effect". If those two ingredients exist, the inserted steps are to be disregarded for fiscal purposes. The Court must then look at the end result. Precisely how the end result will be taxed will depend on the terms of the taxing statute sought to be applied.

Applying that approach to the *Furniss v. Dawson* case, Lord Brightman said that the inserted step was the introduction of Greenjacket as a buyer from the Dawsons and as a seller to Wood Bastow. That inserted step had no business purpose apart from the deferment of tax, although it had a business effect.[29]

Lord Bridge distinguished the *Westminster* case from *Furniss* by saying that it was legitimate for the Court in that case not to apply the "substance of the matter" doctrine given that the transaction was between individuals. However, with regard to a series of inter-dependent transactions designed to produce a result, it is legitimate to draw a distinction between the substance and the form of the composite transaction. This has been the approach in the United States, and it has enabled federal courts to develop a doctrine whereby the tax consequences of the composite transaction are dependent on its substance, not its form. This approach frees the courts from the shackles which have for so long been thought to be imposed by the *Westminster* case. With respect to the *Ramsay* and *Eilbeck v. Rawling* cases, Lord Bridge concluded that neither of the schemes in those cases was designed to achieve any substantial effect in the real world and that the elaborate steps designed to manufacture a tax-deductible loss in each case was purely formal in character.

Further clarification on the new approach to anti-tax avoidance is to be found in other British House of Lords cases, *Craven v. White*, *IRC v. Bowater Property Developments Ltd*, *Baylis v. Gregory*,[30] – which were all decided together. The transactions in these three appeals all displayed[31] the same basic pattern as the *Dawson* transactions in the sense that there was, in each, an ultimate purchase of property originally in the beneficial ownership of the taxpayer. Before the completion of the purchase, this property had been vested in an intermediate company or companies controlled by the taxpayer or by the parent company of the taxpayer. In each case, however, one or more of the salient features present in *Dawson* transactions was missing. In particular, the transactions

29. c.f. *Floor v. Davis*, *supra* n.11
30. [1988] 3 W.L.R. 423, 453; [1988] 3 All E.R. 495 [1988] STC 476; Ashton, R.K. [1988] *British Tax Review* 482; Manfield, G. [1989] B.T.R. 5; Berg, A.G.J., "Avoidance Schemes after *Craven v. White*" [1989] *Journal of Business Law*.
31. summary by Lord Oliver, [1988] STC 476 at pp. 494-495

which, in each appeal, the Revenue sought to reconstruct into single direct disposal from the taxpayer to an ultimate purchaser were not contemporaneous. Nor were they pre-ordained or composite in a sense that it could be predicted with certainty, at the date of the intermediate transfer, what the ultimate destination of the property would be, what would be the terms of any ultimate transfer or even whether an ultimate transfer would take place at all. However, in each appeal the appellant, the Revenue, claimed tax from the taxpayer in reliance upon the decision in *Dawson* and yet in none of them, do the facts match the criteria set out in Lord Brightman's speech.

In the course of judgment, Lord Templeman dispelled the submission by the Revenue that *Dawson* had decided that whenever a taxpayer carried out a tax-avoidance transaction, that transaction must be ignored for the purpose of computing the liability of the taxpayer to tax. He felt that this approach would prevent a taxpayer from "availing himself of the fiscal immunities, privileges, allowances and other mitigating factors provided by Parliament... Parliament intends that a taxpayer shall be free to place an asset out of reach of the taxing provisions." In this case courts do not interfere. He clarified[32] that *Ramsay*, *Burmah* and *Dawson* decided that there was a distinction between an independent transaction carried out to avoid the gambit of a taxing statute in a manner authorised by Parliament and a transaction which is not an independent transaction but forms part of an artificial tax-avoidance scheme designed to enable the taxpayer to carry out a taxable transaction and to avoid a tax assessment. In this vein Lord Oliver of Aylmerton further clarified:

> *Ramsay* as developed by *Dawson* merely established that the fiscal consequences of a pre-ordained series of transactions carried out to their pre-ordained conclusion are generally to be determined by looking at the pre-ordained end result of the series. The emphasis, was, throughout, on the unbroken and pre-destined chain from start to finish and, in the ultimate analysis, the divergence of view ... comes down to the meaning to be attributed ... to the expressions "pre-ordained" and "a composite transaction."[33]

He explained that the wider view interprets "pre-ordained" simply as "pre-conceived" or "Planned to take place in the future" so that *all events* which occur sequentially, which contain a tax-saving element and which result from the same initial conscious volition or contemplation on the taxpayer from the part of "a scheme," are therefore "pre-ordained" and accordingly fall to be construed as part of, and indivisible from the ultimate disposition whether or not at the time of the transaction in question the ultimate disposition was certain, uncertain, anticipated or merely hoped for, provided that there was some particular type of disposition in view.[34] On this footing, the concept of the "single composite transaction" is a Procrustean bed into which events or transactions are forced even at the expense of a total distortion of their actual nature. The decision in *Dawson* did not fall within this wider view for four reasons. First, no such novel general proposition was expressed in terms. All that *Dawson* did was to apply the *Ramsay* principle of construction to a different chain of events. Furthermore, *Ramsay* is not authority for any proposition wider than this: that where it can be shown that successive

32. [1988] STC 476 at p. 487
33. *Ibid* p. 503
34. *Ibid* pp. 503-504

transactions are so indissolubly linked together, both in fact and in intention, as to be properly and realistically viewed as a composite whole, the Court is both bound and entitled so to regard them. Second, if the wider proposition was intended, the meticulous analysis by Lord Brightman in *Dawson* of the steps taken, the way they were carried out and the close relationship between them was unnecessary. Third, the question dealt with in *Ramsay*, *Burmah* and *Dawson* was essentially one of statutory construction – to wit, "when is a disposal not a disposal within the terms of the statute." Fourth, there was no rational basis for the wider proposition given its uncertainty.

Finally, Lord Oliver summarised the current position by formulating four essential elements emerging from the *Dawson* case thus:

(1) that the series of transactions was, at the time when the intermediate transaction was entered into, pre-ordained in order to produce a given result;
(2) that the transaction had no other purpose than tax mitigation;
(3) that there was at that time no practical likelihood that the pre-planned events would not take place in the order pre-ordained, so that the intermediate transaction was not even contemplated practically as having an independent life; and
(4) that the pre-ordained events did in fact take place.[35]

He concluded that "in these circumstances the Court can be justified in linking the beginning with the end so as to make a single composite whole to which the fiscal results of the single composite whole are to be applied."

The House of Lords, by a majority of three to two dismissed the three appeals (Lords Templeman and Goff dissenting) by the Revenue on the main ground that the *Ramsay* principle was inapplicable to the transactions before it since it could not be said that there was sufficient practical certainty that the final transaction would take place at the time when the potentially tax-saving transactions were concluded.

C. Tax Avoidance in the Ugandan Context

Prior to the promulgation of the Income Tax Act, 1997, capital gains tax did not exist in Uganda. The cases discussed above had limited application since they are largely concerned with capital gains tax and surtax. With the passage of the Income Tax Act, which has introduced a limited form of capital gains tax,[36] such cases are now relevant to Uganda, especially in relation to what constitutes "a disposal,"[37] the formulation of schemes which have no substantial economic effect[38] or are insubstantial generally[39] or have as their main purposes the avoidance or reduction of liability to tax.[40]

35. *Ibid.* p. 507. For other subsequent cases applying these principles see *Shepherd v. Lyntress Ltd*; *News International PLC v. Shepherd* [1989] STC 617: *Gordon v IRC* [1991] STC 174. For East African cases on tax avoidance see *Associated Contractors Ltd v. Commissioner of Income Tax* [1958] E.A. 676 C.A. (Kenya); *Commissioner of Income Tax v. C.W.Armstrong* [1963] E.A. 505 C.A.
36. ITA, Ss.18(1)(a) 49-54 discussed *supra* chapter 4
37. See further ibid s.51
38. *Ibid* s.91(1)(a)
39. *Ibid* s.91(1)(c)
40. *Ibid* s.91(2)

D. Necessity for Anti-Avoidance Legislation

The necessity for anti-avoidance legislation arises from the legislature's desire to effectively enforce tax legislation. When the legislature introduces provisions designed to impose tax, it also seeks to ensure that such provisions are effective, and it tries all possible means to block all potential "loopholes" in the taxing legislation. The methods include specific provisions, specific anti-avoidance provisions and general anti-avoidance provisions. These will briefly be considered, in turn.

1. Specific Provisions

Specific provisions to block loopholes in taxing legislation are the most common. For this purpose, the charge to tax is imposed in certain circumstances or upon certain transactions, whether or not the intention of the taxpayer is to avoid tax. A typical provision is one related to settlements of income.[41] Such a provision, as we have seen,[42] is aimed at dealing with tax avoidance measures whereby under a trust income is transferred from a higher-rate taxpayer (the settlor) to a lower-rate taxpayer (beneficiary) and where a scheme is designed to ensure that the income belongs to nobody as in the case of a discretionary trust. The purpose of such schemes is to make *bona fide* dispositions to give the appearance of making the income not attributable to the settlor or disposer. To block such schemes the legislature introduced specific provisions.[43]

In *IRC v. Plummer*[44] Lord Wilberforce explained the effect of the British provisions thus:

> Part XVI of the [Income and Corporation Taxes] Act 1970 which includes Sections 434 to 459 is headed "settlements."[45] It includes a number of provisions which have been enacted at different times, the general effect of which is to cause income of which a person has disposed in various ways to be treated, in spite of the disposition as the income of the disposer... Chapter I of Part XVI is headed "Dispositions for short periods", exempting dispositions for valuable and sufficient consideration; it treats dispositions of income for a period which cannot exceed six years as the income of the disposer.[46] Chapter II deals with settlements on children - the general purpose being to prevent (i.e. to tax if they are made) dispositions the effect of which is to spread income among the children of the settlor.[47]... Chapter III deals with revocable settlements, settlements in which a settlor retains an interest and capital payments made to a settlor or his spouse, the effect of which is to tax income from which a settlor or his wife, may benefit as the settlor's income.[48]

---

41. See e.g. ITA, 1997, Ss 70, 71(5); discussed *supra* Chapter 8; Income & Corporation Taxes Act, 1988 Pt XV, Ss. 660 - 694 (U.K.); *Kanjee Naranjee v. Income Tax Commissioner* [1964] E.A. 257 dealing with S. 25 ITD; discussed *supra* Chapter 8; *B.H. v. Commissioner of Income Tax* 3 E.A.T.C. (Pt I & II) 192
42. see Chapter 8 *supra*
43. ITA, Ss 70, 71(5); ICTA, 1988, Ss 660-669 (U.K.)
44. [1980] A.C. 896 H.L. (E)
45. See now ICTA Pt XV, Ss. 660-685
46. ICTA, 1988, Ss. 660-62 (U.K.) See also ITA, Ss. 70, 71(5)
47. ICTA 1988, Ss 663-670 (U.K.) See also ITA, Ss. 70, 71(5) and cases cited at n. 41
48. ICTA, *Ibid* Ss 671-682; ITA, S.70 (definition of "Settlor Trust" discussed *supra* Chapter 8)

2. Specific Anti-Avoidance Provisions

Specific anti-avoidance provisions are aimed at particular types of transaction and when such transaction is entered into for the purpose of tax avoidance. Provisions in United Kingdom legislation fall into this particular category and are designed to cancel a tax advantage obtained from transactions in securities.[49] There are no corresponding provisions in Uganda. However, with the introduction of the capital market,[50] there may be need to introduce similar anti-tax avoidance provisions to address malpractices in securities dealings already identified in the Ugandan legislation.[51]

3. General Anti-Avoidance Provisions

A general anti-avoidance provision seeks to nullify the effect of tax avoidance in general. Such provisions exist in a number of jurisdictions, including Uganda. Thus it is provided[52] that for the purpose of determining liability to tax under the ITA, the Commissioner may recharacterise a transaction or an element thereof that was entered into as part of a tax-avoidance scheme.

Decisions of courts and the Privy Council in appeals from Commonwealth countries in relation to general anti-avoidance provisions are instructive with regard to the interpretation of particular provisions, but they are also significant for the consideration of recent developments in the judicial approach to tax avoidance in the United Kingdom.[53] Thus in *C.I.R. v. Challenge Corporation Ltd*,[54] by an agreement Merbank Corporation Ltd ("Merbank") sold to the respondent taxpayer, the whole of the issued share capital of a company, Perth Property Developments Ltd ("Perth") at a price equal to 222 of the amount of the tax loss of $5.8 million incurred by Perth, which proved to be deductible from the assessable income of the respondent taxpayer, whichever price should prove to be higher. The purpose of this agreement was to reduce the liability to income tax of the respondent taxpayer by $5.8 million.

By Section 99 of the Income Tax Act, 1976, of New Zealand any "contract" shall be "absolutely void as against" the Commissioner of Inland Revenue "if and to the extent that, directly or indirectly... its purpose or effect" is to reduce "any liability to income tax."

In this case, the taxpayer asserted that, notwithstanding Section 99, it was entitled to treat the agreement as valid against the Commissioner because Section 191 of the Act allowed losses to be transferred, in certain circumstances, between members of a group of companies. In other words, the taxpayer claimed that his action amounted to tax mitigation and not tax avoidance.[55] The Privy Council advised that the appeal should be allowed. In delivering the majority opinion, Lord Templeman said:

---

49. ICTA, ibid Pt XVII, Ss. 703-709. See also *Bird v. IRC; Beam Nominees Ltd v. I.R.C.* [1988] 2 All E.R. 670; [1988] S.T.C. 312
50. Capital Markets Authority Act, Cap. 84
51. Ibid Ss 82, 83, 84, 87, 88 For an attempt at doing this, see ITA, s.90 dealing with transactions between associates.
52. ITA, S. 91(1)(a), (2)
53. See *supra* under Section B
54. [1987] 2 W.L.R. 24; [1986] S.T.C. 548 P.C. (New Zealand)
55. Emphasis emphasised.

> The material distinction in the present case is between tax mitigation and tax avoidance. A taxpayer has always been free to mitigate his tax liability to tax. Income tax is mitigated by a taxpayer who reduces his income or incurs expenditure in circumstances which reduce his assessable income or entitle him to reduction in his tax liability. Section 99 does not apply to tax mitigation because the taxpayer's tax advantage is not derived from an "arrangement" but from the reduction of income which he accepts or the expenditure which he incurs. Section 99 does apply to tax avoidance. Income tax is avoided and a tax advantage is derived from an arrangement when the taxpayer reduces his liability to tax without involving him in the loss or expenditure which entitles him to that reduction. The taxpayer engaged in tax avoidance does not reduce his income or suffer a loss or incur expenditure but nevertheless obtains reduction in his liability to tax as if he had.[56]

In an arrangement of tax avoidance, the final position of the taxpayer is unaffected (save for the costs of devising and implementing the arrangement) and by the arrangement the taxpayer seeks to obtain a tax advantage without suffering reduction in income, loss or expenditure which other taxpayers suffer and which Parliament intended to be suffered by the taxpayer qualifying for a reduction in his liability to tax.

He concluded that:

> Most tax avoidance involves a pretence. In the present case the taxpayer and its taxpayer subsidiaries pretend that they suffered a loss when in truth the loss was sustained by Perth and suffered by Merbank. In New Zealand Section 99 would apply to all English cases of income tax avoidance.[57]

From the above case, it can be inferred that Section 91(1)(a) of ITA of Uganda, which is equivalent to Section 99 of the New Zealand Income Tax Act, 1976, is a general anti-avoidance provision and applies to all English cases on income tax avoidance already discussed.[58] Additionally, it is intended as an anti-avoidance provision to nullify the effect of tax avoidance generally – that is, transactions which are employed by taxpayers to avoid tax which they are liable to pay under the statute, but for the pretence to create a tax advantage.

---

56. [1986] S.T.C. 548 at pp. 554-555 Emphasis supplied. See also discussion under Section B *supra*. See also ITA, s.91(1)(b)(c)
57. *Ibid.* p. 556 referring to the *Ramsay* case [1979] 1 W.L.R. 974, 979. See also ITA, s.91(1)(b).
58. See Section B of this chapter

10

Administration of Income Tax

This chapter attempts to outline administrative procedures relating to the assessment and collection of income tax, appeals, fines and penalties as well as other miscellaneous matters thereto. A more detailed treatment of tax appeals appears in Chapter 11.

A. Administration of Income Tax Act

1. Commissioner-General

The Commissioner-General appointed under the Uganda Revenue Authority Act[1] is empowered together with other officers[2] to administer the Act and in particular the efficient operation of the Department of Internal Revenue in the Uganda Revenue Authority which administers income tax. In practice he has delegated his powers to the Commissioner for Internal Revenue.[3] The Commissioner-General's powers and duties may be exercised, apart from those relating to compounding of offences, by a revenue officer.[4] The Commissioner-General is also authorised to delegate his powers, other than those under ITA Section 148 and 156 relating to compounding of offences and delegation, to any officer.[5]

2. Revenue Officers

(a) Official Secrecy

Every officer employed to execute the Income Tax Act is enjoined to observe an oath of secrecy and for that purpose not to reveal documents or information acquired in the exercise of his duties other than for the purpose of executing the Act.[6] However, such information may be released to any other officer appointed under the URA Statute or to the Minister of Finance.[7] He may also reveal documents or information solely for revenue or statistical purposes to a government statistical department for official purposes.[8] A revenue officer under the ITA may also reveal documents and information to the Auditor-General or his designate for official purposes.[9] Information may also be released to a government official for purposes of determining any relief or allowance sought by a taxpayer under a double taxation agreement.[10]

---

1. Cap. 196 S. 9 read together with ITA, Cap. 340, S. 156
2. Appointed under URA Act, S. 11 (1).
3. See instrument signed by the Commissioner-General in 1993. See also ITA, S.156
4. ITA, S. 156 and the Human Resource Management Manual of URA designating officers as Revenue Officers
5. ITA, S. 156
6. *Ibid.* S. 157(1), (2)
7. *Ibid.* S. 157 (3) (a), (b)
8. *Ibid.* S. 157 (3) (b)
9. *Ibid.* S. 157(3) (c)
10. *Ibid.* S. 157 (3)(d)

(b) Offences

Any revenue officer executing the ITA who solicits a bribe or engages in an agreement whereby tax revenue may be defrauded is guilty of an offence and liable to a fine not exceeding Shs500,000 or imprisonment for a term of at least three months.[11] A similar penalty is imposed on an officer who breaches the oath of secrecy mentioned above, except that the term of imprisonment is limited to one year and both a fine and imprisonment may be imposed.[12] Conversely any person who offers a bribe or entices a revenue officer to engage in acts likely to lead to defrauding of tax revenue is also liable to a similar fine and term of imprisonment.[13] The ITA has, however, introduced provision for lenient treatment of an officer or any other person involved in bribery who volunteers information to the Commissioner on the bribery. Such persons may be exonerated from prosecution and may be entitled to receive 20 percent of the fine imposed in the case of an officer or reduction in tax payable in the case of another person.[14]

B. Returns and Notices

1. Return of Income

Every taxpayer is required to file a return of particulars of his income, including a declaration that the return is complete and correct by 31 October of the immediately succeeding year.[15] However, if the accounting period of such person does not coincide with the assessment year, the return should be submitted not later than four months from the end of the accounting date to which such a person makes up his accounts.[16] An employee whose tax has been recovered under Sections 4(4) and 116 or whose income is solely from emoluments is not required to file a return.[17] Similarly a non-resident person whose tax is recovered under Section 87 of the ITA by withholding is not required to file a return.[18] The Commissioner-General may by written notice require any taxpayer, executor, administrator, or liquidator to furnish a return of income at any time.[19] This power caters for situations in which affected persons did not file returns.

Upon application by an affected person, the Commissioner-General may extend up to 90 days the period of filing a return, if he is satisfied that the delay was due to absence from Uganda, sickness or some other reasonable cause.[20]

A taxpayer may submit a return of income for the year which is treated as an assessment.[21]

11. *Ibid* S. 145 (1)
12. *Ibid* S. 157(1)
13. *Ibid* S. 145 (2)
14. *Ibid* S.145(3),(4),(5)
15. *Ibid* S. 92(1),(3)
16. *Ibid.* S. 92(1) read together with S.2
17. *Ibid.* S. 93(b) (i)
18. *Ibid* S. 93(a)
19. *Ibid.* S. 92 (8)
20. *Ibid* S. 94(1) (3)
21. *Ibid* S.96(1),(2)

A person whose business has ended, an executor of a deceased person or a liquidator of a company is required to file returns within four months of the date of discontinuance of the business. The person becomes executor of the deceased person, or liquidation of the company commences on the first day of the year of income in which such event occurred and ends on the date on which such event occurred.[22]

Without prejudice to the requirement to furnish a return by 31 October,[23] it is provided that any resident person who is about to leave Uganda permanently in any year of income, shall furnish to the Commissioner-General a return of income for such year of income or part thereof up to the date of his departure.[24]

2. Provisional Tax

A person who derives or expects to derive any income during a year of income which would not be subject to withholding tax at source[25] or rental tax is obliged to[26] pay provisional tax.[27] For taxpayers other than individuals (invariably companies), the tax is payable in two installments on or before the last day of the sixth and twelfth months of the relevant year of income in which tax liability arises.[28] For this purpose the amount of each Instalment of provisional tax is calculated using the formula[29]

$$50\% \times A\text{-}B$$

A is the estimated tax payable by the provisional taxpayer for the year of income, while B is any tax withheld before the due date for payment of the installment from any amounts earned by the taxpayer during the relevant year of income and which will be included in the gross income of the taxpayer for that year.

With respect to a provisional taxpayer who is an individual, provisional tax is payable in four installments on or before the last day of the third, sixth, ninth and twelfth months in the relevant year of income in respect of which the liability for income tax arises.[30] For this purpose the amount of each installment of tax for the year of income is computed according to the formula[31]

$$25\% \times (A\text{-}B)$$

A is the estimated tax payable by the taxpayer. B is the amount of tax withheld before the due date for payment of the installment in respect of the taxpayer's income during

22. *Ibid* S. 92 (8)
23. *Ibid* S. 92 (1)
24. *Ibid* S. 92 (8)
25. See ITA SS 116, 117 and 118 relating to withholding tax from employment, interest and dividend payments.
26. ITA, S.5
27. *Ibid* S.111 (1)
28. *Ibid* S.111(2)
29. *Ibid* S.111(3)
30. *Ibid* S.111(4)
31. *Ibid* S.111(5)

the year of income which is included in the gross income of the taxpayer. The date of payment of an installment may follow written application and for good cause shown may be extended by the Commissioner.[32]

Installments of provisional tax are a debt due to the government and may be collected and recovered in the normal way.[33]

Furthermore, each installment of provisional tax shall be credited against the income tax assessed on the provisional taxpayer for the relevant year of income to which it relates.[34] If total installments for the year exceed the tax assessed for that year, they will offset any tax due from the taxpayer and make provisional tax payments during the year in which the refund thereof is to be made.[35]

3. Particulars of Return

a) General

The repealed law gave detailed particulars to be included in a return of income required to be filed with the Commissioner.[36] However, the Income Tax Act, Cap 340, simply indicates that "a return of income shall be in the form prescribed by the Commissioner ... state the information required, and be furnished in a manner prescribed by the Commissioner."[37] Presumably such particulars may be specified in regulations made by the Minister of Finance under the Act.[38] However, some particulars are specified in the Act. For instance, the return of income should be signed by the taxpayer and include a declaration that the return is complete and accurate.[39] If a taxpayer is legally incapacitated, the return should contain a declaration as to completeness and accuracy and be signed by the taxpayer's legal representative.[40] Additionally, where the taxpayer carried on business, the return should include a statement of income and expenditure and one of liabilities and assets.[41] An accountant or auditor who, for remuneration, prepares or assists in the preparation of a return of income, balance sheet, statement of income and expenditure or any other document in support of the return is required to sign the return certifying that he has examined the books of accounts and other relevant documents of the taxpayer and that to the best of his knowledge, the return or document correctly reflects the data and transactions to which it relates.[42] If such person fails or refuses to sign the certificate, he should furnish the taxpayer with a written statement of the reasons for such refusal. The taxpayer should include this statement with the return of income to which the refusal relates.[43]

---

32. *Ibid.* S.111(6)
33. *Ibid* S.111(7) read together with SS103-110. See *infra* discussion on collection and recovery
34. *Ibid.* S.111(8)
35. *Ibid* S.111(9) read together with S.113(3)
36. Income Tax Decree, 1974, Ss.59-78
37. *Ibid* S.92(2)
38. *Ibid* S.164
39. *Ibid* S.92(3)
40. *Ibid* S.92(4)
41. *Ibid* S.92(5)
42. *Ibid* S.92(6)
43. *Ibid* S.92 (7)

b) Special Cases

When the taxpayer has died, become bankrupt, or gone into liquidation, or is about to leave Uganda permanently or is about to cease activity in Uganda, or in any case considered appropriate by the Commissioner, the letter may by written notice require the taxpayer or his trustee to furnish, by a specified date, a return of income for the taxpayer for a period less than 12 months.[44]

c) Failure to Furnish a Return/Additional Information

Where a person fails to furnish a return of income, the Commissioner may by written notice appoint a person to prepare and furnish the return and such return shall for the purpose of the ITA be attributed to the person originally required to furnish the return.[45]

The Commissioner is also empowered to require, in writing, the person who has furnished the return to provide a fuller or further return of income.[46]

d) Rental Income

A resident individual who is charged tax under Section 6 is required to furnish a return of gross rental income for each year of income not later than four months after the end of that year.[47] For this purpose the Commissioner shall prescribe the form of return of gross rental income.[48]

e) Exemptions

Except upon the Commissioner's written request, no return of income is required to be furnished under the ITA by

i) a non-resident person in respect of Uganda-source income derived from dividends, interest, royalty, natural resource payment or management charge; public entertainment and sports contracts and professional engagements; and shipping, air transportation and telecommunications.[49]

ii) a resident individual engaged in employment, presumptively assessed or whose total income is subject to the zero rate under Part I of the Third Schedule of the ITA.[50]

f) Extension of Time for Filing and Reform

A taxpayer who is required to file a return may, upon written application to the Commissioner, be permitted extension of time to furnish the return.[51] Such application should be made by the due date for furnishing the return to which it relates.[52] The Commissioner will normally permit such extension if he is satisfied that the taxpayer is unable to furnish a return by the due date owing to absence from Uganda, sickness or

44. *Ibid* S.92(8)
45. *Ibid* S.92(9)
46. *Ibid* S.92(10)
47. *Ibid* S.114(1)
48. *Ibid* S.114(3)
49. *Ibid* S.93(a) read together with Ss 83-87
50. *Ibid* S.93(b) read together with S.4(4), (5) and Part I Third Schedule
51. *Ibid* S.94(1)
52. *Ibid* S.94(2)

other reasonable cause. An extension is limited to 90 days.[53] A person who is dissatisfied with the Commissioner's decision may object to or appeal it in the normal way provided for under the ITA.[54]

g) Offence for Failure to Furnish a Return

If a person is so convicted and fails to furnish a return or document to which the offence relates within the period prescribed by the court, an offence is committed. On conviction, this offense attracts a fine of up to Shs400,000.[55]

In *K et al. v. Commissioner of Income Tax*,[56] the two appellants, N.K. and C.K., were brothers and co-directors of K & Co. Ltd. The appellants omitted to make returns made by K & Co. Ltd. Thereafter correspondence passed between the Commission and the appellants or their accountants with regard to the income of the appellants but there was an appreciable delay before the information required was an supplied by the appellants. The Commissioner imposed on each of the appellants the full amount of the additional tax under the then Income Tax Ordinance No. 27 of 1950. The appellants appealed to the local committee on the ground that the evidence did not justify the imposition of the full additional tax. The committee reduced the additional tax for both appellants. The appellants appealed to the High Court. The court held that where a taxpayer defaults in furnishing a return or omits from his return any amount which should have been included therein, the full additional tax is imposed by law, but the Commissioner thereafter has power to remit the additional tax in whole or in part.

C. Assessments

1. Normal Assessments

The Commissioner-General is empowered to assess every person who has taxable income as expeditiously as possible after expiration of the time allowed for such person to furnish a return of income. For that purpose the assessment may be based on the return submitted[57] or on the judgment of the Commissioner-General where he has reasonable cause to believe that the return is untrue and incorrect.[58] In the event of a return not having been furnished, the Commissioner-General may determine the taxable income of a person and assess him accordingly and without prejudice for failure to file a return under the ITA.[59]

In *Mandavia v. Commissioner of Income Tax,*[60] the appellant resided in Kenya since 1921. Prior to 1953 he had not been served with notices calling for any return of income, and he had made no returns. He claimed that he had approached the revenue authorities in 1943 and that in 1950 he gave oral notice that he was chargeable to tax for that and

53. *Ibid* S.94(3)
54. *Ibid* S.94(4)
55. *Ibid* S. 137(2)
56. 1 E.A.T.C.94 (1951) (Tanganyika)
57. ITA, S.95(1)
58. *Ibid.* S. 95 (2) (b)
59. *Ibid* S. 95(2)(b) See also Section 138 discussed *supra*
60. [1958] E.A. 696 P.C. See also [1958] E.A. 407, 410 C.A. (Kenya)

eight previous years. This was followed by some correspondence involving request for information, some of which was given. Thereafter on 26 May 1953, the Commissioner sent notices by post requiring returns of income to be made within a specified period [which time could not under S. 59 of the E.A. Income Tax (Management) Act 1952 be less than 30 days after service of notices]. The appellant, who was in England, asked for an extension until he returned to East Africa, which might be the end of July. In reply to this letter, the Commissioner indicated his intention to issue, immediately, estimated assessments with relevant penalties added thereto. The assessments were issued on June, 26, which was less than 30 days after the date of service of the notices and the penalties added were triple the tax. The appellant appealed and claimed that the assessments were ultra vires and void because they were made before the time allowed under Section 71 of the East African Income Tax (Management) Act 1952.[61] Both the Supreme Court of Kenya and Court of Appeal for Eastern Africa held that the assessments were properly made under Section 72 of the Act,[62] which was an alternative to Section 71 and under which an original assessment could be made, whether or not a notice requiring a return of income had been issued.

The Privy Council, in allowing the appeal, advised that an opportunity to make a return should be a condition precedent to assessment, that Section 71 of the 1952 Act[63] provides how all original assessments are to be made, and that Section 72[64] deals with the reopening of cases which had been settled under normal procedure. The council further advised that before making assessments, the time allowed under Section 71 must elapse. Since it had not done so, the assessments were *ultra vires*.

2. Objection to Assessment

A person assessed normally or provisionally under sections 95 and 97 is permitted within 45 days of service of notice of assessment to submit to the Commissioner General an objection to the assessment.[65] The Commissioner General, upon being satisfied with the objection, may cancel the assessment objected to and substitute it with another.[66] If the assessee is aggrieved by the Commissioner General's refusal to cancel the assessment objected to, he may within 45 days of the service of such refusal appeal to the High Court or apply for review thereof to the Tax Appeals Tribunal.[67]

3. Assessment of a Person about to Leave or Having Left Uganda, Ceased Activity, Died or of a Company Liquidated

The Commissioner General may assess a person who is about to leave Uganda or who has left Uganda on a permanent basis, or who is about to cease activity. He may also assess the trustee or a liquidated company.[68]

4. Exemption from Assessment

61. equivalent to ITA, S. 95 (Uganda)
62. equivalent to ITA S. 97 read together with Ss 95 (1)
63. See note 62 *supra*
64. See note 63 *supra*
65. ITA, S.99(1)
66. *Ibid.* S. 99(5)
67. *Ibid.* S. 100 (1) (2).
68. *Ibid* S. 95(4) read together with S.92(8)

(a) Employee
An employee whose income consists only of emoluments and whose tax has been recovered by deduction under Section 4(4) of the ITA is exempted from assessment.[69]

(b) Non-Resident Person
A non-resident person chargeable to tax shall not be assessed if he had no income other than income at the non-resident rates and if the tax chargeable at such non-resident rates was recovered on a withholding basis under Section 87 of ITA.[70]

(c) Small Business
A person assessed by virtue of Section 4(5) shall not be assessed again.[71]

5. Additional Assessment
Where the Commissioner-General determines that a person has been under-assessed relative to assessable income or to tax payable, he may issue an additional assessment in respect of the additional amount to his best judgment.[72]

6. Service of Notice of Assessment and Time for Making Assessment

(a) Service of Notice
The Commissioner-General is required to cause a notice of an assessment or provisional assessment to be served on each assessee. The notice should state the amount of income assessed and the amount of tax payable, the amount of tax paid (if any), and the time, place and manner of objecting to the assessment.[73] A notice of assessment need not be served in a case where a person is deemed to have been assessed under Section 96 of ITA when he has furnished a return of income.[74]

(b) Time for Making Assessment
A time limit of seven years after the year of income to which the assessment relates is given for making the assessments. However, in the case of fraud or wilful neglect committed in relation to tax for any year of income, an assessment in relation to such year may be made at any time.[75]

In *D.A. Pritani v. Commissioner of Income Tax*,[76] the court held that if the Commissioner seeks to maintain that any particular assessment was made more than seven years after the end of the year of income to which it relates and is not statute-

69. *Ibid* S. S.95(5) read together with S.93(b)(i)
70. *Ibid* S. 95 (5) read together with S.93 (a)
71. *Ibid* S.95(5) read together with S.93(b)(i)
72 *Ibid* S.97(1)
73. *Ibid* S.95(6) read together with S.99(1)
74. *Ibid* S.96(1)
75. *Ibid* S. 95 (1) read together with S.98(2)

barred, he must establish that there was a preponderance of probability that the taxpayer, in relation to his income tax for the relevant year of assessment, either acted fraudulently or was in gross or wilful default.[77]

7. Assessment Lists

Following submission of returns, the Commissioner General is required to prepare a list of the names and addresses of persons assessed tax for the relevant year of income, the amount of income upon which the assessment had been made, and the amount of tax payable.[78] An extract from the assessment list duly certified by the Commissioner General for the purpose of any legal proceedings shall be *prima facie* evidence of the matters therein contained.[79]

8. Effect of Mistake, Defect or Omission in Assessment

A mistake, defect or omission in an assessment, warrant or document issued under the Income Tax Act shall not render the assessment, warrant, or document void or voidable, if in substance it is in conformity with the Act.[80]

D. Objections, Appeals and Relief for Mistakes

1. Objection to Assessment

(a) Right to Object

Any person who disputes an assessment made upon him under the ITA has the right to object, by notice in writing, to the Commissioner General, to the assessment.[81] To be valid and acceptable, the notice must state precisely the grounds of the objection to the assessment and should be received by the Commissioner General within 45 days of the date of service of the notice of assessment.[82] However, the period may be extended if the Commissioner General is satisfied that owing to absence from Uganda, sickness or other reasonable cause, he was prevented from giving the notice within the prescribed period and that there had been no unreasonable delay on his part.[83] Thereafter the notice out of time is admitted as a valid notice of objection. A person aggrieved by the Commissioner General's refusal to admit a notice of objection out of time may apply to the Tax Appeals Tribunal for review of the decision within 45 days of service of notice of decision.[84]

In *Commissioner of Income Tax v. B.O.*,[85] the Commissioner assessed the defendant to tax for the years 1953 to 1957. The defendant did not object to the assessments within 30 days under Section 109 (1) of the East African Income Tax (Management) Act 1958.[86]

---

76. [1961] E.A. 671 (Kenya)
77. *Ibid* p. 675 per Mayers J.
78. ITA, S. 98 (1)
79 *Ibid* S. 98 (2)
80. *Ibid* S. 98 (3) Emphasis added.
81. *Ibid* S. 99 (1)
82. *Ibid* S. 99(1) (2)
83. *Ibid* S.99(3)
84. *Ibid* s. 99(4). For detailed account of the Tribunal, see chap. 11 *infra*

Since no timeous objection was made, the assessments became final and conclusive under Section 114 of the Act. Thereafter an Assessor in the Income Tax Department agreed at the defendant's request to accept a notice of objection out of time and agreed to issue amended assessments based on new figures submitted by the defendant. Although no amended assessments were issued, the defendant started making payments under the agreement. The plaintiff sued for the tax due on the original assessments, contending that although his employee had indicated that he would accept certain figures as the defendant's income and had issued amended assessments, he was not estopped or prevented from subsequently refusing to do so and relying on the original assessments. The defendant contested the suit on the grounds that the plaintiff was estopped by the agreement to vary the original assessments and to issue amended assessments based on agreed figures.

It was held that where the Commissioner accepted a notice of objection made after the statutory period, he must be deemed to have been satisfied under Section 109 (1) of the Act,[87] that the objector was prevented from giving notice within the period and that it is not open to the Commissioner to say later that he was not so satisfied. Additionally, it was held that the burden on the person assessed to satisfy the Commissioner under S. 109 (1) of the Act[88] that there is just cause to admit a notice of objection after the statutory period is discharged when the Commissioner later admits the late notice. Furthermore, it was held that the Commissioner's acceptance of late notice of objection after the statutory period under Section 109 (1) of the Act[89] was not *ultra vires* his statutory powers. Therefore the notice was valid.

(b) Commissioner-General's Powers

Upon receipt of a notice of objection, the Commissioner General is empowered to amend the assessment in accordance with the objection or according to his best judgment or to refuse to amend the assessment.[90] When he refuses to amend the assessment, he should issue a notice confirming the assessment, which should be served on the assessee.[91] If an objection decision is not made within 90 days of lodgement by the taxpayer, the taxpayer may by written notice to the Commissioner elect[92] to treat the Commissioner as having allowed the objection.

---

85. 4 E.A.T.C. (Pt 1) 10 (Kenya) See also *Sardah Mohamed Maherally Shroff v. Commissioner of Income Tax.* 4 E.A.T.C. (Pt 1) 89
86. equivalent to ITA, S. 99(1)
87. equivalent to ITA, S. 99 (1)
88. *Ibid*
89. *Ibid*
90. *Ibid.* S. 99 (5)
91. *Ibid.* S. 99 (6)
92. *Ibid* S. 99(7),(8)

E. Collection, Recovery and Repayment of Tax

1. Collection

(a) Time for Payment

(i) General

Tax charged in any assessment is payable within 45 days of the date of notice of such assessment.[93] However, where a return of income is required to be submitted under Section 96, the due date of payment of the tax payable in accordance with that return or estimated assessment shall be the date when a return for such year of income should have been submitted, and the provisions relating to the collection and recovery of tax shall apply with effect from that date.[94]

(ii) Provisional Assessment on Companies

In the case of provisional assessments on companies and partnerships, the tax charged shall be payable in two equal installments. In the case where the accounting period does not coincide with the year of income as provided under Section 40 (9), the tax shall be payable not later than 6 months and 12 months, respectively, after the commencement of the accounting period and in any other case not later than 30 June and 31 December, respectively.[95]

(iii) Provisional Assessment on Individuals

In a case where provisional assessment is made on an individual pursuant to Section 111, the tax is payable in four equal quarterly instalments. In the case where the accounting period does not coincide with the year of income, the tax shall be payable not later than 3 months, 6 months, 9 months and 12 months, respectively, after the commencement of the accounting period.[96]

(iv) Effect of Notice of Objection

Where a valid notice of objection to assessment has been given under Section 99 of ITA, irrespective of the determination of the assessment, the tax payable is 30 percent of the tax assessed or that part of the tax which is not in dispute.[97]

(vi) Payment in Installments

The Commissioner General may,[98] upon written application by the taxpayer and where good cause is shown, allow payment of tax in installments of equal or varying amounts as he may determine.[99] However, where the taxpayer defaults in paying the installments,

93. *Ibid* S.103(1)(b)
94. *Ibid.* S. 103 (1)(a)
95. *Ibid.* S. 111 (2) discussed supra under Provisional Tax
96. *Ibid.* S. 111 (4)
97. *Ibid* S.103(2)
98. *Ibid* S. 103 (3)
99. *Ibid* S.103(4)

the whole balance of the tax outstanding becomes immediately payable.[100] Permission to pay in installments does not preclude liability for interest arising under the ITA.[101]

(b) Interest on Unpaid Tax

Where any amount of tax remains unpaid after the due date, interest at a rate of 2 percent per month or part thereof shall immediately become due and payable thereon and similar interest shall so become due and payable upon the expiration of each succeeding period of one month on any amount of tax still remaining unpaid at each such expiration.[102] Such interest is deemed to be tax for purposes of collection and recovery under ITA.[103] Additionally, the Minister may on the advice of the Commissiner remit the whole or any part of any interest charged under Section 136.[104]

2. Recovery of Tax

(a) Collection by Agent

The Commissioner General may, in his discretion and by written notice addressed to any person, appoint that person agent for another person for purposes of specifying, collecting and recovering tax due from such person.[105] Thereafter, the agent is required to pay the tax specified in the appointment notice out of moneys which may, be held by him for or due to him to, his principal.[106] If he is unable to comply, he should notify the Commissioner General in writing of his reasons. Thereafter the Commissioner General may accept the notification and cancel or amend the appointment notice accordingly or if he is not satisfied by the reasons given, he may reject the notification in writing.[107]

In *Shah Jivraj Kira & Sons v. Gohl,*[108] the main issue was whether a notice appointing an employer as agent to collect tax due from an employee to the Commissioner of Income Tax takes priority over a subsequent court order for attachment of the salary of the employee. It was held that the notice of the Commissioner of Income Tax, when served on the employer, takes effect in the nature of a statutory assignment. In respect of that portion of the employee's salary which is specified in the notice, the employee becomes a trustee for the Commissioner. Second, the notice has the effect of curtailing the amount payable to the employee at the source. Accordingly, the notice by the Commissioner has priority over a subsequent court order for attachment of salary.

In *C.C. v. Commissioner of Income Tax,*[109] the appellant acquired a plot of land in Nairobi in 1960 and developed it with the aid of a loan. In 1962, the appellant sold the

---

100. *Ibid* S.103(5)
101. *Ibid* S.103(6) read together with S.136
102. *Ibid* S. 136 (1)
103. *Ibid* S. 136 (1) (b)
104. *Ibid* S. 136 (3)
105. *Ibid* S. 106 (1)
106. *Ibid*
107 *Ibid* S. 106 (4), (5)
108. [1960] E.A. 922 Supreme Court (Kenya). See also *C.B. & Anors v. Commissioner of Income Tax* 4 E.A.T.C. (Pt II) 1
109. 4 E.A.T.C. (Pt II) 9 (Kenya). See also *Mulji Jetha Ltd v. Commissioner of Income Tax* [1966] E.A. 259; *Commissioner of Income Tax v. C.W. Armstrong* [1963] E.A. 505

property to an investment company, with the result that the investment company owed the appellant a sum in excess of Shs200,000/=. In early 1962 a formal declaration of trust was made by the appellant which recited that the land was purchased for, and was held by the appellant on trust for, certain named beneficiaries, who were for the most part, directors and shareholders of the appellant company. The Commissioner issued a notice, under the equivalent of Section 106 ITA, to the investment compan, requiring it to pay over to him Shs200,000/= from the amount owed to the appellant in respect of tax due to the Commissioner by the appellant. The appellant appealed to the High Court as a "person aggrieved" by the notice served on the investment company. The sole ground of appeal was that the appellant was entitled to the payments from the investment company in its capacity as a trustee and not in its personal capacity. The Commissioner conceded that this was a legitimate trust, but it must be ignored as it was a scheme conceived with the intention of putting the appellant's property out of reach of the Commissioner. Furthermore, the Commissioner held that the trust was invalid in law and that the appellant must show that the purchase price for the property was provided by the beneficiaries under the trust.

It was held that the declaration of trust could not be disregarded merely because it may have been designed to put the property of the taxpayer beyond the Commissioner.

The agent is subject to enforcement measures under the ITA relating to recovery of tax as if he was a taxpayer[110] if he fails to pay the tax specified in the appointment notice – either within the period specified by the Commissioner or on the date on which any moneys come into his hands for or become due by him for payment of the principal — whichever is the later and if he has given no notice of inability to pay or such notification has been rejected by the Commissioner. In *B.X. v. Commissioner of Income Tax*,[111] it was held that the Commissioner, by virtue of a notice served under the equivalent of Section 106, ITA, steps into the shoes of the taxpayer and acquires no more than the rights of the taxpayer. Furthermore, the appellant was not entitled to set-off against the amount claimed by the Commissioner the amount of damages he was claiming from the lessor for breach of the terms of the lease.

However, an agent who has made payment under an agency collection notice under Section 106 is deemed for all purposes to have acted with authority of his principal and of all other affected persons and is indemnified in respect of such payment against all legal proceedings, irrespective of any contrary provision in any written law, contract or agreement.[112]

A person who fails to comply with an agency notice issued under Section106 commits an offence and is liable on conviction to a fine of up to Shs500,000/=.[113]

b) Persons Leaving or Having Left Uganda

The Commissioner General may by written notice require a person who is leaving or who has left Uganda to pay the tax remaining unpaid or to provide security for such payment.[114]

110. ITA, S. 106 (8)
111. 4 E.A.T.C. (Pt I) 234 (Kenya)
112. ITA S. 106 (7)
113. *Ibid* S.138 (1) (a)
114. *Ibid* S.105

The payment of the tax specified in the certificate to a customs or immigration office or the production of a certificate issued by the Commissioner stating that the tax has been paid or secured shall be sufficient authority to allow the person to leave Uganda.[115]

(c) Tax Clearance Certificates

A taxpayer who is involved in providing a passenger transport service or freight transport service or a freight transport service for which the goods vehicle has a load capacity of more than two tonnes, or who supplies goods or services to the government or transfers funds in excess of Shs 50 million from Uganda to a place outside Uganda should obtain a tax clearance certificate from the Commissioner.[116]

(d) Withholding Tax on Imported or Exported Goods

Withholding tax at the rate of 4 percent of the value of goods is payable in respect of consignments of goods imported into or exported from Uganda.[117] This is invariably collected by the Department of Customs and Excise of the Uganda Revenue Authority at ports of entry or exit. The value of goods is determined by the Customs Department relative to valuation for Customs duty purposes.[118] Payment of withholding tax is regarded as advance income tax for the relevant year of income in which the payment was made, and credit thereof is given for purposes of determining final tax liability at the time of assessment.[119]

Payment of withholding tax does not apply to persons exempted from payment of income tax under the ITA. Nor does it apply to[120] petroleum products (apart from cosmetics, fabrics or yarn made out of petroleum products); capital goods including plant, machinery, spare parts and raw materials; building materials; human and animal drugs; scholastic materials; importations by approved religious or charitable organisations; any case or person exempted by the Minister of Finance by Statutory Order; and any goods imported or exported by or on behalf of a person whose tax affairs are up to date.

A local authority, Government of Uganda, government institution or company controlled by the Government is required to withhold tax at the rate of 4 percent on payments made by it which in aggregate exceed shilling one million to any person who supplies it with goods, or services, or water.[121]

(e) Collection by Suit

If tax has not been paid on or before the due date, the tax owed may be sued for and recovered as a debt due to the Government in a Court of competent jurisdiction[122] by the Commissioner-General in his official name,[123] subject to general directions of the

115. *Ibid* S.105(3)
116. *Ibid* S.134
117. *Ibid* S. 119 (3)
118. *Ibid* S. 119 (4)
119. *Ibid* S. 119(b) read together with S.128(1),(3)
120. *Ibid* S. 119(5)
121. *Ibid* S, 119(1), (2)
122. Tax worth Shs 5 million or less would be sued for in Magistrate's Courts, while that exceeding Shs5 million is sued for in the Commercial Division of the High Court.
123. This must now be read subject to Section 3 of URA Act Cap 196 which requires the URA to sue in its Corporate name.

Attorney General.[124] In such a suit, a certificate signed by the Commissioner General or his designate (invariably the Commissioner for Internal Revenue) giving the name and address of the affected taxpayer and the amount of tax due from him is sufficient evidence that such amount of tax is due and payable by him.[125]

(f) Collection of Tax by Distraint

Instead of suing for the tax due under Section 104 of ITA, the Commissioner General may recover it by distress by issuing a written order specifying the person against whose property the proceedings are authorised, the location of the property and the tax liability to which the proceedings date and also requiring a police presence.[126] In the event that the full tax due is not recovered by distress, the deficiency may be recovered by suit under Section 104.[127] Where the tax is recovered prior to execution of distress, the Commissioner-General may recover any costs or expenses incurred prior to execution as if it were tax using recovery measures under the Act.[128]

In executing distress, the authorised officer and his assistants may break open during day time any premises with the assistance of the police.[129] The distress may be continued for 10 days.[130] When the person distrained against does not pay the tax and relevant costs within 10 days, the goods and chattels distrained may be sold by public auction.[131] The proceeds are applied first to meet the cost of securing, keeping and selling the goods, then the tax due. The remainder are restored to the owner.[132]

(g) Security of Property for Unpaid Tax

An income taxpayer who defaults in paying due tax, but owns land or buildings, may be given notice in writing by the Commissioner-General of the Commissioner-General's intention to apply to the Chief Registrar of Titles for such land or buildings to be the subject of security for tax specified in the notice.[133] If the person so notified fails to effect payment of all the tax specified in the notice, the Commissioner-General may, by written notice direct the Chief Registrar of Titles that the land or building, to the extent of the interest therein of such person, are subject to security for the tax due. The Registrar is then obliged to register such interest without fee as if it were an instrument of mortgage or charge on the affected property, which has the effect of a legal charge or mortgage during its subsistence to secure the tax due.[134] Upon payment by the taxpayer of the whole of the tax due, the Commissioner-General may direct the Chief Registrar, in writing to cancel the direction for security, which the Chief Registrar then records with the result that the direction for security ceases to subsist.[135]

124. ITA, S. 104 (1), (2)
125. *Ibid* S. 104 (3)
126. *Ibid* S.107(1)
127. *Ibid* S. 107 (6) read together with S.104(2)
128. *Ibid* S. 107 (7)
129. *Ibid* S.107 (1)(2)
130. *Ibid* S.108 (3)
131. *Ibid* S.107(4)
132. *Ibid* S. 107 (5)
133. *Ibid* S. 110 (1)
134 *Ibid* S. 110 (2)
135. *Ibid* S. 110 (3)

(h) Collection of Tax from Agent of a Non-Resident Person

i) General

The collection of tax from agents of non-resident persons is governed by Section 108 of the Income Tax Act, Cap 340, which empowers the Commissioner to request any person who is in possession of an asset, including money belonging to a non-resident taxpayer, to pay tax on behalf of the non-resident person up to the market value of the asset but not exceeding the amount of tax due.[137] For this purpose, the captain of any aircraft or ship owned or chartered by a non-resident person is deemed to be in possession of the aircraft or ship.[138]

ii) Partners

Furthermore, the tax payable on the gross income of a non-resident partner attributable to Ugandan sources will be assessed in the name of the partnership or of any resident partner of the partnership and may be recovered out of the assets of the partnership or from the resident partner personally.[139]

iii) Trust Income

The tax payable in respect of the gross income of a non-resident beneficiary is assessable in the name of the trustee and may be recovered out of the assets of the trust or from the trustee personally.[140]

iv) Deemed Authority

A person paying tax on behalf of a non-resident taxpayer is deemed to have been acting under the authority of the taxpayer and all other affected persons and is indemnified in respect of the payment against all legal proceedings.[141]

v) Enforcement

The tax due from a non-resident taxpayer may be recovered in the manner provided by the ITA.[142]

(i) Collection from Receivers

A receiver is required to notify, in writing, the Commissioner, within 14 days of being appointed to the position of receiver or of taking possession of an asset in Uganda, whichever occurs first [ITA, S.109(1)]. The Commissioner may, in writing, notify the receiver of the amount of tax due by the person whose assets are in the receiver's possession [ITA, S.109(2)].

---

137. *Ibid* S.108(1)
138. *Ibid* S.108(2)
139. *Ibid* S.108(3) read together with S.67
140. *Ibid* S.108(4) read together with Ss 72-73
141. *Ibid* S.108(5)
142. S.108(6). See also Ss 104-107.

A receiver should dispose of no asset held by him in the capacity of receiver without prior written permission of the Commissioner [ITA, S.109(3)].

A receiver is required to set aside out of the proceeds of sale of an asset the amount of tax payable by the person whose assets he holds as notified by the Commissioner [ITA, S.109(4)(a)]. For this purpose, the receiver is liable to the extent of the amount set aside for the tax of the person who owned the asset, although the receiver may pay any debt that has priority over the tax due [ITA, S.103(4)(b),(c)].

When a receiver fails to comply with Section 109 of the ITA, he is personally liable to the extent of the tax due from the person of whom he is a receiver [109(5)].

A receiver includes a person who, in respect of an asset in Uganda, is a liquidator of a company, a receiver appointed out of court or by any court, a trustee of a bankrupt business or a mortgage in possession, an executor of a deceased's estate or any other person conducting the business of a person who is legally incapacitated [S.109(6)].

3. Repayment of Tax

Refund of Excess Tax

Excess tax paid by a taxpayer, to the satisfaction of the Commissioner-General may be refunded together with relevant interest under ITA to the person entitled to such refund.[143] When the person entitled to refund has outstanding tax due, the amount of tax to be refunded may be offset by the outstanding tax.[144]

All claims for refunds of tax must be lodged within five years of the expiration of the year of income to which the claim relates.[145]

F. Offences and Penalties

Offences and penalties under ITA may be broadly classified into four categories: (1) those which relate to failure to comply with notices, (2) those arising out of filing of incorrect returns, (3) those affecting filing of fraudulent returns, (4) those related to obstruction of officers.

1. Offences

(a) Failure to Comply with Notice

An offence is committed[146] for failure to furnish a return or other document within 15 days of being so required under the ITA. The offender is liable on conviction to a fine of up to Shs300,000/=[147]. Failure to provide a return by a person so convicted within a period specified by the court attracts a fine of Shs400,000/=.[148]

143. *Ibid* S. 113 (1) (4)
144. *Ibid* S. 113 (3)
145. *Ibid* S. 113 (2)
146. *Ibid* S.137(1)
147. *Ibid* S.137 (1)
148. *Ibid* S.137(2)

(b) Incorrect Returns

An offence is committed by a person[149] who (1) makes an incorrect return of income by omitting therefrom or understating therein any income which should have been stated; (2) makes any incorrect statement in any return made in compliance with a notice served on him under the Income Tax Act; (3) gives incorrect information in relation to any matter or thing, including any claim for a personal allowance affecting his or another person's tax liability. A person convicted for this offence could be fined at least Shs500,000, imprisoned of up to one year, or both.[150] In other cases the fine shall not exceed Shs500,000/=.[151]

(c) Fraudulent Returns

An offence amounting to a fraudulent claim for repayment of tax or evasion of tax is committed by[152] (1) making a false return of income by omitting therefrom or understating therein any income which should have been declared; (2) making any false statement in any return provided after service of notice under the ITA; (3) giving false information, including that in relation to any claim for personal allowance affecting his tax liability; (4) preparing or maintaining or authorising the preparation or maintenance of any false books of account or other record, or falsifying or authorising the falsification of any books of account or record; (5) making use of any fraud or authorising use of any fraud. A person who assists in the commission of the above offence in the forms stipulated is also guilty of an offence.[153]

The punishment for the offence is a fine of at least Shs500,000/= when the statement or omission is made knowingly or recklessly and up to that amount in other cases.[154]

(d) Obstruction of An Officer

Any person who, in any way, obstructs or attempts to obstruct an officer in the performance of his duties or in the exercise of his powers under ITA is guilty of an offence and is liable on conviction to a fine of up to Shs500,000/=.

(e) Failure to Comply with Recovery Measures by Taxpayer's Agent/Receiver

Any person who fails to comply with an agency notice for collection of tax on behalf of a taxpayer to whom the person owes or holds money on his behalf is guilty of an offence and is liable on conviction to a fine of up to Shs500,000/=.[155] Similarly, a receiver who fails, upon request by the Commissioner, to pay tax on behalf of the person for whom he acts as receiver commits an offence and is liable on conviction to a fine of up to Shs500,000/=.[156] Upon conviction, the Court may order the agent or receiver to pay to

---

149 *Ibid* S. 142 (1)(3)
150 *Ibid* S. 142 (1)(c)
151. *Ibid* S.142 (1)(d)
152. *Ibid* S. 142 (1),(3)
153 *Ibid* S. 144
154. *Ibid* S.142(1)(c)(d). See also *Alfed Granville Ross v. R.* [1957] E.A 507
155. *Ibid* S.138(1)(a) Read together with S. 106
156. *Ibid* S.138(1)(b) read together with S.109

the Commissioner the amount of tax to which failure to comply relates.[157] However, a person who notifies the Commissioner that he is unable to comply with the agency notice shall be regarded as having complied with the agency notice until the Commissioner issues that person a notice rejecting the notification or amending the agency notice.[158]

f) Failure to Maintain Proper Records

A person who, deliberately fails to maintain proper records under the ITA commits an offence and is liable on conviction to a fine of at least Shs300,000/= or to imprisonment for a up to one year.[159] In other cases, the fine imposed is up to Shs500,000/=.[160]

g) Failure to Furnish Information Required by Commissioner

A person who, without good cause, fails to comply with a notice to furnish information stipulated in the notice or to attend an examination by the Commissioner concerning the tax affairs of himself or any other person commits an offence and is liable on conviction to a fine of up to Shs500,000/= .[161]

h) Improper Use of Tax Identification Number (TIN)

A person who knowingly or recklessly uses a false TIN, including the TIN of another person, on a return or document prescribed or used for purposes of the ITA, commits an offence and is liable on conviction to a fine of at least Shs500,000/=, to imprisonment for up to one year, or both.[162]

2. Interest

A person who fails to pay any tax, including provisional tax, penal tax, or any tax withheld or required to be withheld by the person from a payment to another person on or before the date on which the payment is due is liable for interest on the outstanding amount at a rate of 2 percent per month as calculated from the date on which payment was due until the date on which payment is made.[163] Such interest may be refunded to the person if the tax to which it relates is found subsequently not to have been due or payable.[164] The interest may, for good cause shown in writing by the person liable therefor, be remitted in whole or part by the Minister upon the advice of the Commissioner.[165]

The interest charged in respect of failure to remit withholding tax is borne personally by the withholding agent and is not recoverable from the principal taxpayer in respect of which the tax is withheld.[166] The interest chargeable may be recovered and collected in the manner provided by the ITA.[167]

157. *Ibid* S.138(2)
158. *Ibid* S.138(3) read together with S.106(1),(4),(5)
159. *Ibid* S.139(a) read together with S.129
160. *Ibid* S.139(b)
161. ITA, S.140. Read together with S.132
162. ITA, S.141 read together with S.135
163. *Ibid* S.136(1)
164. *Ibid* S.136(2)
165. *Ibid* S.136(3)
166. *Ibid* S.136(4) read together with Part XIIIi and S.123
167. *Ibid* S.136(6) read together with ss.103-110

3. Penal Tax

a) Failure to Furnish Income Return

A person who fails to furnish a return of income for the relevant year of income within the stipulated period is liable to pay a penal tax equal to 20 percent of the tax payable for that year or Shs20,000/= per month, whichever is the greater, for the period that the return is outstanding.[168]

b) Failure to Maintain Records

A person who deliberately fails to maintain records for a year in accordance with the requirements of the ITA for the relevant year of income is liable to pay a penal tax equal to double the amount of tax payable by that person for the year.[169]

c) Fraudulent Statements

A person who knowingly or recklessly makes a statement to a Revenue Officer that is false or misleading in a material particular or who omits from a statement made to such officer any matter or thing without which the statement is misleading in a material particular so that the tax properly payable by the person exceeds that given in the statement is liable to pay a penal tax equal to double the amount of the excess amount.[170]

The import of the Tax Appeals Tribunal or Court being restricted to issues of fraud or gross neglect in relation to returns may be illustrated by *A.K. v. Regina* [2 E.A.T.C.Pt.1 & II) 139 Kenya]. In that case, the appellant, in his returns for each of the years of assessment 1948 to 1951 and those for 1951 to 1953, made a statement in relation to his income from mortgage interest for the year. At different times he made differing statements as to his income from mortgage interest for each of the years. He was charged under Section 91 (1) (b) of the E.A. Income Tax (Management) Act, 1952, with making a false statement with the intent to evade income tax in his returns for each of the years of assessment and years of income. The particulars of the charge specified merely the amount returned and that the true amount was in excess thereof. The appellant contended that the charges were defective and that prosecution evidence did not disclose an intent to evade tax when the false statements were made. The appellant, who was convicted on each of the charges, appealed to the then Supreme Court of Kenya.

It was held that the onus on the appellant under Section 91 (2) of the East African Income Tax (Management) Act 1952 was only to satisfy the Court of the probability that the false statement had been made innocently, either by forgetfulness or by oversight, but that he had failed to discharge that onus. The Court held that it would have been more satisfactory if the charges had specified a definite sum as having been understated; nevertheless, the omission did not make the charges bad as the essence of the offence was falsity.

---

168. *Ibid* S.151 read together with S.92
169. *Ibid* S.152 read together with ss.129 and 130
170. *Ibid* S.153 read together with Ss.132 and 142(3)

The case of *X v. Commissioner of Income Tax* [2E.A.T.C.(Pt.I &II) 39 (1954) (Kenya)] is also relevant to the application of Section 153 of the ITA. In that case, the appellant, an accountant practising in East Africa, made belated returns of his income for the years 1943 to 1946 and made no returns for the years 1947 to 1951 and for the year 1951. Letters were written to the appellant and he was interviewed, but no income information satisfactory to the Commissioner of Income Tax was obtained. During the years in question, the appellant purchased and sold a number of properties.

For the years of assessment 1943 to 1946, the Commissioner of Income Tax, acting under Section 55 (2) of the then Income Tax Ordinance, refused to accept the appellant's returns and raised estimated assessments in excess of the income returned by the appellant but imposed no additional tax. For the years of assessment 1947 to 1950, the Commissioner, acting under Section 55 (3) of the Income Tax Ordinance, raised estimated assessments and imposed treble additional tax. For the year of assessment 1951, the Commissioner, by virtue of Section 71 (3) of the Act, raised an estimated assessment and imposed treble additional tax. For the year of income 1951, the Commissioner, pursuant to Section 71 (3) of the Act, raised an estimated assessment but imposed no additional tax.

The appellant appealed each of the assessments on the ground that it was excessive. He also appealed against the additional tax imposed the years of assessment 1947 to 1951 on the ground that where no return is made and an assessment is raised under Section 55 (3) of the Income Tax Ordinance or Section 71 (3) of the E.A. Income Tax (Management Act) 1952, no additional tax may be imposed. At the hearing of the appeal, the Commissioner of Income Tax requested that certain of the assessments be increased, that additional tax be imposed for the years of assessment 1943 to 1946 and that no personal allowance be granted for the years of assessment 1947 to 1951 and the year of income 1951.

The Court held firstly that the onus was on the appellant to prove that the assessment for each year was excessive and that he had failed to discharge the onus. Second, the Court held that while it had the power to increase assessments, none of the assessments should be increased as they were estimated assessments. The Commissioner had divulged no basis for arriving at the assessments nor made any request for an increase in the assessments in the statement of facts. Third, the Court held that when no return has been made and an assessment has been raised, no additional tax may be imposed. Fourth, the Court held that double additional tax should be imposed in the years of assessment 1943 to 1946. Finally, it held that no personal allowances should be granted for the years of assessment 1947 to 1951 and the year of income 1951 as they had not been properly claimed.

Furthermore, in *Income Tax Commissioner v. Roshanali Nazerally Merali* [1964] E.A.95C.A. (Kenya)], the Commissioner assessed the respondents as administrators of the estate of a deceased with tax and included therein a sum for additional tax chargeable under Section 40 of the E.A. Income Tax (Management) Act 1952 (equivalent to ITA, S.136). It was not disputed that there had been a default or omission on the part of the deceased before his death that rendered Section 40 applicable, but it was submitted that the additional tax chargeable under Section 40 amounted to a penalty, that under common law a penalty is not recoverable after the death of the person concerned, and that the Act should not override the common law unless that intention was to be plainly gathered. The respondents' appeal to the Local Committee was rejected, but the respondents succeeded on further appeal to the then Supreme Court of Kenya, and the assessment for additional tax was set aside on the ground that it was a penalty and as such recoverable only by a suit instituted for its recovery. The Commissioner appealed to the Court of Appeal for East Africa.

The Court of Appeal held that although the effect of Section 40 of the E.A. Income Tax (Management) Act 1952 was to impose higher rates in cases of default and omission, the important consideration is that whilst the Section is expressed in terms of amount, it is invariably an "amount of tax." The additional tax is plainly within the meaning of the Act and Section 40 enacts that the person concerned shall be chargeable with it. Additionally, though the additional tax chargeable by that Section had been designed as a penalty, there was no distinction in any part of the Act between the treatment accorded to the additional tax and any other tax. Third, the Court held that there was nothing in the Act which suggested that the "tax" chargeable under Section 56 of the Act of 1952 by assessment does not, or ought not, to include all tax with which the deceased would have been chargeable or that some different basis of assessment should apply; the plain intention is to substitute the administrator for the deceased.

In *Executors of the Estate of Sheikh Fazal Ilahi v. Commissioner of Income Tax* [1965] E.A.252 C.A.(Kenya)], the taxpayer was engaged in the business of buying and selling land on a substantial scale. His executors, the appellants, disputed assessments raised in January 1955 based on profits, actual or estimated, from specific sales of property in various years of income going back to 1940. The Commissioner included in the assessment additional tax at twice and, where possible, treble the sum properly chargeable, because the taxpayer had defaulted or was grossly negligent in making tax returns relating to the sales. The appellants contended at trial and on appeal that the sales were capital transactions. However no documentary evidence was produced by the appellants to that effect. The trial judge held that consistent withholding of information requested by the Commissioner and delay enabled him to raise additional assessments on the taxpayer for 1949, 1951, 1952 and 1953, but he rejected assessments for 1940, 1942, 1944 and 1945 as being out of time. (Under ITA, S.95, the period of limitation is seven years.) The Commissioner cross-appealed on the ground that a policy of obstruction within the period of limitation amounted to wilful default.

The Court of Appeal held firstly that the onus of proof on the appellants that an assessment is excessive depends on the particular facts in each case. A suspicion of the Court or of the Commissioner of undisclosed sources of income, not being in issue, cannot be taken into account when the taxpayer is seeking to prove an assessment based on a specific transaction is excessive. The appellant's clarifications may be a convenient method of approach. The appellant's clarifications were that

(1) when the Commissioner has no information and makes a blind assessment, the taxpayer must prove his total income is less than the assessment;
(2) when a return has ignored certain sources or categories of income or is unacceptable to the Commissioner as rendered, only income from the sources in dispute need be proved;

(3) when the Commissioner raises an assessment on a profit on a specific transaction, the taxpayer can prove the assessment is excessive for purposes of Section 78 (5) of the East African Income Tax (Management) Act of 1952 if he satisfies the Court that the Commissioner is wrong in law in his interpretation of the particular transaction.

Secondly, the Court of Appeal held that the appellants had neither discharged the onus on them nor shown that all the sales were capital transactions. The Court should consider each year on its merits. Third, the Court held that when a taxpayer is engaged in a business of buying and selling certain properties, a scheme of reinvestment by sale of those properties will not rebut a presumption that any reinvestment in land would be a revenue transaction. The length of time a property is retained is a factor to be taken into account in deciding whether a profitable sale is a revenue transaction. In this case, retention of a plot for 142 years did not displace the presumption that its sale was a revenue transaction. Fourth, the Court held that "wilful default" in Section 72 of the East Africa Income Tax (Management) Act of 1952 [equivalent to ITA, S.142] meant "intentional abstention from doing something in relation to income tax which the abstainer knows he is under legal obligation to do." Such default must be proved by the Commissioner in relation to each year of assessment and to have occurred during the limitation period. Since the additional assessments had been paid there was no loss to be made good. Furthermore, in deciding whether there had been fraud or wilful neglect the Court would take into account an honest belief that certain profits are not taxable. Such a belief may also be a proper factor in mitigation of the assessment. Equally a policy of evasion or delay would be a ground for imposing the maximum penalty.

d) Understatement of Provisional Tax Estimates

If a provisional taxpayer's estimate or revised estimate is less than 90 percent of the actual chargeable income, the taxpayer is liable to a penal tax of 20 percent of the difference between the revised estimate and 90 percent of his actual chargeable income for the relevant year.[171] A similar penalty may be imposed on the difference between the revised estimate of gross turnover and the taxpayer's actual gross turnover for the year.[172]

e) Collection of Penal Tax

Liability for penal tax is calculated separately for each section dealing with penal tax.[173] Penal tax is imposed in addition to any interest imposed under the ITA and any penalty imposed following a conviction of an offence.[174]

No penal tax shall be imposed on a person who has been convicted for failure to maintain proper records or for making false or misleading statements.[175] However, if penal tax has been imposed for those offences, it shall be refunded if the person is subsequently prosecuted therefor.[176]

171. *Ibid* S.154(1) read together with S.112
172. *Ibid* S.154(2)
173. *Ibid* S.155(1)
174. *Ibid.*155(2) read together with S.136
175. *Ibid* S.155(3) read together with ss.139, 142, 152, 153
176. *Ibid* S.155(4)

The penal tax imposed under the ITA is treated for all purposes as an assessment under that Act.[177]

The penal tax may, for good cause shown in writing by the person liable to pay it, be remitted wholly or partly by the Minister of Finance upon the advice of the Commissioner.[178]

4. Miscellaneous

(a) Compounding of Offences

The Commissioner General has the power to compound offences other than bribery under Section 145 rather than prosecuting the person in Court.[179] Upon the taxpayear's written admission that he has committed the offence, the Commissioner General may order the person to pay a sum not exceeding the fine stipulated under ITA for the offence.[180] The compounding order should be in writing, with the written admission of the taxpayer attached.[181] It should specify the offence committed, the sum of money ordered to be paid and the date on which payment is to be made. A compounding order is final; it is not subject to appeal and may be enforced in the same way as a decree of a Court for payment of the amount stated therein.[182] The effect of compounding is that the affected person is not liable to further prosecution for the compounded offence. In case prosecution is brought, the compounding order is a good defence against it.[183]

(b) Trial Venue

A person charged with an offence under the ITA may be tried anywhere in Uganda, where he may be held in custody for the offence and where the offence shall be deemed to have been committed. Notwithstanding, the offender may be prosecuted and tried at a place where he would normally have been tried.[184]

(c) Corporate Offences

If an offence is committed by a corporation, liability, in case of conviction, is attributed to a director, general manager, secretary, or similar officer of the corporation, unless such official proves that the offence was committed without his consent or knowledge and that he exercised all due diligence to prevent the commission of the offence as he ought to have exercised having regard to the nature of his functions.[185]

177. *Ibid* S.155(3) read together with Ss.139, 142, 152, 153
178. *Ibid* S.155(6)
179 *Ibid* S. 148 (1)
180. *Ibid* S. 148 (1)(2)
181. *Ibid* S. 148 (3) (a)
182. *Ibid* S. 148 (3) (c), (d)
183. *Ibid* S. 148(4)
184. *Ibid* S. 149
185 *Ibid* S. 146

(d) Prosecution by Revenue Officer

The Commissioner-General may authorise in writing a revenue officer to prosecute offences on his behalf and for that purpose, subject to the directions of the Attorney General. Such an officer would have all the powers of a public prosecutor appointed under the Magistrates' Courts Act Cap 116.[186]

(e) Payment of Tax Irrespective of Prosecution

Regardless of prosecution or compounding of an offence under ITA, the tax with relevant interest due is payable and shall not abate.[187]

186 *Ibid* S. 147

187. *Ibid* S. 150

11

Tax Appeals

A. Introduction

In the previous chapter, we saw that a person dissatisfied with an assessment may lodge an objection to the Commissioner, who then issues an objection decision.[1] A person who is dissatisfied with an objection decision may either appeal the decision to the High Court or apply for review of the decision to a Tax Appeal Tribunal.[2] Other decisions of the Commissioner may be subjected to review by the Tribunal.[3]

The purpose of this chapter is to consider the mechanism of taxation review under the Tax Appeals Tribunals Act. The establishment of the tribunals arose from concern about the lack of a speedy mechanism for appealing decisions of the Commissioner General of the Uganda Revenue Authority.

B. Composition, Tenure and Qualification of Members of the Tribunal

1. Composition

A Taxation Appeal Tribunal shall consist of a chairperson and four other members appointed pursuant to the Tax Appeals Tribunal Act. The chairperson is appointed by the Ministry of Finance in consultation with the chairperson of the Judicial Service Commission.[4] The other members of the Tribunal are appointed by the Minister of Finance.[5]

2. Qualifications and Tenure

a) Chairperson of the Tribunal

The chairperson of a tribunal must be a person who is qualified to be appointed a judge of the High Court[6] and shall hold office for a term of three years and be eligible for re-appointment.[7]

The appointment of a judge as chairperson does not affect his or her tenure of office as a judge and is deemed for all purposes to be a continuation of service as a judge.[8]

1. ITA, S.99(1),(5)
2. *Ibid.* S.100(1). See also Tax Appeal Tribunals Act Cap. 345 (hereinafter referred to as T.A.T.A.)
3. T.A.T.A.S.2(2)
4. *Ibid* S.3(1)
5. *Ibid* S.4(1)
6. *Ibid* S.3(2) read together with Article 143(1)(e) of the Constitution
7. *Ibid* S.6(1)
8. *Ibid* S.7(2)

b) Member of the Tribunal

To be eligible for appointment to the tribunal, a person must be of high moral character and proven integrity and must not have been convicted of any offence involving moral turpitude.[9] Second, he must be a person qualified in taxation, finance, accounting or law.[10] Third, no officer of the Uganda Revenue Authority can serve as a member of a tribunal.[11]

A member of a tribunal holds office for a term of three years and is eligible for re-appointment.[12]

(c) Termination of Appointment

i) Resignation

A member of a tribunal may resign his or her office by giving notice in writing to the Minister of Finance.[13]

ii) Removal

A member of the tribunal may be removed from office only for inability to perform the functions of the office arising from infirmity of body or mind, misbehavior or misconduct, incompetence, or an undischarged bankruptcy.[14]

However, prior to removal, the issue of removal should be referred to a committee of three persons appointed by the Minister. The committee should give a recommendation on the member's removal.[15] Pending the deliberation of the committee, the Minister shall suspend the member from performing the functions of his or her office.[16] The suspension shall cease upon the committee's recommendation that the suspended member should not be removed from office.[17]

C. Constitution of the Tax Appeals Tribunal

A tax appeals tribunal is constituted to handle proceedings by three members presided over by the chairperson. In the absence of the chairperson, members may elect from among themselves a member to preside.[18]

If in the course of the proceedings a member of the tribunal ceases to be a member or to be available for the proceedings before the matter is determined, the parties to the proceedings may agree to have the proceedings continued with the remaining members.[19] Where they fail to agree, the proceedings shall be adjourned and reheard

9. *Ibid* S.5(1)
10. *Ibid* S.5(2)
11. *Ibid* S.5(3)
12. *Ibid* S.6(2)
13. *Ibid* S.9(2)
14. *Ibid* S.9(3)
15, *Ibid* S.9(4),(5),(6)
16. *Ibid* S.9(7)
17. *Ibid* S.9(8)
18. *Ibid* S.13(1)(2)
19. *Ibid* S.13(3)(a)

after the member who has left has been replaced.[20] In that case the tribunal may take into account the record of proceedings prior to its reconstitution.[21]

D. Review by Tribunal of Taxation Decisions

1. Jurisdiction to Review Taxation Decisions

Any person who is aggrieved by a decision made under a taxing act (which includes the ITA) by the Uganda Revenue Authority may apply to the tribunal for a review of the decision for which an application has been properly made and in doing so shall be independent and not subject to the direction or control of any person or authority.[23]

2. Deposit of Tax Pending Determination of Objection

A taxpayer who has lodged a notice of objection to an assessment[24] is required, pending final resolution of the objection, to pay 30 percent of the tax assessed or that part of the tax assessed not in dispute, whichever is greater.[25]

3. Application

An application to a tribunal for review of a taxation is required to be in writing in the prescribed form, state the reasons for the application, and be lodged with the tribunal within 30 days after the person making it has been served with notice of decision.[26] Where the application for review relates to an objection decision, the applicant is, unless the Tribunal Orders otherwise, limited to the grounds stated in the taxation objection to which the decision relates.[27] Failure to comply with the prescribed procedure for application could amount to an abuse of process and could lead to striking of the appeal.[28] In *Income Tax v. T. Ltd (No.1),*[29] the appellant filed a memorandum of appeal which merely stated that the decision of the local committee was erroneous. The respondent contended that the appeal was incompetent as it was in breach of Income Tax (Appeal to Kenya High Court) Rules 1959, r.4 in not stating the grounds of appeal. The appellant contended that he did not have to set out his grounds. It was held that the grounds of appeal must be given by the Commissioner. However, failure to give grounds of appeal is not a serious abuse of the process of the court which would entitle the court to strike the appeal. Though there was no specific provision allowing the amendment of a memorandum of appeal, the court, in the exercise of its inherent jurisdiction, would allow the Commissioner to amend his memorandum of appeal. Furthermore, in *Commissioner of Income Tax v. A.F. Limited,*[30] while accepting that the notices of appeal

20. *Ibid* S.13(3)(b),(4)
22. *Ibid* S.13(5)
23. *Ibid* S.14(2),(3)
24. Income Tax Act, s. 99(1)
25. T.A.T.A., S.15(1)
26. T.A.T.A, S.16(1)
27. *Ibid* S.16(4)
28. *Vincenzini v. Commissioner of Income Tax* [1963] E.A.162
29. [1971] E.A.560
30. 2 E.A.T.C.104

did not contain the minimum information necessary in that they did not state the body to which the appeal was directed, the failure by the Commissioner to inform the company of the invalidity of the notices and his acceptance of them as notices of appeal to the local committee had the effect of curing the defect.

The tribunal may, upon written application, extend the time for making the application for review of a taxation decision.[31] In *Sardah Mohammed Maherally Shroff v. Commissioner of Income Tax,*[32] the appellant filed his memoranda of appeal 2 days after the statutory 75 days from the notice of the local committee's decision. At the time he filed the memoranda of appeal, he applied to a judge for an extension of time within which to file the memoranda. The applications were supported by affidavits in which he stated that he suffered a recurrence of high blood pressure and that during the period that the 75 days were running he was severely stricken with hypertension and was unable to instruct his advocate. A certificate to that effect from a doctor was annexed to the affidavit. The Supreme Court dismissed the appeal on the grounds that the appellant had not shown that he was "prevented" by sickness from presenting the appeals and that there was an unreasonable delay as the appellant could have instructed his advocate either before or after his illness. This was upheld by both the Court of Appeal for Eastern Africa and the Privy Council.

An example of "reasonable cause" may be gathered from Section 99(3) of the ITA which permits an extension of time if the tribunal or court is "satisfied that owing to absence from Uganda, sickness ... he was prevented from giving notice of appeal within such relevant period and that there was no unreasonable delay on his part."

In *Esso Standard v. Income Tax,*[33] the Court of Appeal held that extension of time to file the notice of appeal would be allowed because the case involved points for decision which were on a matter of public importance viz "the circumstances in which foreign investors have to pay income tax on loans made abroad for the purpose of development in Africa."[34] In *Northern Province Labour Utilization Board v. Commissioner of Income Tax,*[35] it was held that since the error of an advocate had been held not to be "sufficient reason" for granting an extension of time under rule 9 of the Eastern Africa Court of Appeal Rules, it was arguable that such an error could not be a "reasonable cause" under Section 111 (3) of the Eastern African Income Tax (Management) Act, 1958. Furthermore, the words "other reasonable cause" in Section 111(3) of the Act should be construed *ejusdem generis* with the words "absence from the territories" and "sickness" in that subsection,[36] Both absence and sickness connote a physical impediment preventing notice of appeal being given, whereas there is no such element in the slip of an advocate. However, in *M v. Commissioner of Income Tax,*[37] it was held that what constitutes "other reasonable cause" is a question of fact in each case and should not be construed *ejusdem generis* with absence from country or sickness and that an error by an

31. T.A.T.A., S.16(2)
32. 4 E.A.T.C. (Pt.1)89 [1964] 484 P.C.(Kenya)
33. 4 E.A.T.C. (Pt.1)89 [1964] E.A.484 P.C. (Kenya)
34. *Ibid* p.141, per Duffus P.
35. [1960] E.A.1015 (Tanganyika)
36. C.f. *M v. Commissioner of Income Tax* [1969] E.A.671 Kenya
37. *Ibid*

advocate is a reasonable cause for extension of time. To decide otherwise would deprive a blameless appellant of the right to appeal.

In *Income Tax v. R.M. & Another,*[38] the Commissioner General of Income Tax applied to extend the time for filing an appeal against the decision of a local committee. He had not given the respondents notice of appeal in writing within 45 days. The respondents objected that no appeal would lie, and the applicant argued that a notice had been sent, but out of time. The court held that a notice of appeal means a valid notice and that no extension for giving notice of appeal is given to the Commissioner General as distinct from the taxpayer and this effect must be given. Furthermore, the Court held that extending time would have no effect when no valid appeal could be filed. The applicant to the tribunal should serve a copy of the application on the revenue decision maker within five days of lodging the application.[39] The decision maker should, within 30 days of being served with such copy, lodge with the tribunal the notice of the decision, a statement giving the reasons for the decision, and relevant documents.[40] The tribunal may require the decision maker to furnish it with other documents under his control, irrespective of whether they are privileged.[41] The application should be accompanied by a prescribed fee.[42]

4. Procedure on Review

The chairperson of the tribunal is required to fix the day, time and place for hearing of the application and shall give notice thereof to the appellant and to the officers against whose order the application is preferred.[43] At the actual conduct of the review proceedings, the applicant may appear in person before the tribunal, be represented by an authorized agent or make written submissions covering the grounds of the application on the day and time and place for hearing the application.[44] The tribunal has power to adjourn the hearing of the application from time to time.[45] In addition from the Tribunal may take evidence on oath and proceed in the absence of a party who had reasonable notice of the proceedings. It may also summon persons to give evidence or produce relevant books and documents in their custody. It may also receive evidence by affidavit or interrogation and commission or request to examine witnesses abroad. The tribunal may make orders for costs against any party enforceable as an order of the High Court [T.A.T.A.S.21(5)].

The order of the tribunal disposing of the application shall be in writing and shall state the point for determination, the decision thereon, and the reasons for decision.[46] Upon disposal of the application the tribunal is required to communicate the order passed by it to the parties to the proceedings.[47]

38. [1972] E.A.459 (Kenya)
39. T.A.T.A., S.16(3)
40. *Ibid* S.17(1)
41. *Ibid* S.17(2),(3)
42. *Ibid* S.16(5)
43. *Ibid* S.12(2)(b),(3)
44. *Ibid* S.23
45. *Ibid* S.21(1)(c)
46. *Ibid* S.19(2)
47. *Ibid* S.19(3)

In *O et al. v. Commissioner of Income Tax,*[48] the local committee, to which an appeal had been made, gave no reasons for its decision. In considering an appeal, the High Court made certain assumptions from the decision of the local committee and held that the High Court was obliged to make its own assumption, regardless of any findings of the local committee. It is submitted that in a similar situation where the Tribunal has not given reasons for its decision, the High Court may make it own findings. It has also been held[49] that the onus of proving that an assessment is excessive lies upon the taxpayer, but the decision rests upon a balance of probabilities. Similarly in *Commissioner of Income Tax v. C.W. Armstrong*[50] it was held that the onus of proving that a direction that certain income be deemed to be of the taxpayer is invalid.

5. Powers of the Tribunal

In disposing of an application, the tribunal has the following powers: (1) affirming the decision under review, (2) varying the decision under review, and (3) setting aside the decision under review. In the last case, the tribunal could make a decision in substitution for the decision set aside or remit the matter to the decision maker for reconsideration in accordance with its directions or recommendations.[51]

6. Effect of Tribunal Decision

A decision of the tribunal is effective from the date it is made or on such date as the tribunal may specify.[52] Furthermore, the tribunal's decision which varies or substitutes a taxation decision under review shall for all purposes, except for purposes of making an application to the Tribunal for review or lodging of an appeal against the decision, be deemed to be a decision of the decision maker. Unless otherwise ordered by the tribunal, it has effect on and from the day on which the decision under review had effect.[53] Such a decision by the tribunal is enforceable as if it were a court decision.[54]

7. Publication

All decisions of the tribunal and all evidence received by it, including a transcript of the report of the hearings, are public records open to public inspection and should be availed by the tribunal for publication, provided that in so doing the tribunal shall ensure protection from disclosure of trade secrets or other confidential information.[55]

8. Informal Procedure

The tribunal may determine its procedure, which may be as informal as possible or in line with the procedure of any Court in respect of which it may enforce lawful writs, processes, orders, rules or commands available to a court.[56]

48. 1 E.A.T.C.124(Tanganyika)
49. *Maria Godinho v. Commissioner of Income Tax* [1960] E.A 977 (Uganda). See also T.A.T.A., S.18
50. [1962] E.A.505 C.A. (Kenya). See also T.A.T.A *ibid*
51. T.A.T.A., S.19(1) See also *O et al. v. Commissioner of Income Tax,* supra n.48
52. T.A.T.A.S.19(4)
53. *Ibid* S.19(5)
54. *Ibid* S.19(6)
55. *Ibid* S.19(7),(8),(9)
56. Ibid S.22

In addition, the tribunal should give reasonable opportunity to every party to a proceeding to present his or her case and the relevant documents which it proposes to consider and also to make submission in relation to such documents.[57]

9. Discontinuance, Dismissal or Reinstatement of Application

An applicant may, by written notice to the tribunal, at any time, notify it that he/she has discontinued or withdrawn the application, in which instance the tribunal shall dismiss the application without reviewing the decision sought to be reviewed.[58] Similarly, an application may be dismissed if the applicant fails without reasonable excuse[59] to appear at the hearing.[60] The tribunal may also dismiss an application if an applicant fails, within a reasonable time, to proceed with the application or comply with a direction of the tribunal relating to the application.[61] However, the applicant may in cases of non-appearance at the hearing or failure to proceed with the application, apply, within 30 days of being notified of the dismissal of the application, for the reinstatement of the application. The tribunal may, if it considers it appropriate, reinstate the application and give appropriate directions.[62]

10. Agreement between the Parties

Where, at any stage during the review proceeding, the parties to the proceeding agree in writing to the terms of a decision of the tribunal therein, the tribunal may make a decision in accordance with those terms without holding a hearing or where the hearing was started, without completing the hearing.[63] Where the agreement relates to a part of the proceeding or arising out of the proceeding in its decision, the tribunal shall give effect to the terms of the agreement without dealing at the hearing with that part of the proceeding or matter arising out of the proceeding to which the agreement relates.[64]

E. Appeals to Court

A party to a proceeding before a tribunal may, within 30 days of being notified of the decision or within such additional time as the High Court may allow, lodge a notice of appeal with the Registrar of the High Court. The party so appealing shall serve a copy of the notice of appeal on the other party to the proceeding before the tribunal.[65]

An appeal to the High Court may be made on questions of law only, and the notice of appeal shall state the question(s) of law that will be raised on appeal.[66]

57. *Ibid* S. 24
58. *Ibid* S.25(1)
59. See discussion supra as to what constitutes "reasonable excuse" and ITA, S.99(3)
60. T.A.T.A. S.25(2)
61. *Ibid* S.25(3)
62. *Ibid* S.25(4)
63. *Ibid* S.26(a)
64. *Ibid* S.26(b)
65. *Ibid* S.27(1)
66. *Ibid* S.27(2)

The High Court is required to hear and determine the appeal and make such order as it thinks appropriate by reason of its decision, including an order affirming or setting aside the decision of the tribunal or an order remitting the case to the tribunal for reconsideration.[67]

F. Effect of Tribunal or Court Proceedings on Implementation of Taxation Decision

The tribunal or court may stay the operation or implementation of the taxation decision under review or part of decision as it considers appropriate for purposes of securing the effectiveness of the proceedings and determination of the application or appeal.[68]

G. Refund of Tax

In the event of the decision maker (invariably the Uganda Revenue Authority) being required to refund tax to a person as a result of the decision of the Tribunal or the High Court, such tax shall be repaid at a rate specified in the relevant law[69] on the amount of the refund for a period starting from the date the person paid the tax refunded to the last day of the month to which the refund is made.

H. Offences

The Tax Appeals Tribunals Act contains penal provisions[70] relating to failure to comply with summons to appear as a witness before the tribunal and to produce a book, document or other item ordered to be produced. In addition, failure to answer questions as requested or giving false or misleading evidence is punishable.[71] Contempt of the tribunal is also criminally punishable.[72] In each of those cases[73] a person so convicted is liable to a fine of up to Shs500,000/= in the case of contempt and up to Shs1,200,000/= or imprisonment of between six months (in case of contempt) and two years or both.

---

67. *Ibid* S.27(3)
68. *Ibid* S.28(1)
69. See e.g. *Ibid.* ITA, S.113(4) which provides for interest at a rate of 2 per cent per month.
70. T.A.T.A,S.28(2) s. 31
71. *Ibid* s.32-3
72. S.34
73. *Ibid* S.31-34

Index

www.ingramcontent.com/pod-product-compliance
Lightning Source LLC
LaVergne TN
LVHW080048210926
848481LV00011B/3302

* 9 7 8 9 9 7 0 0 2 5 6 5 7 *